Playing Back
the 80s

Playing Back the 80s

A Decade of Unstoppable Hits

JIM BEVIGLIA

ROWMAN & LITTLEFIELD
Lanham • Boulder • New York • London

Published by Rowman & Littlefield
An imprint of The Rowman & Littlefield Publishing Group, Inc.
4501 Forbes Boulevard, Suite 200, Lanham, Maryland 20706
www.rowman.com

Unit A, Whitacre Mews, 26-34 Stannary Street, London SE11 4AB

British Library Cataloguing in Publication Information Available

Library of Congress Cataloging-in-Publication Data

Names: Beviglia, Jim, author.
Title: Playing back the 80s : a decade of unstoppable hits / Jim Beviglia.
Description: Lanham : Rowman & Littlefield, [2018] | Includes index.
Identifiers: LCCN 2018016713 (print) | LCCN 2018017698 (ebook) | ISBN
    9781538116401 (electronic) | ISBN 9781538116395 (hardback : alk. paper)
Subjects: LCSH: Popular music—1981-1990—History and criticism.
Classification: LCC ML3470 (ebook) | LCC ML3470 .B49 2018 (print) | DDC
    782.4216409/048—dc23
LC record available at https://lccn.loc.gov/2018016713

Printed in the United States of America

To Chuck, Art, and Mike

The only thing better than the music in the 80s
was the friendship

Contents

Acknowledgments

When I first decided that I was going to attempt to base this book around the artists of the 80s telling their stories about their finest songs, I truly thought I would be lucky to get a handful of people to cooperate and I would then have to go back to the drawing board. Instead, the response blew me away. I was able to speak—via telephone, Skype, or e-mail—with sixty-four artists, songwriters, and producers. It blew me away.

What was even more amazing was the cordiality, graciousness, and forthcoming nature of the participants. They say you should never meet your heroes. When I was a kid growing up listening to this music, these men and women were my heroes, and I was not the least bit disappointed in any of them. If anything, my appreciation of them grew deeper.

So I need to start my acknowledgments by thanking each of those sixty-four folks for their time and friendliness. That extends also to the publicists, managers, agents, and other workers who helped set up these interviews for me. They made my job extremely easy with their tirelessness and diligence.

I also must say that even the artists who decided not to participate expressed that decision in a manner that was unfailingly polite and respectful, and that goes for their representatives as well. Hopefully, I'll get a chance to speak to them all down the line.

Beyond that, I of course have to thank Rowman & Littlefield for sticking with me on a somewhat unconventional project, and my editor, Natalie Mandziuk, for seeing its potential even when others doubted it. My agent, Amelia Appel, made it clear almost immediately with her hard work and advice why I should have had an agent all along. I'd also like to thank all the folks who have read my previous books, Drew Pisarra at *CultureSonar* and Caine O'Rear at *American Songwriter* for not only publishing my music writing but also promoting my books for no reason other than that they're good guys, and Trish

Stevens at Ascot Media for publicizing my work so well. Frankie Warren has always promoted my work on local radio and was an excellent sounding board for the write-ups in the book; I thank him for that and, more than anything, for his friendship.

That makes for a good segue into my personal circle, without whom none of this would have been even imaginable, let alone possible. That means my mom, my brothers, all my relatives and friends (special shout-out to the guys at Old Man Hoops), coworkers, and too many people to mention, even though they deserve it. My daughter, Daniele, remains my favorite musician of all, and she endured her dad's insistence on listening to 80s music in the car as "research" for the past year or so with her usual good nature. What an amazing kid. And finally, there's my wife, Marie, who made the suggestion that broke this book open for me. It's only fitting that she save my work, since she's already saved my life.

Finally, I wanted to elaborate a bit on the three gentlemen named in the dedication. Art and Mike Lucarelli were my next-door neighbors, and Chuck Sweeder, my cousin, lived less than a quarter of a mile away. I know people have a tendency to blow the friendships they had as kids out of proportion, but that's not possible for me, because these three were—and I consider them still— my third, fourth, and fifth brothers. The times spent with them will always be among the best of my life. Now we're all married and have eight children between us, but when we get together, we're right back in the 80s again. Listening to the music from that time to prepare to write this book often led to me getting lost in memories of those times with those guys. If not one person buys this book, it will still have been worth it for that.

Introduction

It's probably natural that one defends the decade in which one grew up, and I grew up in the 80s. I turned eight in 1980 and eighteen in 1990. That means the decade spanned from third grade to my senior year of high school. People use the term "formative years," and I suppose it doesn't get much more formative than that.

Up until 1980, I can remember liking music, but only in a kind of second-hand way, absorbing it alternately through what my father and mother played in the car or my brothers played in their bedroom. Then John Lennon was killed, my family bought a bunch of Beatles records—which I pretty much memorized the day after we purchased them—and I became an instant musical omnivore. As much as I wanted to go back and listen to everything that came before me, I also wanted to imbibe everything that was going on at the time.

What timing. I didn't get MTV on local cable until 1985, but the presence of it made videos a big deal, and you could see them on various outlets even if you didn't have that be-all and end-all channel. With videos came all-new artists: ones who might not have had the chance to bust out in previous years, ones who belonged to my generation. What I couldn't yet wrap my young brain around was that this coincided with a drastic change in the way artists made records; the use of synthesizers was a kind of democratizing agent on music, allowing anybody to try to make hit records even if they weren't expert musicians—or musicians at all, for that matter.

It's impossible to adequately explain how much music was a constant companion for me as a kid and teen. I listened in the car, I listened on cassettes and 8-tracks and eventually CDs at home, or on boom boxes hooked up in our rec room and tuned in to the local Top 40 channels. On weekends, I made it a point to listen to Casey Kasem's countdown show pretty much from start to finish.

Once I did get the chance to see MTV, I tuned in immediately every day after school and the minute I woke up every summer morning.

Needless to say, as someone who's lucky enough to write about the music he loves, it was natural that I would one day devote myself to an in-depth excavation of those 80s days. And what I've found as I've gone back is that there isn't much of a guilty aftertaste or a feeling that my eight- to seventeen-year-old self was way off base with the music that he loved so dearly. I had a feeling that would be the case, but I must admit surprise, even after listening to these songs a trillion times or so, at how fresh they still sound to me.

The 80s was a time when people were doing bold things, innovative things, taking the pop song structure and filtering it through fascinating new sensibilities. It was also perhaps the last time the charts were a pretty good representation of quality. There was certainly still music under the radar that was worthy of greater attention, but for the most part the 80s felt like the last time when the stuff you heard and saw was generally the best stuff that was being made.

When I interviewed Huey Lewis for this book about his song "I Want a New Drug," he shared an interesting take on why the 80s felt like such a peak for popular music (and when I use that term, I'm talking about whatever made it to those charts, be it rock, R&B, country, rap, heavy metal, novelty, etc.):

> Popular music is like a haiku. It's not music. Music is jazz or classical. Pop music, since Day One, has pretty much followed the formula. Most of it is in 4/4 time, there's like an eight-bar intro, verse, chorus; or verse, B-section, chorus; or verse, chorus, and then bridge, and then verse, chorus, out. And I mean since time began, all the popular songs adhere to that formula and so do the 80s.
>
> But shortly after the 80s, that formula got busted, for the most part. And now these are like sound collages. That's one of the reasons those 80s tunes stand out. They were the last decade that really did adhere to the audio formula that was popular music.

What also happened as the 80s wore on was that genre fragmentation became even more extreme. That eventually meant that you couldn't always rely on the best music being found on the Top 40 countdown; you had to search a little bit for it sometimes. Thus it felt like the 80s were a pretty convenient time, in that sense, to be a budding music fan.

When I decided to write about the 80s, I originally intended to do a kind of combination of critical look back at the decade's music and memoir of sorts. But when I started to put it together, the feedback I was getting was that it was neither one thing nor the other, and I had to agree. It was my wife who had the idea to reach out and talk to the artists who made the music (one of the many things for which I have to thank her).

On that note, I'd like to explain a little bit about how the book was put together. I began making lists of the best songs from the decade and reaching out to as many of the available artists as possible. I decided that the songs I would attempt to profile had to be ones a reasonable number of music fans from the era would know, either because they were hits or because they've had an enduring shelf life.

Early on in the process, I realized there was going to be enough response that I would be able to exclusively include songs for which I had fresh interviews and still have a book-length project. I simply thought—and my editor agreed—that it was more compelling for these artists to tell their own stories rather than for me to spend twelve hundred words or so opining on what I thought was great about each song. There is a little bit of that in each entry, but for the most part the book is intended to be a showcase for the amazingly talented men and women who were such an integral part of making this music.

Since this was the structure, the songs included were determined by the responses I got. Unfortunately, a couple genres turned out to be underrepresented. I can't possibly explain what a huge fan I was of the rap explosion in the late 80s, and I contacted practically every one of the rap pioneers with hits from that time, with no success. I also tried hard to get interviews with some of the artists behind the best songs from the so-called hair metal era, also to no avail. Again, this wasn't for lack of trying; it's just how it worked out. Maybe next time.

I also ended up with a selection that is weighted heavily toward the first half of the decade. This could certainly be a reflection of personal taste. I've always contended that "We Are the World" was a kind of demarcation line in the decade; after that, the quality tailed off somewhat, in my estimation. That said, the songs that I chose from the second half of the decade, like all of the songs found here (listed chronologically), are ones that I enjoyed then, enjoy now, and will defend with every ounce of my being to the naysayers.

Which, I suppose, brings me to another reason why I did this book. For a long while, I've sort of silently gritted my teeth while some cultural critics have labeled the music of the 80s as campy, kitschy, or even downright embarrassing. Sometimes I think they conflate the music with the fashion.

Some of the era's music—as is the case for the music of any decade—may sound dated and might not hold up too well today. But as someone who lived through it all, I will defend, in general, the music of the 80s to anyone who would write it off. In my previous books, I've always tried to maintain objectivity about songs regardless of how they affected me in my personal life. While I hope that the write-ups in this book give some objective indication of why these songs deserve as much critical love as they have enduring popularity, I won't even try to pretend: This book was personal for me, and I hope that for all those who love 80s music as I do, it's personal for you as well.

When I was still trying to include aspects of memoir in the book, it had the working subtitle "How the Music from the 80s Warped My Brain and Saved My Life." There may have been some artistic license in there; it's not like I was out on a ledge at some point, heard the distant strains of "One Night in Bangkok" wafting through the air, and decided that life was worth living. But, as any kid does between the ages of eight and seventeen, I dealt with a lot of tumult and turmoil. In my case, there was even an unfortunate amount of tragedy as well. At my lowest points, I could always turn to the music as a salve, a pick-me-up, a distraction. Even if only in the smallest increments, it always improved my mood—or, when I wanted it to, it allowed me to wallow without asking anything in return.

For that, I will be eternally grateful to the music of the 1980s. Consider this book my humble attempt at repaying that massive debt.

"Cars" by Gary Numan
PLEASURE PRINCIPLE (1979)

This is supposed to be a book about the 1980s, but our first song was actually released in 1979. Technically, it belongs because it didn't hit the US charts till the following year, when it made it all the way to number 9. But musically, Gary Numan's "Cars" is a 1980s song in the way that it anticipates an era where machines would occasionally trump instrumental dexterity, when anti–rock stars could give guitar heroes a run for their money.

Numan had already started to spread his synthetic sound and vision in his native England on a pair of albums with his band Tubeway Army, even scoring a number 1 hit with the song "Are 'Friends' Electric?" in 1979. The synthesizer was his weapon of choice, and he wore the fact that he wasn't technically a musician with pride. "I was following my interest in sound rather than songwriting, although they are obviously connected," Numan says about his MO. "When I first started to use electronic instruments in 1978 an entire world of sound creation opened up to me. I was absolutely fascinated by noises, be they synth-created or otherwise. I still am. I have a feeling that my songwriting was done as much as a vehicle to explore sounds [as] anything else."

For the first single off his 1979 album *Pleasure Principle*, which would be the first released under his own name, Numan chose a song that he dashed off rather quickly. "I wrote the bass line first," he remembers. "In fact I'd been to London that day to buy my first bass guitar and the 'Cars' riff was the very first thing I played when I took the guitar out of its case. The music took ten minutes at the most, the lyrics another half an hour, tops. Quickest song I've ever written."

From there, Numan applied his usual touch, seconding the bass guitar with a thunderous part on the synths, while some icy high notes swooped over the top. Following the bass line robotically, Numan sings the praises of automobiles and their seeming safety. But ambivalence creeps into the lyrics as the song progresses. "When the image breaks down/Will you visit me please?" he queries. In the final verse, he plots escape, but isn't sure about the outcome: "I know I've started to think/About leaving tonight/Although nothing seems right/In cars," he sings in closing. The vocals are finished about a minute-and-a-half into the song, leaving just the wash of the synthesizers and the occasional white-noise crash of the drums. "Cars" is catchy, danceable, and eerie all at once and remains forever futuristic. You could sneak it into a playlist in 2080.

Hearing the song now, its simultaneous embrace and fear of technology seemingly wrapped up in an uneasy package, it's tempting to read it as Numan's view on the oncoming computer age. But he warns against that:

> Remember, I wrote that song in early 1978. There was very little technology at the time that gave much of an insight into what was coming. Home video had only just appeared, no CDs, no DVDs, no mobile phones or internet. Home computers were still pathetic for the most part and video games were, at best, a white dot and two white lines pretending to play tennis.
>
> I was very aware of human beings becoming closer to technology, becoming bound to it, and I saw that as a potentially frightening, but still exciting, thing. Other songs on the *Pleasure Principle* album look at the thoughts of the last thinking machine as it dies, centuries after humans have died off; a factory where synthetic humans are built; a culture that lives entirely underground, never seeing daylight, so that they can keep the city above running without even knowing if anything is still alive above them; all kinds of tech related topics. "Cars" really isn't one of them, though. It's simply about why I felt safe in a car. I have Asperger syndrome, so I don't interact well with people, generally speaking. I find people unnerving, they make me uncomfortable, and I see the car as a bubble that allows me to drift through this dangerous world of people in relative safety.

Yet "Cars," with its stateside success, thrust Numan into the role of international pop star, one he wasn't always comfortable fulfilling:

> As a young Englishman, only just poking my head out from my parents' security blanket, I had no idea what was on American radio until I came to the US for the first time to promote "Cars" and the *Pleasure Principle* album it came from. I felt as out of place as you can possibly feel. On almost every radio show I went on my music would be squeezed in between things like Rush and the rest of that old US rock-style music. My music sounded nothing like any of that and I felt horribly uncomfortable.
>
> I have never been confident about what I do, regardless of any success or otherwise, and I wished I'd felt proud of how different my stuff sounded back then. But I didn't. I felt like the new boy in school

that everyone was laughing at and picking on. When it started to hit the charts, though, and people started stopping me in the streets, I began to realize that it was doing something, changing things. Then it felt cool.

Numan was also okay with the fact that "Cars" signaled a sea change in how popular music could be made:

> The entire *Pleasure Principle* album, from which "Cars" is taken, was my reaction to the early negativity towards electronic music. For all of its huge and rapid success, a great many people didn't get it at all for a while, and the music press got it last of all in the UK. They still seemed to think that music not centered around the guitar wasn't real music. The Musicians Union in the UK tried to ban me as they said I was putting "real musicians out of work," so the reaction against it was pretty strong.
>
> To answer that, I decided to make an album that revolved entirely around synths. The live show that I toured that album with also revolved around synths as the primary instrument. Guitars still had a place, but it was very secondary. That entire album and tour was meant to show that another way existed for rock music now, that didn't have the guitar at the heart of everything, both on record and on stage.

Although "Cars" became the song that helped initiate this revolution and maintains its relevance all these years later (no easy feat for a groundbreaking track), Gary Numan—who is still pushing music into the future with every new release—took awhile to make peace with its place in his career. But he got there eventually:

> I've had a rather uneasy relationship with it strangely enough. It's one of those songs that tended to overshadow everything else I did, or certainly did for a very long time. Because of that I actually grew to resent it.
>
> It's only more recently, as the newer albums have gained widespread acclaim, although not the commercial success, that I've felt that I've moved out from under that shadow. Having done that though I've been able to look back at "Cars" with different eyes and now I'm very proud of it. I think it's true to say that most songwriters dream of writing something that well known and that long lasting. My previously resentful feelings about it now seem a little childish.

"Escape (The Piña Colada Song)" by Rupert Holmes

PARTNERS IN CRIME (1979)

Rupert Holmes is what is commonly known in modern parlance as a hyphenate: Tony winner on Broadway, long-running television show creator, acclaimed novelist whose works have been turned into equally acclaimed motion pictures, and on and on. It is somewhat unfair, then, that some people know him only for a song that he wrote and recorded that ended up being both one of the last number 1 hits of the 70s and the first of the 80s.

But Holmes has come to terms with the legacy of "Escape (The Piña Colada Song)":

> I can have a friendly conversation anywhere in the world. If they ask me what I do, and I say, "Well, I'm a writer, sometime of novels, plays, musicals or just pop songs," and they ask, "Anything I'd know?" I can answer, "Well, did you ever hear that song, 'If you like piña coladas'?" And I will have a connection with a total stranger, who will tell me that invention of mine has resided, like it or not, in his or her brain for years. What a remarkable thing for a writer to have in one's life.

Before we can explore the legacy of "Escape," it's important to map just how Holmes got there. When he began his career, he thought it would be a fine thing to write songs for other singers to perform, and indeed, many of his compositions have become fodder for others, ranging from Barbra Streisand to the Jets, who had a number 3 hit in 1986 with Holmes's sweet ballad "You Got It All." But he soon found that many of the cover versions of his material weren't matching what he was hearing in his head, in terms of arrangement or vocals. He thus began a career as a singer-songwriter, releasing four albums of well-regarded material in the 70s.

Leading up to his fifth release, 1979's *Partners in Crime*, Holmes underwent a record label switch to Infinity Records, whose strategy was based more on singles than the album-oriented rock for which the artist was known. Luckily, he felt that he had one such killer single in his holster, the brooding love-triangle saga "Him," which indeed hit the Top 10 in 1980. But even that song would be superseded by the eleventh-hour composition that transformed Holmes's life and career.

As he approached the end of recording *Partners in Crime*, Holmes felt the album contained a lot of ballads but was lacking in material that was a bit more peppy. In his many years in the music business, Holmes had learned never to give up on a recording, and a piece of music he had written as a joke five years earlier came back into his head. "The melody had a singsong quality, and the accompanying riff I played on the electric piano had a nice 'trademark riff' feel to it, a bit chunky-reggae in nature," Holmes recalls.

Holmes and his band set out to record the song, and they laid down a ragged first take. Unfortunately, one of the two drummers who played on the track became too inebriated to continue, leaving Holmes to try to make do with what he had. "Listening carefully to the track, I realized that there were sixteen bars in a row that we had recorded that were tight, had a good groove," he remembers. "So we did something that is commonplace in the world of rap music now in the digital age, but which was highly unusual in 1979. We duplicated those sixteen bars from one 24-track master machine to another. And then we edited those sixteen bars together, over and over again."

Holmes's primitive form of sampling had provided him with a basic music track, but now he needed lyrics. Inspired by the personal ads in a copy of the *Village Voice* that was lying around, he devised a scenario whereby a man, bored with his wife, answers an ad with specifications he feels he possesses but are overlooked by his wife, only to find that his wife is the one who had placed it. "The plot line reminded me of something that the author O. Henry might have come up with had he lived in the sordid 1970s rather than a hundred years earlier," Holmes muses.

Holmes knew that the key to the song's success was that audiences not be able to guess the song's twist ending. To that end, when he went in to record it the next morning, he asked to sing a first vocal all the way through to see if he could fool guitarist Dean Bailin. That decision led to some crucial, on-the-spot changes to the song.

The lyric that he had penned the previous night included a chorus that began, "If you love Humphrey Bogart." But right before he laid down the vocal, Holmes had second thoughts. "Much as I was a devotee of old Bogart films, watching a black-and-white movie seemed inappropriate to the sense of escape that the woman placing the personal ad was seeking," he says. "She wanted to let some color into her life. I pictured a tropical beach with pink sands, palm trees, and the ocean sweeping in."

Hence, piña coladas replaced Bogey. And Holmes not only fooled the people listening; his animated first take proved to be unmatchable and turned out to be the one that he used. An instrumental connecting piece with a suitably tropical feel was tacked on, and "Escape" was complete. Holmes marvels at how much of it emanated from the spur of the moment: "In those five minutes, I made a series of instant decisions having no idea that they would change the course of my life forever."

"Escape," which managed to straddle the decades by hitting the top spot at the end of 1979 and the beginning of 1980, is one of the last in a long line of 1970s story songs, marvels of economy wherein a complete tale is laid out, from setup to denouement, in the course of three or four minutes. The wonder of Holmes's creation is that it manages to wrap up the story so neatly and yet still presents a series of thorny moral dilemmas to ponder long after the song is over: Does what happens to this couple constitute a happy ending? Do they even deserve one?

Holmes doesn't judge his characters—"'Escape' is not about good guys or bad guys," he says—but he does have ideas about the resolution:

> The two do not have a happy ending. They have a comeuppance, a realization of what they have become. When I sing, "We laughed for a moment," it is surely not uproarious or celebratory laughter, but the nervous kind that quickly runs out of steam and grows silent. Two people look at each other and realize they are now both flawed in each other's eyes.
>
> Can they start again? If they are to have a happy ending, they will have to make that happen for themselves, each with the knowledge that they once were willing to betray each other's trust. Some people can grow from a misadventure or "near-miss." Others repeat or compound their errors.

Pretty heady stuff for a pop hit, and one that Rupert Holmes can appreciate, even with the unlikelihood of it all. "Growing up, if someone had told me I'd have a number 1 record amongst the hundred-plus songs I've written, I'd have been overjoyed," he surmises. "As it turns out, 'Escape' wasn't perhaps the song I would have chosen, had that choice been left to me. But still, what a privilege my life and career have been, and how grateful am I to have been given both."

"Whip It" by Devo

FREEDOM OF CHOICE (1980)

The third album is often the one where artists either elevate their game to another level, producing a classic in the process, or stagnate, and perhaps as a result never garner the same public attention again. Devo had certainly gained a lot of attention heading into their third release in 1980, with their low-budget sci-fi costumes and their compellingly robotic songs that took New Wave precision to an extreme.

But according to Gerald Casale (who, along with his brother Bob, brothers Mark and Bob Mothersbaugh, and Alan Myers, formed Devo in Akron, Ohio), at the time they were recording the album that contained "Whip It," their first Top 20 hit single, they had actually exhausted the patience of their record company:

> We were critical darlings with no airplay, basically. Warner's was very disappointed with the second record, *Duty Now for the Future*, because coming off of the explosion of the first record, going on *Saturday Night Live* and having suddenly a national platform, they were seeing dollar signs. And it didn't happen.
>
> While we are on tour for *Duty Now for the Future*, someone from the record company showed up in New York before we played a show, and they huddled in the back room with our assistant manager, Ron Stone. And basically, they told Ron Stone that unless this record that we were starting to write was some kind of breakthrough or represented some aesthetic change of course, they were going to renege on their deal. They didn't give a shit what the deal said; that would be the last record. I don't think that it really had the effect that they had hoped for, but what it did was just make it clear to us what we were really a part of in the most unvarnished, Machiavellian way.

Regardless of their disillusion, Devo had already made plans for a slight change of course. "We were starting to explore and experiment in a new direction," Casale says. "We had made some basic decisions that I was going to play bass on a Minimoog, for instance. And we were going to do some twisted version of Devo R&B. In other words, rhythm and blues would be a starting point for inspiration, since Bob Mothersbaugh and I particularly loved all of that growing up. So those were the marching orders." To that end, the band hired producer Robert Margouleff, who had gained renown for his work on Stevie Wonder's string of classic 70s albums, to co-helm 1980's *Freedom of Choice*.

"Whip It" was a collaboration in the truest sense of the word. Mark Mothersbaugh devised the chorus melody from a synthesizer piece he had demoed at home. Gerald Casale came up with the bass line that he calls "basically a twisted version of 'Pretty Woman.'" Meanwhile, the staccato stops in the bridge were sourced from yet another song the group had been formulating. Once drummer Myers hit upon the lockstep beat that would unify all the parts, the music cohered into what you hear on the finished version.

"We really prided ourselves as being the robot version of James Brown," Casale laughs. "We really tried to play our instruments as if we were machines, without a sequencer line as a metronome. We were human metronomes. You hear that in 'Whip It.' And what Mark and I shared most was a love of parts fitting together in a contrapuntal way, rather than some wall of sound where everybody's playing the same thing on different instruments at the same time. We liked the interlocking geometry and mathematics of it. And you hear that in 'Whip It' too."

The song still needed lyrics, and Gerald Casale pulled out a bunch he had tucked away in a notebook that, in typical Devo fashion, cast a sideways glance at something familiar. "I had been reading *Gravity's Rainbow* by Thomas Pynchon," he says. "I wrote those lyrics in December of 1979 and was sitting on them wondering what to do with them. I was making an attempt to do his kind of parody of Horatio Alger: 'You can do it, there's nobody else like you.' This kind of narcissistic, American exceptionalism. 'You're number one, everybody's special.'"

When *Freedom of Choice* was released in 1980, the song 'Girl U Want,' was chosen as the lead single, but it failed to make an impact. Warner Bros. was considering not even releasing a second single when a radio station in Florida put "Whip It" into heavy rotation out of nowhere. "And we got the word and it just exploded." Casale remembers. "It went up the East Coast. Once it hit New York, it was over. Then it went everywhere. We had to stop the tour, recalibrate everything, because suddenly, instead of playing to five hundred or seven hundred people, we were going to play to three to five thousand people."

"Whip It" is still as subversive a pop hit as you'll ever hear, with Mark Mothersbaugh and Gerald Casale shouting out bizarre slogans such as "Crack that whip/Give the past a slip" as if they were members of Up with People in a particularly surly mood. "No one gets away/Until they whip it" is a couplet that hints at the parody of blind conformity the song was always meant to be. But you need not go that deep to sink into the lockstep grooves and get lost in the pinball synths and white-noise percussion cracks.

As a matter of fact, Casale came to accept that many would misinterpret his lyrics, even steering into the curve when the band did a belated video for the song once it took off. "When these jerk-off DJs with their baseball jackets would go, 'Whip it, dude!' and make a whipping motion, we'd just grin and laugh and go along with it," he admits. "Let them leeringly thing it was about whacking off or S&M. That's exactly why I made the video that I did. I thought, why not, in a parody way, live up to their expectations. Give people exactly what they think, but not really."

Devo has made a career out of giving the people what they want, but not really—but it only could have happened to the extent that it did because of their biggest hit. "It turned everything around," Casale says. "That dire warning that the plug was about to be pulled in the fall of '79 just went away. They were totally on board with the next three records."

And "Whip It," as if it has somehow heeded its own ironic advice and become a supercharged version of itself, has turned out to be persistently timeless and always ready to parody a new generation's excesses. "You'd like to think when you're making something, if there's ideas behind it, it there's substance to it, that it goes beyond the moment of trendiness," Casale says today. "That's what you hope, as a creative artist, that you would make something like Picasso, where they look at it a hundred years later and they still find it relevant or see something in it that's universal. 'Whip It' achieved that. It's become a cultural meme."

"Everybody's Got to Learn Sometime" by the Korgis

DUMB WAITERS (1980)

The synthesizer was beginning to truly make its mark on the pop scene at the end of the 1970s, democratizing the process of making music. You didn't need to know how to play any instruments or have the money to hire those who did to make riveting sounds. At least in the early postpunk and New Wave period, most artists who employed the instrument did so in the service of up-tempo songs, as it provided frenzied electronic beats and Day-Glo keyboard colors to those futuristic-sounding recordings.

But "Everybody's Got to Learn Sometime," a somewhat unlikely hit by the British band the Korgis, tried something a little different. The Fairlight synthesizer utilized by the band cast a hazy reverie over the entire song, which proceeded at a tiptoeing tempo. Every word sung by Korgis' songwriter and lead singer James Warren seemed to take on more meaning thanks to the simulated strings poured over the track. The end result was a ballad that somehow hinted at mysteries too vast to be encompassed by normal analog instruments; the synthetic, in this case, was much more authentic than the real thing.

The Korgis were formed by Warren and Andy Davis out of the ashes of a more experimental group called Stackridge. But when their self-titled 1979 debut album as the Korgis included a British Top 20 hit in "If I Had You," they were inspired to shoot for the cheap seats. In particular, Warren had overseas success in mind:

> I'd been toying with the idea that it'd be great if I could just come up with a Transatlantic rock ballad, something that would appeal to the States, to the Americans as well as English listeners. So that's when I started playing the piano intro. Just that one chord, which is C-sharp minor seventh. And everything just sort of happened very easily, effortlessly from that. I think the whole tune was written in

about ten minutes. I got straight down to writing the words. So it was a very fast thing.

The lyrics were minimal, but suggested profound possibilities nonetheless. Warren recalls,

> At the time, I was very into Buddhist philosophy, and also there was a particular Indian spiritual teacher called [Jiddu] Krishnamurti. He had his very individual philosophy, but it was basically a Buddhist approach to life. I used to read his books constantly at the time. So the lyrics to that song were really his kind of idea which I had imbibed. This thing about changing fundamentally the way we look at life, the way we look at other people. Change your heart and look at the world with completely fresh eyes, not with the eyes of our social conditioning. Break away from your social conditioning and look at the world as if you were looking at it for the first time without any preconceptions. All that kind of stuff. As simply as possible, I made that the lyric of the song.

Originally, Warren thought that the song would work best in the vein of Paul McCartney's original idea for the Beatles' "The Long and Winding Road" (before Phil Spector added heavy strings, to McCartney's dismay). "I did the same thing with 'Everybody's Got to Learn Sometime,' and thought I could perhaps get away with it just like that, with just piano, voice, bass and drums," Warren explains. "And that was about it really. But David Lord, our producer, it was his idea to make it big and luscious. He thought it really lent itself to that sort of approach. I think he was right with the synthesizer strings thing he came up with. I think it definitely increased the magical feel of the song."

When Warren urges listeners to "Change your heart, look around you" in the song, the import of the plea is emphasized by the vulnerability of his vocal. That voice takes on a bit more desperation when he looks to connect with someone else: "I need your loving like the sunshine," he sings, the girl's love becoming an almost elemental necessity, like water or air. Then those synths wash all over him, and he resignedly sings the title refrain. It's as if he's conceding that there will be infinite mistakes made by people in the pursuit of triviality before they finally realize what is important in their lives. You can find uplift in "Everybody's Got to Learn Sometime" if you look hard enough, and you can also find despair, making it kind of one-size-fits-all song for listeners, depending on whatever mood strikes them on a particular day or time.

Touching on all of those big ideas is a pretty amazing feat for a song with essentially a single verse and a chorus, but such is the strange magic conjured by "Everybody's Got to Learn Sometime," magic that was immediately evident to all in its vicinity. "I thought it was something special actually," Warren says.

"I thought, 'Yeah, this will be played on the radio.' And that was reinforced as soon as we sent the track up to the record company in London, because they immediately got back and said, 'Wow. That's the one. That's gonna be a hit; that's gonna be a single.' And people around us, who were coming to the studio when we were recording that song, the reaction just seemed to be the same from everyone."

All of that was reinforced by the song's soaring to hit single status all over the world, including, as Warren had originally intended, in America. It has also been the subject of many a cover version over the years, which Warren attributes to its simple structure. "This idea that if I could come up with very simple musical phrases coming in occasionally with lots of space in between, I think that was part of my original concept," he says. "That's why it invites cover versions. It's just sort of this simple thing for people to put their own take on it."

The Korgis' star faded almost as fast as it rose; Davis left the band before the next album, stunting their momentum. But Warren admits that this song of his stumbled onto a formula that would have been difficult to repeat even in the best of circumstances. "It was one of those unusual, magical things that just seemed to have a life of its own," he explains. "It just seemed to work. It's not a repeatable kind of thing. I don't think I've ever been able to write 'Everybody's Got to Learn Sometime, Part II.' It's just sort of one of those one-off things.'"

"Once in a Lifetime" by Talking Heads

REMAIN IN LIGHT (1980)

Perhaps no story better indicates the unfamiliarity of the methods employed by Talking Heads and producer Brian Eno on their 1980 album *Remain in Light* than the one Chris Frantz tells about one of the project's initial stewards.

"The first engineer we had was a great British engineer named Red Davis," Frantz remembers with a laugh. "He had done a lot of work with Eno and had mixed [Talking Heads' 1978 album] *More Songs about Buildings and Food*. We knew Red and we liked him. But after a few days of basic tracks, Red quit. He threw up his hands and said, 'Every time you come up with something that sounds like it might be a popular song, Brian says, "No, that's no good!"'"

Red was right, in a way, about "Once in a Lifetime." The album's first single, it left mainstream radio a tad dumbfounded and didn't even crack the US Top 100, let alone the Top 40. But popularity and greatness are two very different things, and there are few greater songs in the era than this musically visionary and lyrically trenchant piece. And it eventually insinuated its way to classic status, to the point where it has become one of Talking Heads' most well-known tracks, as well as perhaps its most beloved.

By 1980, Talking Heads had already established themselves as fearless and innovative. Although they ran in the same circles as the bands in the nascent New York City–based punk movement of the late 70s, the only characteristic they shared with those groups was a willingness to shake up the status quo. Talking Heads achieved this with songs complex enough to send musicologists scurrying for sources, yet, thanks to the married couple of Frantz on drums and Tina Weymouth on bass, still eminently danceable. Jerry Harrison on guitar also concerned himself more with the groove than any showoff playing, while singer David Byrne was a truly unique frontman, his nebbishy appearance unable to hide his twitchily explosive vocals.

Yet the band wanted to push the boundaries even further with *Remain in Light*. "It was the first set of recordings that we made that had not been written prior to the recordings," Frantz says. "It was also the first time we were ever actually composing in the studio. There was talk that this was something that Miles Davis had done, just recorded bits of music that were later edited together to make songs. That was the approach. The idea was that it was going to be an experiment. And we were gonna see if it worked. Everybody in the band and Brian Eno were on board with that idea."

To pull this off, the band needed a modicum of solitude. Frantz explains,

> We recorded those basic tracks at Compass Point Studios in the Bahamas, where we had worked before. We liked to work there. That was our second time there. We returned because we loved the ambience. It was very conducive to woodshedding. There weren't a lot of distractions. There was the studio and the beach. That was about it.
>
> It wasn't like in New York where you had people dropping by to see what's happening, record company people popping in to make sure they were getting their money's worth. The last thing we wanted was somebody who was going to come in and say, "I don't hear any hits." Those things we did not have to worry about in Nassau.

In terms of "Once in a Lifetime," the band started by jamming away, but not in the sense of trying to immediately work their way to a completed performance. "I wanted to construct parts that didn't necessarily sound like traditional rock-and-roll drum parts," Frantz says. "But I had to construct them in such a way that they were like loops, so that they could be edited at any point. I had no idea where the vocals would be, I had no idea where the verses and choruses would be. So I played parts that were basically human loops. Tina did the same."

All four members and Eno are credited with writing "Once in a Lifetime," and all ideas were considered, including Harrison's late-in-the-game brainstorm. "After we were actually ready to call it a day for the actual recording," Frantz recalls, "Jerry said, 'There's one part that I've always wanted to add on to a song.' It was an organ part that he wanted to lift from a Velvet Underground song called 'What Goes On.' We put that organ part on the outro of the song. And we all thought it sounded great."

From those looplike instrumental parts, Eno and the band could then pick and choose the most effective moments. "When it came to mixing, it was challenging because you didn't have a situation where the songs were already arranged in the way that they were played," Frantz says. "There was a lot of muting and unmuting that had to be done. Flying this part over there and that part over here. It was more challenging than it was on our previous albums. But Brian Eno and Dave Jerden, the engineer, did a great job." (Nineteen-year-old Steven

Stanley also did supplemental engineering on the basic "Once in a Lifetime" track once Red Davis bailed.)

For lyrics, Frantz remembers that Byrne knew he had to rise to the occasion of the impressive instrumentals:

> David said, "Well, I don't have any words right now." He thought, and we had to agree with him, that the tracks were very original and unique and they required very original and unique lyrics and melodies. So when we finished the basic tracks in the Bahamas, there were no vocals. We went back to New York and David took some time off.
>
> According to legend, and I believe it's true, he rented a car and basically drove around the American South and listened to Pentecostal preachers on the radio. Fire and brimstone that you can still hear on certain radio stations in the South, particularly on a Sunday morning. That type of preaching and messaging was the big inspiration for his lyrics on "Once in a Lifetime."

The end result is a song that would have been a winner had Byrne not uttered a word. Frantz's kicky beat anticipates hip-hop, while Weymouth thumps along at gut level. Harrison's synthesizers evoke the aquatic turn that Byrne's lyrics take, while the organ closing part is a fitting finishing touch for such a massive song.

All of that serves as a frame for Byrne's musings on the possibility that one can almost inexplicably find oneself in a life one doesn't recognize. The preacher-like tone of his vocals is contrasted by the existential tenor of his message. Byrne intended it as a commentary on middle-class values, but the song inadvertently touches on a malaise that's anything but exclusive: the feeling the time is ebbing away from your life while you can't get your head above water to stop it. That Eureka moment when Byrne shouts out, "My God, what have I done?" cuts almost terrifyingly deep.

Even though it wasn't bound for hit status, the feeling the song engendered in the band was something that couldn't be taken away. "We're very proud of our work on that record," Frantz recalls. "It's not every day that one experiences such an afterglow."

You might even say it occurs "Once in a Lifetime," but songs this good might be even rarer than that.

"All Out of Love" by Air Supply

LOST IN LOVE (1980)

They had a number of rotating instrumentalists play with them throughout their career, but for all intents and purposes Air Supply was Graham Russell and Russell Hitchcock, with the former often writing the songs and the latter usually singing them. The word "love" featured prominently in many of their song and album titles, but that was just a matter of the duo playing to their strengths. With Russell's knack for heartfelt melody and Hitchcock's acrobatic vocals, they effortlessly delivered both the joy that accompanies love and the agony of being denied it.

Their success in their native Australia was immediate, as they posted charting singles barely a year after they first formed in 1975. Their first attempted crossover to America, however, proved a humbling experience. "In '77, we opened for Rod Stewart on his world tour," Graham Russell remembers. "We thought that it was a no-brainer that we were gonna break, because we'd had so much success in Australia very quickly in the first months of being a band. And we thought, 'Oh, we're unstoppable.' The tour was a great experience for us, but when nothing happened, it brought us way back down to Earth. And I think we needed it at that point."

Air Supply dusted themselves off and kept churning out songs. One of them, "Lost in Love," caught the attention of no less than Clive Davis, leading to an Arista recording contract. In 1980, that breezy track busted down the formerly resistant American doors, rocketing to the top of the pop charts. And this time around, they were not going to let stateside success escape their grip, as it had once before.

"When 'Lost in Love' broke, because of how we were kind of knocked off our perch a little previously, we were ready," Russell explains. "We knew what we had. 'Lost in Love' came, and we knew we had 'All Out of Love' in the can, and we had another half dozen songs that were ready to go. So we were kind of ready for it. Although I must state, I don't think we were ready for the success that was about to explode for us."

That explosion, ignited by "Lost in Love," was further fanned by "All Out of Love," one of the all-time weepers. It's a song that began with Graham Russell putting some piano movers through a difficult day. "I lived in a tiny apartment in Sydney at the time," he recalls. "And I wanted to write a song on piano, but I didn't have one. So I rented this piano. I lived up four flights of stairs, and these guys, they toiled with this piano; it was an upright and it was really heavy. They brought it in. And I ended up just writing one song on it, but that was 'All Out of Love.' I wrote it the same afternoon they delivered it. And I thought, 'Oh, that's great,' but I felt for these guys who did all this work bringing this piano up."

It's unclear whether any of those piano movers realized their place in music history. But it was clear that Russell had written another winner, which ordinarily meant that Hitchcock would be called upon to sing the stuffing out of it. But a division of labor turned out to be the right call for the song. Graham Russell explains,

> Originally Russell [Hitchcock] was supposed to sing it. In those days, he was the lead singer. He still is; he gets the first shot at everything. And I said to him, "You need to sing this song." And I played it for him on piano and he said, "Oh, it's great."
>
> We went in the studio with producer Harry Maslick. It was right in his [Hitchcock's] range, but there was something about it that didn't sound right when he sang it, and he knew it. He said, "Come in here and sing this." And I said, "I can't. It's too high." But I started to sing it and Harry said, "That's it. You've got to sing the verse and Russell [Hitchcock] has to sing the chorus." And, of course, as soon as we put it together, it was just magic.

The fact that Graham Russell has to strain just a bit to hit those notes in the verses actually helps "All Out of Love," playing into the narrator's urgency for a reunion with the girl he's addressing. His anguish is palpable, as he longs to hold on to a memory of the girl because "It would make me believe what tomorrow could bring/When today doesn't really know." As her absence becomes more of a reality he can't change, he pleads desperately, as the music swells, "Please love me or I'll be gone." And then, like a secret weapon waiting in the shadows, Russell Hitchcock emerges for the chorus and starts hitting notes somewhere up in the stratosphere, as the narrator makes his apology and prays it's not too late. There's no need to know the details of the separation; all that's needed is for the duo to conjure vast reserves of sorrow, which they do in gut-wrenching fashion.

There was just one more tweak that needed to be made before the song was ready to conquer America. Clive Davis provided it, gaining a songwriting credit in the process. According to Graham Russell,

> Clive got "Lost in Love" first, which he loved. And he said, "We're gonna go with 'All Out of Love' next, but for the American market, there's a lyric change that needs to happen." And I wasn't very happy about it. It was originally, "I'm all out love/I want to arrest you." In that context, I meant to get one's attention. But he said, "No, in America, people will think getting arrested by the police."
>
> So he said, "What about 'I'm so lost without you?'" This was Clive Davis, and I couldn't say no. And he said to me, "If you make that lyric change, it will be one of the biggest songs of the year." So I said, "Okay, let's do it." And he got credit for that, quite rightly, 'cause it was his line.

Davis proved right; "All Out of Love" rolled to the Top 5, earning cathartic teardrops all the way. And Air Supply was then two songs into a stunning streak of seven straight Top 10 singles, putting them in quite rarefied air. "It was uncharted territory at that time," Graham Russell says. "The only other band to do that at that point was the Beatles. So we were in great company. It gave us a great beginning to a great career, and we're in our forty-second year now. And those early songs are a great part of that. The fact that we've become kind of the romantic band for the world was never by design. It was just the way it happened."

For that brilliant single, they may have been "All Out of Love." But in the 1980s, Air Supply always had a love song to spare.

"(Just Like) Starting Over" by John Lennon

DOUBLE FANTASY (1980)

John Lennon's death in 1980 was one of the most impactful events of the twentieth century, something that stretched beyond the obvious effect that someone's death has on the people who personally know and love the individual. One of the side effects may have been that, by denying the world any hope for a true Beatles reunion, it forced radical innovations in rock and rock-leaning pop music after tentativeness held sway in those genres throughout much of the 70s. Without Lennon, the Beatles could not come riding back in to usher in the same wave of musical energy that the 60s embodied. It's understandable, then, that the British New Wave, the ascendancy of Michael Jackson and Prince, and MTV all pretty much took hold in the immediate months and years after Lennon's death; big events had to fill the mammoth void.

But Lennon left us with one more shining example of what made him so special with the album *Double Fantasy*, a joint effort with his wife Yoko Ono, the two trading off on songs. That what was meant to be his triumphant return turned out to be a bittersweet farewell is one of the harshest ironies music fans have ever had to endure, but at least he went out with something that was benevolent, wise, and worthy of the towering standard of his previous work, with "(Just Like) Starting Over" serving as the perfect reintroduction to his unassuming genius and undeniable charisma.

For the album, Lennon assembled an impressive group of studio veterans to bring his songs to life, including Andy Newmark, who had previously drummed on sessions for big-name artists ranging from Sly Stone to David Bowie. Even though he was getting a call from an ex-Beatle returning to work after being out of the studio for five years, Newmark's experience helped him keep the butterflies at bay. "I don't think there were too many nerves because the players that were there were all asked to participate based on the way they played," Newmark says. "So you're basically getting paid to be yourself."

Newmark had never met Lennon prior to the sessions. What he found when he arrived was a guy who loved being back in the thick of it. "John seemed to be in a very good mood," he says. "I heard in earlier years he was a lot darker when he was getting high, but then, that would apply to anyone, including myself. He seemed very upbeat, happy, and straight as an arrow. Aware, awake, tuned-in, and just really excited to be making music again. And that was quite contagious and spread to all of us."

The drummer also remembers that Lennon was very hands-off with the players, although he did give Newmark one specific piece of instruction: "His overall direction to me in general was 'Andy, play like Ringo.' And you couldn't give me clearer instructions than that because I knew how he played and it was very familiar to the way I approached drumming. So I had my overall remit for the entire session: Keep it simple and play like Ringo. He said, 'Ringo is my favorite drummer.'"

"(Just Like) Starting Over" is an example of Lennon's unique ability to bring what he was hearing in his head to bear, even if it may not have jibed with typical pop song structures. The song begins with a dreamy solo section, kicks into a bluesy, Fats Domino–like shuffle, incorporates that opening into the main beat, endures a false ending, then triumphantly returns for the fade-out, Lennon's vocal soaring into falsetto exultation. As a result, what could have been a straightforward track turns into something much more satisfying.

Newmark was a key component in this process. His snapping snare drums serve as the bridge from the intro to the first verse. And his mini-solo also heralds the song's closing moments, although he was aided by some snare drum sampling, something he always cops to when asked. "A lot of people say to me, 'Wow, that fill you played. It was like you had a third hand or something.' And I have to say, 'It wasn't me, brother.' There was a third hand, and it was manufactured after the fact."

Lennon, never the one to let things get overly somber, also seemed to be channeling a hero of his in the vocal. "There was evidence from day one that he was doing his Elvis Presley impersonation in that song," Newmark recalls. "When he does that 'Well-a, well-a, well-a,' it's no secret that it's clearly Elvis."

Newmark says that Lennon didn't even realize just what he had in the song:

> When we went into the control to hear it, we were just there in front of the mixing console listening to the playback. And I think everyone will agree it's quite a perky, funky little groove. It has like a snap-your-fingers, sexy shake-your-hips groove to it that's quite sassy. Different than all the other songs on the record.
>
> I remember listening back to it and the playback was over and I looked at John and said, "This is special." Because, as a drummer, it had a vibe to it, setting aside the song's content. If you took the

vocals off that track, it's still really grooving. So I was getting off on it in my own particular self-centered way. He looked at me and said, "Really, you think so?"

"(Just Like) Starting Over" is fascinating for how it manages to be nostalgic and eschew nostalgia all at once. Lennon references the early days of his love affair with Ono but also makes clear that things have changed, albeit for the better. "We have grown," he sings in the opening moments, twice as if to emphasize it. It's one of the most directly affecting songs he ever did as a solo artist, free of any burden to change the world, just two people "falling in love again."

Of course, Lennon was too savvy not to know that people would hear it many other ways. There was the obvious import of this being his return to the public eye for the first time in what seemed like an eternity, especially in an era when rock stars were expected to churn out product on the regular. And Newmark says that it seemed Lennon was indeed leaning toward truly revving up his career again, and not just because he, Ono, and the band recorded enough material for almost two complete albums in their month or so together in the studio (the extra tracks would appear on the posthumous release *Milk and Honey* in 1983); Lennon was also hinting at a fuller schedule in the near future.

"He definitely wanted to be active again," Newmark says. "He talked about going out and playing. And threw it out very lightly to us in a noncommittal way, 'Would you guys be up for going out and playing live?' He was thinking he wanted to get into it again. He was having fun."

That we were deprived of that possibility is one of the myriad tragedies attached to Lennon's death. Context makes "(Just Like) Starting Over" sound quite different than what it was intended to be. John Lennon meant that he was getting ready to start over with his music, his fans, and, most of all, his wife. Now we hear the title as what we all somehow had to find the strength to do in the wake of losing him.

"Take It Easy on Me" by Little River Band

TIME EXPOSURE (1981)

Some people might consider the Australian collective Little River Band an odd choice for a book highlighting the songs and artists of the 80s. After all, they are often associated with the previous decade, in part because they indeed had some big hits in that era, highlighted by "Cool Change" and "Reminiscing," songs that lived on the more laid-back part of the musical spectrum that one might associate with the 70s.

But their run of thirteen Top 40 hits in a nine-year stretch took them from 1975 to 1983. They even put together a span in 1981 and 1982 of four straight singles in the Top 15, including "Take It Easy on Me," the song being profiled here, at number 10. It's worth noting that their music in the 80s possessed a tougher musical feel, no doubt allowing them to ride the wave away from the softer side that was falling out of vogue.

Another reason that Little River Band doesn't quite seem like an 80s band is that, in an era where personality was everything, they were a largely faceless group. They churned through members at a pretty high rate for a hit band, and they traded off the writing and singing responsibilities so that there wasn't any true frontman in the group. The one defining characteristic found on all their best tracks was the prominent featuring of their pristine vocal harmonies.

The band steered clear of trendiness and just churned out singles that were mercilessly free of flab and delivered the intended message with no-frills efficiency, while those harmonies cast a golden glow on all of it. For 1981's *Time Exposure* album, by which point the band featured founding members Graeham Goble, Beeb Birtles, Glenn Shorrock, and Derek Pellicci along with Wayne Nelson and David Briggs, Little River Band even had the chance to be produced by someone who knew a little something about groups with nice vocal blends: George Martin.

The esteemed Beatles producer's reputation helped get him the gig, as did his preferred location for working. "Somehow we met George backstage at one of our gigs and put it to him to produce the next album because we were looking around," Graeham Goble remembers. "We were aware that he had just opened the AIR Studios in Montserrat. There had been Paul McCartney, the Police, and Stevie Wonder before us that recorded there. We were about the fourth or fifth band in there. And so we just liked the idea. Because at that point we were all married with children and things, we liked the idea of going away onto an island, concentrating on the band and recording."

Goble was one of the group's chief songwriters, and he had penned "The Night Owls," the first hit single to come from *Time Exposure*. While writing and performing for a band at the top of their game might have seemed like a great position to inhabit, he was actually struggling. "I was going through incredible amounts of personal issues both at home and in the band," Goble remembers. "It was tough, because there's no rest from it. You're in the band 24/7, and you have to deal with the personal issues. And then you've got to be creative, although the creativity saves your head, it keeps you sane. I also wasn't in a happy marriage at that point."

Often songwriters channel inner turmoil into their material, which is what occurred when Goble churned out "Take It Easy on Me." "I think it sort of all mixed in, with the personal relationship and the situation in the band," he says. "Because I had as much frustration in the band as I did in my personal life."

One of the band issues was a growing fissure between Goble and Shorrock, who was as close to a lead singer as the band possessed. Goble was writing more songs tailored for Wayne Nelson because he felt Nelson had a better range, and Shorrock was vetoing most of the songs that Goble was writing. It became so divisive that a third party was needed to make the decisions. "We got to the point where the producer would pick the songs," Goble remembers.

Ironically enough, that situation actually ended up working in the favor of "Take It Easy on Me":

> I had written "Take It Easy on Me" and "The Night Owls" with Wayne's voice in mind. The first vocal to go on "Take It Easy on Me" was Wayne's, because he had sung "The Night Owls." George Martin felt that Glenn should put a vocal on it as well. So we had two lead vocals and both were mixed and both were sent to the record company.
>
> The record company chose Glenn's version, which I strongly opposed. I even went and had a meeting with the head of Capitol to say that I didn't agree. But now, in retrospect, I was completely wrong and they were right. Glenn's version is infinitely better. It's got more soul and was a big component in it becoming successful.

But Nelson wasn't completely out of the picture, as his higher range was suited to the high-arcing melody of the bridge. "Some of the middle eights in songs can be the most exciting parts," Goble muses. "I think in this particular song, the middle eight really kicks the song into another gear."

The song also benefits from a unique arrangement, as it begins with just piano player Peter Jones and singer Shorrock performing the opening verse as if it were a torch song. It makes the moment when those harmonies arrive even more special. "When I'm writing something, I can hear the harmonies already there," Goble says. "That's what gives a chorus some lift. In a chorus, there's gotta be a lift. And when you have a band that could harmonize like we could, it just makes it so much easier."

You could look all day to find some fault with the construction of "Take It Easy on Me," and you'd be left wanting. As great as those harmonies are, Shorrock centers the song with his lead vocal, both proud and wounded. Goble's lyrics succinctly convey that awful period when a relationship is imploding, as the narrator prepares to go off on that "minstrel road," knowing that occasionally his brave facade will crumble without his love by his side.

"Be kind to each other" is Goble's explanation for the song's ultimate message. "That's really what you want. Let's try and acknowledge the good times and the fact that it's falling part. Just take it easy on me. It's a plea."

Little River Band eventually tailed off, perhaps due more to the continued exodus of key band members than anything else. After all, impeccable songs like "Take It Easy on Me" are largely immune to the whims of changing tastes. Graeham Goble believes that the longevity of their best work is due to that time-tested combination of skill and hard work.

"I think it is a testament to the incredible talent of the band members," Goble says. "We took so much care on everything from the kick drum to the high hat pattern to the bass. Which meant hours and hours and hours of making sure that every component of a record was adding to it, not just fluff around the place. It was really important that it contributed to the arrangement. And I think we made some timeless records, records that will live for many, many years."

"Jessie's Girl" by Rick Springfield

WORKING CLASS DOG (1981)

Although it arrived more than a year into the decade, "Jessie's Girl" feels like one of the first smash hit songs to truly represent and even define the music of the 80s as fans of that era would come to know it. It was devoid of any of the lifelessness of some of the more soporific 70s soft rock or the beats-without-a-soul issues plaguing the laziest disco. Passion and dynamism are the main traits of this 1981 killer, a song that pulls you in close and then blows you away.

"Bette Davis Eyes," a song that barely preceded it in the top spot on the *Billboard* charts, could make a similar claim as an 80s standard bearer, ironic since Kim Carnes had built her career up in the previous decade. The Australian man who made "Jessie's Girl" was also a celebrity of sorts in the 70s. Rick Springfield's early recording career included some successful singles, especially in his home country, but had stalled by the turn of the decade, in part because of his struggles to define himself as a mature artist while saddled with a youngish fan base. He even took up acting in case things didn't turn around.

And so, as Springfield explains today, he decided it was time for a drastic change. "I was pretty sure, after six years of teen magazine coverage, that the world didn't need to hear another Rick Springfield album," he says. "Punk was just exploding and guitars were starting to be heard on the radio again as disco, and ballads, while not dead yet, were coughing up blood. So I set about writing my version of punk: two-minute-and-thirty-second songs that were fast and furious."

He also initially thought that his next album would be one best suited for a collaboration with a small band, inspired as he was by the songwriting chops and stripped-down approach of burgeoning artists like Elvis Costello and the Police. But an unexpected breakout acting stint on *General Hospital* changed his plans. "It was my intent to release *Working Class Dog* as a band project so as to avoid any bad taste in anyone's mouth form the whole TeenBeat fiasco," Springfield recalls. "But I happened to land a dopey soap opera gig just before the record's release and I was starting to get a little attention from that. So I changed it back to a solo record at the last minute."

The song that emerged as his signature emanated, as many great songs do, from a case of unrequited affection. "I hadn't had much record success and was thinking about some other career to make up the financial difference between life and what I was making as a musician," Springfield remembers. "Unbelievably, I thought that becoming a stained-glass artisan would make up that difference. Naive shit for sure. I started going to a stained glass–making class in Pasadena in 1979, and there was a girl there who was hot and got my motor running, but she had a boyfriend and didn't have any time for me. So I went home and wrote a song about her from the perspective of my sexual angst."

Springfield doesn't get enough credit for the clever way in which the lyrics to "Jessie's Girl" unfold. He lays down all of the particulars by the end of the first verse: the girl, the guy, and the lust-struck narrator watching helplessly in the wings. From there, it's a matter of righteously defending his qualifications ("I've been funny, I've been cool with the lines") even when undercutting them somewhat ("moot" is not a word you would expect to hear out of a smooth lothario's mouth). He tortures himself with imaginings of what they're doing when they're alone in the frantic build to the chorus, which then charges ahead with power chords blazing, a lashing-out that's ultimately ineffectual.

As for the music, it's important to note that Springfield made detailed demos of his newest songs. His process indirectly led to the quiet-loud dynamic that predated grunge, the genre that often gets credit for that approach, by about a decade:

> I did pretty thorough demos on my TEAC 4-track, even using pillows for drums and a pawn shop bass, so the song arrangement and dynamics were already in the demo. I'd been heading towards the small verse/big chorus thing for a while and it crystalized with "Jessie's Girl," I think. Some of that was due to my low-fi recording techniques, because I wanted all the choruses to explode. The only way to do that on my limited equipment was to totally break the verses down, so that when the cushions and the bass kicked in, it had a bigger impact.

The impact "Jessie's Girl" left on the listening public was undeniable, as it slow-built its way to the top, something that surprised its creator even after he received positive feedback about it from recording studio employees. "I thought it sounded really good and modern, for 1980, but the real shift came when people around Sound City started saying how much they liked the song," Springfield says. "That didn't really happen with studio personnel. So I thought we might have something, but I wasn't overly optimistic, having had three previous albums that had flopped. I was surprised when it took off. It wasn't the selected single, but radio DJs started playing it because they liked the song, and RCA was kind of pressured into releasing it as a single."

Much has also been made of the fact that "Jessie's Girl" was the number 1 song at the time that MTV made its debut, but connecting one to the other is a stretch. As Springfield says about the video, which he storyboarded himself, "I honestly didn't see the point of a video, as there was no MTV, but it was one of those serendipitous things that just was the right thing at the right time. It looks so cheap and cheesy to me now, but I think that's part of its charm."

Regardless of what the reasons ultimately were, "Jessie's Girl" lent Springfield the kind of renown he'd begun to doubt he would ever achieve on the musical side of his career. "I'd been a fan of so many bands and read all about them, so I knew how that first big song can launch a career," he says. "I was starting to think I might not have one in me after a bunch of failed attempts, but it was not so. I am very persistent and I think that had a lot to do with any success I have had. I went down but I never went out for the full ten count."

Amazingly, Springfield never has been able to track down the mystery girl who inspired the song, even with some pretty impressive folks trying to help. ("Oprah got close," he muses.) Wherever she might be, she jump-started a song that became a signifier for an entire decade, a decade he proudly defends, odd appearances notwithstanding. "I think the haircuts put people off. Oh, and the ridiculous clothes," he laughs, before admitting, "It was exciting, experimental, bombastic, cool, and amazing to be a part of."

And an integral part, at that.

"Bette Davis Eyes" by Kim Carnes

MISTAKEN IDENTITY (1981)

Irony of ironies, the song that many consider to be the unofficial kick-off of 80s pop music in America (although I contend that it shares that title with Rick Springfield's "Jessie's Girl") was written in 1974 and eventually recorded by an artist that made her bones in the soft-rock 70s. But Kim Carnes had ears venturing into the future when she made "Bette Davis Eyes" a single for the ages in 1981.

The song was written by Donna Weiss and Jackie DeShannon; DeShannon, known for being a 60s hitmaker as well as a pioneering female songwriter, released her version in 1974. What you hear when you listen to that take on "Bette Davis Eyes" is something light and bouncy, distinguished by saloon-style piano but lacking any of the danger and intrigue that the song would eventually possess once Carnes got a hold of it.

One wonders if the musical landscape might have been altered that much more quickly if Carnes had recorded the song when she first intended, on 1980's *Romance Dance* album. "I immediately loved the lyric," Carnes remembers. "I just thought, 'This is brilliant.' The way in which it was recorded was very different. It was not in a minor key, like we eventually made it, and it was up-tempo. I knew I would want to change that drastically, but the lyrics just killed me. I didn't have to listen twice to know how special and how cool it was."

But her producer at the time had been trying to acquire some of the publishing from Weiss and DeShannon, which scuttled the deal. A year later, Weiss explained to Carnes what had occurred and asked if she'd like to record the song for her 1981 album *Mistaken Identity*. She jumped at the chance, but then ran into problems trying to transform the somewhat tame original into what she was hearing in her head. "I was very much into what was going on in Britain," Carnes explains. "I've always loved synthesizers. And I loved all the sounds coming out of there, all these English groups, I loved their records. That was instrumental in not only the song, the album, and the next album, but also the video was inspired by the New Romantic movement in England."

Carnes and her band toiled for three days trying to find that sound, until finally a breakthrough arrived. "Bill Cuomo, my beyond-brilliant keyboard player, was working on the Prophet, which was a wonderful analog keyboard," Carnes recalls. "He was kind of by himself rehearsing all these days and finally he came up with the signature lick. And I looked at him and went, 'Oh my God! That's it!' The rest of the band knew now we were onto something."

The other elements fell together thanks to a misheard instruction. Carnes explains,

> I asked the band, "You know the 'Cars' record?" And I meant the record by Gary Numan called "Cars." There was a keyboard lick that went throughout the record. And Craig Kramph, my drummer, thought I meant the group the Cars. He ran out of the room, came back with the Synare, which became the trash drum.
>
> And then Goldie [Steve Goldstein], my other keyboard player, came up with a really cool signature lick a la the Gary Numan record. My whole band were so brilliant and they all were so into taking it in this dark minor [key] direction. What they played was brilliant and we knew by the end of the day we'd found a way to cut it. We went in the studio and the record is the second take, all live, live vocal.

That record is a prime example of how writing the song is only half the battle. "Bette Davis Eyes" is a sketch of a character, who, in DeShannon's version, sounds bawdy but is ultimately harmless, not someone who is going to leave a lasting impact beyond the first night together. Carnes, inspired by the cold mystery of the music, turns her into someone much more alluring. Her vocals, somewhat spaced-out in the verses yet full and passionate in the chorus, make the references to Garbo and Davis sound not like Golden Era tributes but testaments to how those women were compellingly ahead of their time. The narrator's words, ostensibly meant to warn you away from this girl, only pull you in closer.

Carnes didn't have to wait long for positive feedback about the song. "People who were working in the studio on other projects, we'd play it for them," she remembers. "And then they would come back every night and say, 'I want my fix. Could you play it again for me?' Everybody who heard it beforehand said, 'Do you know how huge this is?'"

Oddly enough, the brain trust at EMI seemed to be the only ones unimpressed by it. "My record company were the first people who didn't feel that way," she says. "And I was given every excuse under the sun, like, 'The public won't buy a lyric by a woman singing about another woman.' Other people said, 'It's not you.' I heard, 'The trash drum will never get played on the radio.' I said, 'Put it all on me. I'll take the full responsibility. Please release this.' I begged every day because I thought if I didn't, somebody else is gonna hear it, do it, and it'll just be horrendous if I lose this. So finally, I think they got tired of me begging."

There are big hits and then there are songs like "Bette Davis Eyes," which launch into another atmosphere. It spent eight weeks on top of the American pop charts, even dipping to number 2 at one point before returning to the summit. "As a songwriter, I'd written hits for other people, I had hits on my own," Carnes says. "But this record had a life of its own. And what it did was open up the world to me. It just was such a huge record everyplace."

Meanwhile, Bette Davis, perhaps shockingly to some considering her Grande Dame image, enjoyed the notoriety the song brought. "We developed the most wonderful friendship, a surprise that I never could have imagined," Carnes says. "She wrote a letter asking, 'How did you know so much about me?' Here she is, this gigantically huge movie star, and she said, 'Finally, this got my grandson's attention. He thinks I'm pretty cool.' When the record went platinum, I took over an album and she got up on a ladder, got a hammer and nail, and put it up on the wall. She was just so wonderful to me and she really loved the record, appreciated what it was and how it made her feel."

That's "Bette Davis Eyes" in a nutshell: lyrically looking back to icons of the first half of the twentieth century, musically insinuating its way into the future, and overall finding a sweet spot between that helped launch the decade of its present.

"Lunatic Fringe" by Red Rider

AS FAR AS SIAM (1981)

The debate about whether or not pop music, in all its various permutations, should tackle serious issues or just stick to frivolity is one that likely won't be settled anytime soon. What can't be debated is that, if you are going to do it, you should do it right. And "Lunatic Fringe," the 1981 stunner dropped by the Canadian band Red Rider that actually came up against that age-old debate in its own way, does it thrillingly right. It addresses societal plagues that, sadly, never go out of fashion, but leaves us believing, if only for the time the song is blasting through the speakers, that we have it within ourselves to conquer those plagues once and for all.

Red Rider was far from a household name in the United States when they released their second album, *As Far as Siam*, in 1981. According to Tom Cochrane, the band's lead vocalist and chief songwriter, their goal at the time was similar to many other up-and-coming bands: just make it to the next album intact. "With every record you made, you were like applying for a job," Cochrane says. "You write the songs, you record the songs, you produce the records. You go out and you tour. You finish up the record and you hope you have enough of a hit with that record that it validates you carrying on with your job to make another one. And luckily we did [with their 1979 debut, *Don't Fight It*]. It was enough to justify us carrying on."

As he began writing the songs for the second album by Red Rider (whose other members at the time were Ken Greer, Jeff Jones, Peter Boynton, and Rob Baker), Cochrane took a cue from some reading material that had intrigued him:

> I read a book by Raoul Wallenberg, and I eventually gave him a tribute in the liner notes. He was a Swedish diplomat who helped well over ten thousand Jewish people escape [during World War II] by forging documents and whatnot. He was captured after the war by

31

the Soviets. They couldn't believe that somebody would be helping in the way that he was, so he ended up in a Gulag.

He was part of the inspiration for it, but the song kind of came from a lot of places. It came from my attitude about racism, about violence, those who abuse their power and position and affect democracy. And it has a defiant edge to it because it talks about how we're not gonna let this happen again.

"Lunatic Fringe" speaks directly to the kind of unsavory element that lurks on the edges of society, hoping to ultimately upheave it by gathering enough like-minded individuals into a powerful group. But the song lets them know that the jig is up: "I can hear you coming," Cochrane sings. "I know what you're after/We're wise to you this time." Cochran is astute about what would drive a person to such terrible thoughts and plans: "Cause you've got to blame someone/ For your own confusion." The final words let the "Lunatic Fringe" know that they're in for a fight: "Can you feel the resistance/Can you feel the thunder?"

Cochrane explains that it was important that the song leave listeners with an inspired feeling at the end of it. "It wasn't nihilistic," he says. "The irony is it's positive in a way. It's saying the good will eventually overcome the bad stuff. And that's the positive thing that I hope people get out of it."

The lyrics alone were a great foundation, but Cochrane needed music to rise to the defiant challenge of the words. He had three inspirations for the instrumental part of the song: composer Aaron Copland's "Fanfare for the Common Man" (for the thundering connecting sections), JJ Cale's guitar work (for the main riff underpinning the verses), and the post-Beatles work of John Lennon (for the bluesy rhythms the song conjures).

Speaking of Lennon, his death came when "Lunatic Fringe" was being demoed; many people would hear the finished song and think that Red Rider was referring to his killer with the title. The shock of it caused both record label higher-ups and Cochrane to rethink whether the song was worth it. Cochrane remembers,

The record company and everybody was saying, "Let's forget about this. Just write some pop songs. We'll get on with making some money." And so I was going through a bit of a crisis of identity at that point. I thought, "Well, okay, maybe they're right."

But [Lennon's death] was one of those things that really hit me hard. I thought here's a guy, with all the success, all the stuff he had gone through, he wore his heart on his sleeve. He called it the way he saw it. And that's what an artist is. I didn't think the song would see the light of day. But I said, "For better or for worse, this song is gonna stand the way it is. Because this is how I feel, and this is what I want to say."

Some technical difficulties nearly felled "Lunatic Fringe" before it could be released. "When I was driving from Vancouver to Toronto with my girlfriend, I was listening to the cassette [of the album]," Cochrane remembers. "I said, 'Something's wrong with this.' There was some crackling on there. It turns out the master tape started to oxidize and fall apart. So we had to totally rerecord it in Los Angeles, which was a huge expense. I was depressed because we'd spent all this time and money on this record and we had to do it again because of some bad tape."

The snafu actually turned into a positive, however, especially in terms of the contributions made by Los Angeles–based session keyboardist Peter Wolf to the song's unforgettable opening moments. "The basic parts were there, and we had initially done it on a Minimoog," says Cochrane. "And it was kind of primitive how we had done it, even if there was a certain charm to it. So Peter Wolf came in. He listened to what we had. And he kind of took this stuff and pumped fifty pounds of air in it, worked his magic."

That intro, which has become the fodder for stadiums, arenas, and any-where a crowd needs energizing, sets the tone for "Lunatic Fringe." It's like the sound track for some sci-fi/western hybrid where the hero is preparing for his final showdown in a vast wasteland. And Tom Cochrane realizes that it's a show-down that—metaphorically, anyway—keeps playing out in the world, which is why Red Rider's classic endures.

"Maybe it needs to be heard more," Cochrane says of the song. "It's one of those things that's bad and good. The song at least gives us a feeling of empow-erment. But it's unfortunate that stuff carries on that way. We have a hard time getting along on this crazy planet of ours. In the music lies a certain amount of documentation, a time line of our lives. Sometimes we're documenting history, and sometimes history keeps repeating itself, so you have to keep reminding people to be vigilant about that."

And as for the way "Lunatic Fringe" overcame the initial skepticism: "Very often the stuff where everybody says, 'No that's not gonna happen. You can't do that,' those are the songs and that is the art that actually hits home. It seems to make an impression on people and the times. So you always have to follow that inner voice, no matter how lonely it gets."

"Baby, Come to Me" by
Patti Austin and James Ingram
EVERY HOME SHOULD HAVE ONE (1981)

The 80s proved a wonderful decade for duets, perhaps the apex era for that unique pop-song art form where two vocal points of view make more of a lyric than one could possibly manage. Right at the beginning of the decade, "Endless Love," by Diana Ross and Lionel Richie, set the tone with an emotive, histrionic style that swung for the fences at every step. Just a few years later, "Baby, Come to Me" played it a little bit cooler and yet turned up the heat all at once, soaring to the top of the pop charts.

Although they were surrounded by proven greatness, with Quincy Jones as producer and Rod Temperton as songwriter, the two singers responsible for it, Patti Austin and James Ingram, came in with track records that didn't exactly portend huge pop success. Austin, for one, wasn't even sure that she wanted such a thing:

> I never really aspired to major stardom. I'm a private person. I love what I do; I've been doing it since I'm four years old. I have worked with everybody in the world. Dinah Washington is my godmother and Quincy Jones is my godfather. And I grew up looking at people in show business and I saw the ravages of what the industry can be. I realized that there were aspects of it I adored and other aspects of it that I was going to try to avoid. So "Baby Come to Me" was not anything I was particularly lusting after. I was not one of those people that sat around and said, "Oh my God, I wish I could make a hit."

As a matter of fact, Austin was content with a lucrative gig singing jingles at the time she was making her 1981 album *Every Home Should Have One*. As for her duet-mate, Austin recalls sitting with Jones listening to demos when one in particular, written by the legendary songwriting team of Barry Mann and Cynthia Weil, struck them, both for the quality of the song and for the powerhouse

34

vocalist bringing it to life. "That's all Quincy," Austin remembers. "He called Cynthia and said, 'Yes, I want the song and who is that guy singing the demo?' 'Oh, that's James Ingram.'"

From that point, Jones decided that it was time to bring in his ace song-writer to make the connection foolproof. Temperton had already proved an unerring writer of suave rhythm and blues, scoring first with the band Heatwave on "Boogie Nights" and "Always and Forever" before Jones hooked him up with Michael Jackson for the *Off the Wall* album and the massive single "Rock with You." Jones and Temperton developed such a rapport that it was a simple request that put the pieces of "Baby, Come to Me" all together. "Quincy went to Rod and said, 'I want you to write a duet for Patti and James,'" Austin says. "And I'd never met James. Quincy said, 'I just know this is gonna work. It's gonna be like King Kong and Fay Wray.' Quincy's magnificence lies in his abil-ity to brilliantly cast everything."

"Baby, Come to Me" is all about the slow burn, that intensity that lies below the surface of the most loving couples and ignites when the two are all alone. Temperton's construction is brilliant in the way that it plays up the triumph of this relationship by first calling to mind the lonely times before the union, hence the very first line: "Thinking back in time, when love was only in my mind." It is this knowledge that spurs these two on to never take their romance for granted.

In the hands of less confident performers, "Baby, Come to Me" easily could have become overwrought. But Austin and Ingram underplay the two verses, giving the insinuating melody room to work its magic. By the time the bridge rolls around, they finally uncoil, and when Austin sings, "Don't talk anymore," it's a sign that the passion between these two will speak louder than any words they could possibly say to describe their feelings.

Even with the embarrassment of riches that "Baby, Come to Me" enjoyed with Jones and Temperton behind the scenes and Austin and Ingram on the mike, the song nearly suffered an ignominious fate. "We cut the song and the song came out and the song died," Austin says. "I'd say the record was out for two or three weeks, and in those days that's what you got. You got two or three weeks to live or die after release date. In those days, they were working the prod-uct pretty good, because they were trying to keep Quincy happy at that time. But it dies and it goes away. Maybe a month passes and we've all said, 'Next!' I think Quincy was harboring a little hostility because he felt it was a really strong record."

But fate luckily intervened in the form of Luke and Laura, the 1980s-era hero and heroine of the hugely successful soap opera *General Hospital*. A radio station in Miami recapped the show's exploits and began playing the first eight bars of "Baby, Come to Me" as an introduction. Radio station listeners started requesting the song and the single sold copies rapidly in Miami.

Yet Austin still had to overcome some record company reluctance to get the song over the hump by making a little investment in herself. "Freddie DeMann, my manager at the time, goes to Warner's and says, 'You've got to rerelease this record.' And they said, 'Absolutely not. It came out once and failed. It's gonna cost $50,000 and we don't want to spend this kind of money.'" DeMann asked Austin if the two could split the costs and pay for the rerelease, insisting they had a number 1 record on their hands. Despite some initial worries ("That's a lot of jingles, my friend," Austin remembers thinking), she agreed, and the manager's prediction was borne out.

Austin never made too much of an effort to follow up the success of "Baby, Come to Me," at least in terms of a pop career. "I'd already seen everybody on the hamster wheel and nobody ever survived the hamster wheel," she admits. "And if they did, they were such a hot mess by the end of it, there was not a whole lot to function with."

Luckily, she stuck around on that wheel long enough for her to join Ingram on that sultriest of 80s duets. "I've been singing that song at least three times a month since 1984," Austin says. "It's always kind of like floating on air."

"Don't Stop Believin'" by Journey

ESCAPE (1981)

The 1980s were a prime time for rocking troubadours who identified with the hopes and dreams of their audience and aimed resonant stories at them with their songs. This everyman quality helped make top-selling artists like Bruce Springsteen, John Mellencamp, and Tom Petty critical darlings as well. But with all due respect to those gentlemen, no song in the 80s captured the inner lives of its fans any better than "Don't Stop Believin'" by Journey, a group that was denied that same kind of critical love even as they rolled out hit after crowd-pleasing hit.

Journey had evolved from its jammy origins in San Francisco to become more radio-friendly as the 70s wore on, especially once they handed the microphone to belter supreme Steve Perry. But Perry and guitarist and founding member Neal Schon (other members were drummer Steve Smith and bassist Ross Valory) still felt they needed a course correction, which they hoped Jonathan Cain, a keyboardist formerly of the Babys might provide. And Cain identified what he thought were issues to be addressed.

"I saw the band going a little bit more piano-synth-oriented," Cain says. "I thought the organ was kind of done, let that be the old sound. And I thought the lyrics were kind of precious. I said, 'We need to sing to these people who love you guys. You're not singing about their lives.' I went in there with that and they received it all."

The songwriting troika of Cain, Schon, and Perry immediately hit it off in the studio and churned out much of the material that would make up 1981's *Escape*, including songs like "Who's Crying Now" and "Open Arms," which would become huge hits. But Perry still wanted a little something more, and he asked Cain to go back to his songwriting notebooks to see if there was anything there.

"I went back and I found something my father said to me when I was struggling in Hollywood," Cain remembers. "He said, 'Don't stop believing.' And I had written that as a big title on a page. I looked at the title that night and said, 'Steve Perry would sing this.' So I sat up there with my little Wurlitzer. I remember there was a little skylight and the stars were above me. I was looking up and the melody came to me. 'Don't stop believing/Hold on to the feeling.' I didn't know what the rest of it was. It was basically just the chorus and the chords."

What followed was an example of how a songwriting team-up should work, each member bringing something unique and special to the table:

> I brought it in the next day and showed it to them. Perry said, "I love those chords. And I love the vibe. Let's work on it." Perry was kind of leading the process and he said, "Why don't you play those chords and change the way you play them? Why don't you do your Jonathan Cain thing, that thing you do in the Babys, those rolling chords?" So I started playing them and then Neal, listening to it, came up with the bass line and showed it to Ross. So we had this loop going and Perry starts yodeling on top of it, like he could do, just coming out of the blue with a melody.
>
> We get the melody kind of hammered out and I said, "Well, what about the chorus now?" And Steve said, "No, we're gonna do something else here." So Neal came up with more chords for the next part [which would become the "Strangers waiting up and down the boulevard" connecting section]. And I said, "Chorus now, Steve?" And he said, "No, not now." So we had done a verse, a turnaround, another verse and still no chorus. Then we get to the end of the second verse and he says, "Now we're gonna play the chorus but we're not gonna sing it." I said, "This is ridiculous." But he said, "Neal, play the melody." So we do the whole chorus, no singing, just Neal playing this melody on guitar. I thought this was the craziest form, but I started to follow it and I started to see where this was going. Steve wanted the big payoff. So he said, "Now we're gonna sing the chorus."

The structure that Perry imagined brilliantly delayed gratification, to the extent that when the singer does come charging in with the chorus in the song's closing moments, it's breathtaking. Next came the lyrics, which Cain helped to unlock based on Schon's playing. "I was thinking about this bit on the tape where Neil's guitar sounds like a train," Cain says. "I said, 'Steve, this sounds like a train. I love that song "Midnight Train to Georgia." What if it was a midnight train going anywhere?' The light went on."

Cain and Perry then concocted a tale they both knew well as struggling artists themselves once upon a time. "I see this song being about two kids in Hollywood who meet each other on Sunset Boulevard," Cain remembers telling his songwriting partner. "They're both going to chase down a dream. And when they arrive, it's like a menagerie. I used to live in Laurel Canyon, and I used it to see every dreamer show up on Friday night trying to make a deal. This is the scene. And immediately Steve got on board with me."

The band chose Detroit as the hometown for the kids because it was a location where the band was extremely popular. (And, yes, Cain knows there technically is no South Detroit, but it sounded good.) Once complete, Journey couldn't wait for fans to hear this track. "It was so special that we opened up the *Escape* album with it," Cain explains. "We felt like, 'This is the new sound of Journey.' We went right for the throat with it. I was always fond of it, because putting that needle down and hearing that piano come up, it was like opening a book."

"Don't Stop Believin'" marvelously manages to incorporate both triumph and tragedy in its tale. The song ends before we know whether or not this pair makes it in the big city. It might not even matter; for people "living just to find emotion," any emotion will do, even heartbreak. And the song suggests that even if some people end up on the losing end, simply the act of going for it is a victory in itself. That idea can be heard in the crackling emotion in Perry's voice and in Schon's guitar, heroic and elegiac all at once.

"Don't Stop Believin'" only reached number 9 at the time of its release, which is somewhat surprising considering how it is now generally considered among the decade's best handful of songs. Its second life, however, demonstrates the kind of impact it possesses, whether inspiring the plot of the successful musical *Rock of Ages* or, unforgettably, scoring the closing moments of Tony Soprano's saga.

For Jonathan Cain, the staying power of the song he and Journey created can be put down to a simple notion. "It's a song that gives you permission to dream," Cain says. "It is a movie. It will go on and on. And things will be all right if you make it or you don't."

In other words, hold on to that feeling.

"867-5309/Jenny" by Tommy Tutone

TOMMY TUTONE 2 (1981)

Has there ever been a phone number so ingrained in the public consciousness as 867-5309? Any unlucky soul who has ever been saddled with the number since the 80s has likely been barraged by wise-guy prank callers asking if there is a "Jenny" on the premises. If you were a music fan in the 80s, chances are you knew this number better than your grandparents' or your best friend's.

Of course, none of this would have transpired were it not for a plucky band out of San Francisco sporting bar band energy and New Wave hooks at the turn of the 1980s. When they recorded "867-5309/Jenny" in 1981, Tommy Tutone—consisting of Tommy Heath, Jim Keller, Jon Lyons, and Victor Carberry—were coming off a self-titled debut album released a year earlier that included a single ("Angel Say No") that squeaked into the Top 40 at *Billboard*. As Keller remembers, even this modest success had them pumped. "That was still at that point where major radio stations still had the flexibility to play whatever they wanted," Keller says. "In that little world, we were one of the darling bands at that point. We had just enough success that there was excitement. And we were young. So there was a lot of optimism going into the second record. It wasn't like we had our tail between our legs. We were very excited about where we were headed."

Heath and Keller often wrote the band's songs together, but they would occasionally collaborate with others outside the group for material as well. Alex Call, formerly of the band Clover, was one of those others, and he had the bare bones of "867-5309/Jenny" worked out when Keller arrived for a particular writing session. "I arrived one day and Alex had this riff that he was playing," Keller says. "He had the structure and he had the phone number. We just started jamming it, playing with it and having fun with it. The thing that I have to say about that song is that, from the very beginning, it was instantly fun. There was something about that progression that was just fun to play. And I think that clearly that is still true or else people wouldn't be listening to it anymore."

Next came the words, which originally leaned to the vulgar side of things due to the songwriters' sense of humor, at least until the potential for the song became clear. According to Keller,

> In the beginning, we wrote a bunch of words that were kind of funny, 'cause we didn't really take it seriously. Anything to make ourselves laugh at that point. Shortly after that, I remember taking the song into a rehearsal with the band. We started playing this and I started singing and Tommy immediately stepped up. He, as everybody else, knew a good thing when they heard it.
>
> Alex and I, shortly after writing that first batch of lyrics, clarified them so that they weren't graphic and stupid, because we were clearly intoxicated by the track. And I have to say, every step of the way, when people would first hear it, whether it was the band members or the management or the record label, I mean, it's simplistic and silly to say people's eyes lit up or whatever, but I think it was very clear to everybody that it was a special song.

Once the music and lyrics were in place, Tommy Tutone were then able to bring their combination of precision and propulsion to the act of putting it all together, something that unified Keller and Heath even when they didn't agree on much else. "Tommy and I always prided ourselves in writing parts, and we did that from the very beginning," Keller explains,

> If you go listen to the first record, almost every song is parts. There's no jamming going on anywhere. Tommy and I brought different sensibilities to the table, and we utilized both of them. We spent hours working out the specifics of what we were going to play. With "867," it's not rocket science, whether it's me playing the main riff, or Tommy putting a spy rock lick in. It's him on his Tele and me on my Strat composing parts, although that's a very glorified word to use for pop music. But we loved doing it. That was a big part of the joy that came out of our tempestuous relationship.

"867-5309" does boast an immense musical hook in that chunky chord progression, as well as the obvious lyrical one with the phone number. But the song would become tiresome quickly if that were all it offered. It also features those instrumental gears playing off each other so precisely that they put Swiss watches to shame. And the lyrics, voiced by Heath with lusty gusto, possess a subversive element to them as well; lines like "You give me something I can hold onto" and "I tried my imagination, but I was disturbed" hint that the narrator might have to pleasure himself if he doesn't muster up the nerve to call Jenny. Heller laughs off specific questions about the lyrics. "There's just no point in me clarifying that," he says. "Take a poll from your readers about whatever they think is going on."

The soaring popularity of the song (it rolled to the Top 5 in early 1982) meant that the phone number aspect was destined to cause a ruckus. That ruckus garnered a lot of headlines, which Heller says didn't disturb him at all, even when they threatened to take the focus off the song's merits. "How could that possibly frustrate me?" he asks. "I'm a twenty-six-year-old guy in a rock band. We're getting exposure and we have a song on the radio. For us it was a fantastic ride. All that stuff just added to it. The management and record label loved it because people were writing about it. It's not like Alex and I wrote a classic novella that we were insulted that people were not taking seriously. We wrote an out-and-out pop song."

One could argue that "Jenny" was such a one-of-a-kind creation that it made it impossible for Tommy Tutone to truly escape its long shadow; their 1983 follow-up album *National Emotion* plummeted without a trace and would be their last until 1996, by which time Keller had split. But their greatest hit holds a soft spot in the hearts of many, even today.

"I'm sixty-three years old," Keller says. "There are fifty-year-old gentlemen coming up to me with this look of awe in their eyes. And I'm like, 'What are they doing?' It's so ancient history, in a way. But those guys were fourteen years old when it was a hit and it was hugely impactful in their lives, which is charming. I'm proud to be a part of something that makes people happy like that and to be a part of something that has lasted that long. And I share that with Alex and I share it with Tommy. I don't own it. The world owns it." And it's a world that has known for the past thirty-five years that "867-5309/Jenny" is the ultimate musical number to call.

"At This Moment" by Billy Vera & the Beaters

BILLY AND THE BEATERS (1981, SINGLE RERELEASE IN 1986)

If you're watching television these days and hear a song you like, you need only know the title of the song or even just a few lyrics so that you can go to the internet and find out both who the artist is and where it's available. There are even apps with artificial intelligence that can identify songs that are played in their vicinity.

Yet none of that technology existed back in 1986, which makes the fact that Billy Vera & the Beaters hit number 1 with "At This Moment"—with a little assist from the NBC sitcom *Family Ties*—all the more amazing. The song's success was partly a testament to the show's popularity. But it was also a testament to the sturdiness of Vera's composition and the power with which he and his band performed it.

The story begins a full decade before the song's eventual ascension to the top spot, with a whirlwind romance that left a lasting impact on Vera. "It was the spring of 1977 and I had just met this girl," he remembers:

> I was thirty-three and she was a twenty-year-old college girl. We started seeing each other and she described breaking up with her previous boyfriend in vivid detail, about how it crushed him and how he went off the deep end. So I started writing the song from what I perceived was his point of view. But I couldn't finish it. Usually if I can't finish a song in three or four hours, I toss it. But this one, for some reason, I stuck in my mother's piano bench.
>
> And then a year later, when the girl broke up with me, I was crushed beyond belief. To this day, I've never been as brokenhearted as I was. And that's when I knew how the song ended and I finished it.

Vera's band gained a reputation as an excellent performing act, and their 1981 record *Billy and the Beaters*, which contained the minor Top 40 hit "I

Can't Take It Anymore," was recorded live for this reason. "At This Moment" was released as the second single, but some bad luck with the band's record company helped stymie it. "The head of promotions at Alfa Records got into a disagreement with the guy who ran the company," Vera remembers. "It was the American arm of a Japanese company. And it was staffed by veteran American record people. And he quit or was fired. He was a very good promotion man, but we no longer had his services. So we had nobody to really promote the record, and it stalled at number 79. Shortly after that, the Japanese owners pulled the plug on the American record operations. So we were without a record deal."

Several years passed before Vera, who had turned forty and was barely eking out a living as an actor, received a fateful telephone call: "The guy says, 'Is this the same Billy Vera that has the band?' I said, 'Yeah.' He said, 'Oh, thank God, I didn't know how to get in touch with you. I had my girl look at every phone book. My name is Michael Weithorn. I write and produce for a show called *Family Ties*. And we were at the club the other night and we heard you singing a song that we thought would be good for an episode we're planning.'"

Family Ties, at that point, stood as one of the crown jewels of the NBC Thursday night comedy dynasty, fueled by the breakout performance of Michael J. Fox as conservative teenager Alex P. Keaton. The episode in question called for a slow dance between Alex and his new love interest, played by Fox's future wife Tracy Pollan. Vera rerecorded the song at NBC's request in a studio setting and didn't think anything more would come of it. But he was pleasantly surprised:

> When the episode ran, I got a bagful of mail. That's the first time that ever happened. Maybe that means people like the song. So I thought I'd interest anybody who would pick up the phone to me at record companies to let me rerecord it. And nobody was interested.
>
> And then one day, I'm having lunch with a fellow named Richard Foos, who ran a reissue company called Rhino Records. In the course of the lunch, I said, "How many records do you need to sell to break even?" He said, "A couple of thousand." I said, "What if I guarantee you two thousand? I could sell them in the clubs if need be. Would you license an album of my Alfa material? We'll put it out and maybe get a little play off this TV show when they rerun it." I compiled an album of the songs that the fans loved the best, but by the time they got it out, they missed the rerun.

Yet after so many years of the song just missing the big time, fate finally smiled upon it. "Lo and behold, the next season, the opening episode was the one where the girl broke up with Michael J. Fox," Vera recalls. "And this time the story of the song, boy loses girl, is the same as the story of the episode. And America, for some reason, without any promotion, responded. NBC called up

Rhino and said they had more phone calls than at any time in the history of the network for this little song. So it became this grassroots phenomenon. It spread like wildfire, and before we knew it, we were jumping over Madonna and Bon Jovi and all these pop stars. And bing, bang, boom, we're number 1, man."

"At This Moment" deserves every bit of the popularity it eventually received. Vera captures all of the desperation of the very instant when a breakup is happening, all of the bargaining and pleading. What really stings is that the listener knows all of his efforts are too little, too late long before the protagonist of the song does. "If you'd stay I'd subtract twenty years from my life," Vera promises, and the shaking urgency in his voice makes you believe that he would keep that promise if only he could. It stands on a par with any of the great soul ballads of the 60s, the prime era for such songs.

Vera thinks the template for the song goes back even further than that. "To be honest with you, when I wrote the song, I didn't really think it was that commercial. It didn't have one of those hooks that just bangs away at your brain until you couldn't get rid of it. It's just a classic 32-bar AABA ballad in the classic sense that people were writing in the 1920s."

He also was contacted a few years ago by a woman on Facebook who informed him that the song didn't have any rhymes, which Vera didn't even realize while he was writing it. "I can make rhymes as good as the next guy, but I listened to the song and said, 'Holy shit, she's right!' I didn't write one rhyme in this song. That bugged me, but then I thought maybe it actually helped the song because it made it more conversational."

Whatever the reason, the moment for "At This Moment" finally arrived, almost a decade after it was written, five years after it was first recorded. Yet Billy Vera lives by a motto that succinctly sums up how it all happened: "Let the song do your work for you. Because it will."

"In The Air Tonight" by Phil Collins

FACE VALUE (1981)

He eventually became one of the decade's biggest hitmakers, both on his own and with the band Genesis. Yet when considering "In the Air Tonight," one of the most definitive songs of the 80s, it's important to remember that Phil Collins was very much an unknown quantity to the public at large at the time of its recording. He had only taken over the frontman role in Genesis five years earlier, and though the band had slowly turned away from the art-rock leanings of its Peter Gabriel–led days and had started to earn mainstream radio success with the 1980 album *Duke*, the thought that Collins had built enough credibility to release a commercially successful solo album at that point seemed far-fetched.

Producer Hugh Padgham, however, got an early taste of the goods that would show up on Collins's *Face Value* album and was impressed immediately. "He had been recording his demos for the album," Padgham says. "He had an 8-track, 1-inch analog tape recorder at a desk. It was pretty cool to have that in 1980. So I listened to the songs and he was really into them. And I thought they sounded absolutely fantastic. What we decided to do, pretty well there and then, was to actually use the demos as the basis for the real recordings."

One of those demos was for "In the Air Tonight," containing an atmospheric keyboard bed, an insistent drum pattern, and Collins's vocal. There was something so haunting about this early take that most of it made it onto the finished version. "What you're hearing on the finished master is actually the Roland drum machine pattern and the pad sound from the Prophet 5 synthesizer, which was one of the first polyphonic synthesizers around," Padgham explains. "We actually did try to see if we could re-create the drum pattern, but we never felt that we could re-create the same tempo or even get exactly the same sound. So we just thought, 'Sod it. Let's just use the original from the demo.'"

Collins wrote the songs for *Face Value* in the midst of a divorce from his first wife. There is no linear story to be found in the lyrics for "In the Air Tonight," just the raw feelings of recrimination and hurt that crop up in the early aftermath of a failed relationship. It is a one-sided harangue, no doubt, but the way these emotions are expressed is unique. "Well, if you told me you were drowning/I would not lend a hand," Collins sings in the first verse. The person he's addressing looks at him like a stranger, but he knows her all too well: "It's all been a pack of lies," he barks out, his vocals stretched out and dehumanized by effects conjured by Collins and Padgham.

All the while, the chorus promises something undefined: triumph, redemption, revenge, perhaps even sudden death: "I can feel it coming in the air tonight, oh Lord/I've been waiting for this moment for all my life, oh Lord." That Collins allows the listener to fill in the blanks is to his credit, because the mystery of it all helps make the song endlessly listenable. If it meant that some folks would take the song too literally and eventually create a bizarre urban legend about the meaning of the song, well, sometimes a price must be paid for trusting your audience.

The music stays in this creeping, insinuating mode for most of the way, the tension building to almost unbearable levels. How that tension is released makes for one of the most memorable moments in the history of popular music, a drum break that lifts the song from cool, strange, and curious to shattering catharsis in a flash.

Collins and Padgham had discovered that explosive drum sound on an earlier project. "I first met Phil when I was working on Peter Gabriel's third solo album," Padgham recalls,

> Peter invited Phil to come and play on some of the songs. We were in a studio called the Townhouse and we built a very live drum room, because we had all got a bit fed up with the dry sound of 70s records. This room sounded really live and almost out of control. We had a reverse talkback mike in the studio that was connected straight to a button on the console. And when you pressed the button, the idea was that there was this huge compressor built into the console on this mike so that you could pick up anybody talking in any part of the studio. I had the microphone open and Phil started to play the drums because he couldn't hear that I was trying to talk to him. And the most unbelievable sound came out.
>
> Two things came out of this. First of all, everyone who was in the control room at the time went, "Wow! This sounds great." And secondly, "Oh dear, we can't record it." Because it's only there as a talkback. It's not connected into the console at all. So that night I asked one of the maintenance guys if he could get inside the console, find the output of that compressor that was built in, and wire it into a patch point which I could then input into a channel. He did that, we came back the next day, Phil started playing the drums, and it sounded unbelievable. But the minute you played a cymbal, it

sounded absolutely terrible because the cymbal took over everything in its way. So it's like, "OK, drum sounds great, but no cymbals."

But Padgham wasn't quite satisfied with the effect yet. "I would always just fiddle around," he says. "I put a noise gate on the drum sound, so that when Phil stopped playing, the gate cut the sound off. So it sounded like you were sort of switching off the electricity. There'd be this huge sound when he hit the snare drum or the tom-tom and then it would suddenly shut off. So it made a very dynamic sound."

Gabriel used the effect on a song called "Intruder," and Collins kept it in his mind. When he and Padgham decided to embellish the initial demo of "In the Air Tonight," the gated drum effect was an obvious choice. But, wisely, restraint was the watchword. "It was like, well, because it's such a shocking sound, let's shock everybody by only having them come in at the end when they're not expecting it," Padgham says.

Hearing the song for the first time, a listener can't say for sure what it is that's coming in the air tonight, but when those drums come in, they surely know that whatever it is, it has just arrived. The effect was both immediate and lasting. The song was a worldwide hit upon its release and provided a crucial launching point for Phil Collins's 80s ubiquity. More importantly, it keeps popping up again and again, whether accompanying a stealthy night drive in *Miami Vice* or getting air-drummed by Mike Tyson in *The Hangover*.

So it is that "In the Air Tonight" keeps coming. Innovative at the time and fresh still today, it's no wonder we never want it to leave.

"I Melt with You" by Modern English

AFTER THE SNOW (1982)

This book is not intended to be a ranking of the top songs of the 1980s, but such lists have certainly been compiled by many different media outlets and online scribes. In a great many of those lists, you will find "I Melt with You" by Modern English ranked pretty prominently. The ironic thing about it is that it is often ranked more prominently in those decade-summing charts than it ever managed on the *Billboard* chart (where it reached a high of number 78 in 1982) when it was first released.

There are other songs in this book that have had similar trajectories, but one can often point to a single instance that spiked their popularity down the road from the original release. "I Melt with You" has been included in a few popular movies and some commercials over the years, but none to which you could point and say definitively that it made much difference in the song's lasting appeal. It just seems to be one of those songs that keeps getting rediscovered, with different people falling in love with it on different occasions, either for the first time or all over again. Which is appropriate because the song is about falling in love, set against the backdrop of a very 80s concern: the threat of annihilation via nuclear war.

On paper, such a song would seem like a disaster waiting to happen, some overwrought, melodramatic piece of misguided ambition, instead of the dead-solid perfect pop song that it turned out to be. Perhaps that's because the group that made it simply didn't know any better about what they could or couldn't do, and also that they didn't put any forethought at all into the song's creation.

Modern English had released their debut album in 1981, only a year before "I Melt with You" was recorded for their album *After the Snow*. The band was comprised of five individuals who weren't exactly seasoned music pros, and lead singer Robbie Grey claims that their move to a more commercial sound after their gothic-flavored debut was driven more by who they had surrounding them than by any conscious choice. "A lot of the reasoning behind that was the producer, Hugh Jones," Grey explains. "He polished the sound more. He brought a lot of different ideas to the table that we would normally never have used. Using violins, acoustic guitars, things like that."

Jones also helped the band meld together what would become one of the decade's definitive songs. "Because we weren't brilliant musicians, we used to stick bits of music together while we were rehearsing, and we used to call them 'pieces,'" Grey says. "We would just go from this piece to that piece. We didn't really call them verses and choruses because we didn't really know what that meant at the time. With 'I Melt with You,' we had a few pieces that we were sticking together to make a song with. I remember Hugh heard this rehearsal tape with these pieces of music on it, and he helped us to take it from one part to another."

The lyrics to which millions have sung along over the last thirty-five or so years were constructed in about as much time as it takes to listen to them. "I'd gone home with some of the music being made for 'I Melt with You,' some of the parts of it, and I wrote the lyrics in about three minutes sitting on the floor stoned in my house in Shepherd's Bush in London," Grey says incredulously. "I just wrote these words down on a scrap of paper really quickly."

Grey managed to create a song about the ability of love to withstand even Earth's eradication, even if he only hints at the nuclear aspect of it. For example, the title could refer to the act of two people making love, or it could mean faces melting off once the bombs drop. In fact, the lyrics are so subtle about it that the heavier parts often aren't even noticed by listeners. "It got missed for years until somebody asked me what it was about," Grey says. "I think everybody just thought it was a straightforward love song. It was almost like a metaphor for that time. Using a relationship and people making love as an example of something good against something so dark in the background. So it was never going to get morbid, really. Lines like 'never comprehending the race had long gone by' might be negative, but it's still an uplifting song, I think."

Grey and Modern English—Gary McDowell on guitar, Stephen Walker on keyboards, Michael Conroy on bass, and Richard Brown on drums—added touches to the recording that still stand out today, like the opening whoosh of guitars. "The idea of the acoustic guitars gliding across the track, that was the band's idea as well as the producer's," Grey remembers. "We overdubbed a lot of guitars playing the same parts with different sounds to get that big sound of the choruses or when the song first comes in."

And, of course, no discussion of "I Melt with You" would be complete without mentioning the humming breakdown. "That was another moment where the band kind of stood still and thought, 'Really, should we do this?'" Grey laughs. "Because we'd never done anything like that before. In a way, I suppose it's got some of the same ideas as country-and-western songs, where you get a harmonica player or you get someone whistling sometimes. This idea of having a break that's not really a normal type of rock break. We tried whistling, a few different things, but the humming was the best. I really like that part, and I really enjoy doing that live."

Grey says the band wasn't sure whether or not what they were creating was the direction they wanted to go. "There was a moment where a couple of the band members were hearing 'I Melt with You' and thinking, 'Oh my God, this is too commercial.' Because we'd never written anything like that before, really. But once we started putting this thing together, it grew on us, like it grew on half the planet."

What half the planet heard is a musical construction that is unstoppable once it revs up, yet just as compelling as when it slows down. And it hears Grey's deadpan verses about the threat all around him, his valiant efforts ("I made a pilgrimage to save this human's race") coming up just short ("I saw the world crashing all around your face"), set against his steadfast promise in the exhilarating refrain: "There's nothing you and I won't do/I'll stop the world and melt with you." It's the old love-conquers-all scenario, and in this case, it conquers doomsday.

Grey, for one, can't understand how some artists have a cross relationship with their most famous work. "We don't have a problem with it," he says:

> The band loves playing the song live. Generally, when we do it live, there'll be a few minutes where I don't have to sing it really. The crowd will do it for me.
>
> We loved the song from the minute we started writing it and we still love it now. It's really a fantastic thing to have such a great reaction from the crowd when you're playing it live. People all tell us that they've made love to it for the first time, they married to it. I don't understand why a member of a band wouldn't enjoy those reactions. For us, it's been a fantastic ride.

"Someday, Someway" by Marshall Crenshaw

MARSHALL CRENSHAW (1982)

There were some artists who rose to prominence in the 1980s that music critics seemed desperate to characterize, no matter how much of a stretch or how
incomplete the characterization might have been. Marshall Crenshaw was one
such artist, a singer-songwriter who was sometimes lumped in with everything
from New Wave to rockabilly to power pop. That kind of pigeonholing might
have made it difficult for him to break out of preconceived notions and score
the kind of commercial success that his endlessly catchy songcraft truly deserved.

But Crenshaw is sanguine about it now, even if it did chafe at him a bit
back in the day. "People always wrote about the stuff at least," he says. "My
name would be in the magazine or whatever. That's a good thing, on one hand,
that anybody's paying attention or thinking about it. But I would bristle at the
characterizations sometimes."

His lone Top 40 hit from the era—"Someday, Someway," from his 1982
self-titled debut album—enjoyed a kind of dry run to prepare it for its eventual
success, as Robert Gordon's cover reached the Top 100 a year before Crenshaw
did his own take. Crenshaw, however, wasn't interested in being a songwriter
for hire. "I was definitely thinking about songs that would be good vehicles for
myself," he recalls. "I was compiling a body of work for myself. The Robert
Gordon thing kind of came out of left field. But that was really a stroke of good
luck because his version of 'Someday, Someway' was really huge in New York
City. And that helped sort of get me to the point where I was getting offers from
record labels. But I wasn't thinking about writing for anybody else. I was utterly
focused on wanting to have a recording career of my own."

Crenshaw's career to that point was a bit on the unusual side, as his biggest
recognition came from a stint playing John Lennon in the touring company of
the musical *Beatlemania*. Perhaps he learned something from his exposure to
the Fab Four's catalog that rubbed off on his own work. "I wanted to write hit

singles," Crenshaw explains. "I was in love with the idea that hit singles were art. That was my medium, my platform, and that was really what I was going for with everything I did back then."

He also felt very much at home with the direction music was taking at that time. "I was picking up on a lot of things that were on the radio at that moment," Crenshaw remembers. "I was hearing a lot of people in my age group [who] were drawing inspiration from music that they loved when they were growing up. And that's what I wanted to do. There was a New Wave/rockabilly thing that was going on right then with the Stray Cats and Dave Edmunds and Rockpile and stuff like that. I felt really connected at that time to the music of the moment."

His own hit single, written in a two-day burst, struck a sweet spot in the middle of all of those genres. "The writing process took the least amount of time that it could take," Crenshaw muses. "It was just a flash of inspiration with the music. It just wrote itself. I was in Boston staying at the Copley Plaza Hotel. The next morning, I was walking around Copley Square. It was freezing cold. I had the tune in my head. All the lyrics instantly appeared in my mind. I didn't really think about what it meant until later on. I didn't labor over it at all."

Those lyrics that came all at once turned out to be quite telling, in their simple way, about the frustration that comes when two people can't communicate in a relationship; even the far-off future suggested by the title isn't a promise, as Crenshaw sings, "Someday, someway, *maybe* I'll understand you." "I knew that the words had some substance to them," Crenshaw says. "And that they suggested layers of meaning. But I didn't analyze it at all. The main thing was just to have the words fit the groove and fit the melody, just to push the song along. But on the other hand, I never wanted to write throwaway lyrics."

Pushing the song along was something that Crenshaw originally had a hard time doing in the studio, at least until his drummer brother Robert and an alert set of ears helped him crack the code. Crenshaw recalls,

> When we were cutting the basic track, I didn't feel like we were getting it. We played it three dozen times or something. When we were doing the basic track, I think they were trying to get drums and bass at the same time. I was doing a scratch guitar and scratch vocal. That's how the producer wanted to do it. I wasn't sure about it. And then finally, somebody said, "Let's come back to it tomorrow and try it again." We gave up, is what happened.
>
> When we came in the next morning, the assistant engineer, Jim Ball, he'd listened to all the tapes and he put a star next to number 17 out of 36, or something. And he put it up on the 2-inch machine and I said, "Take out everything except the drums." And when we listened to just the drums, there it was. It really is beautiful to me,

just the way that thing feels. My brother just really killed it on this
one take. It's got a lot of nuance to it and it swings and it's really cool.
It's got a magical groove to it.

Crenshaw then played the remainder of the instruments himself, including
the buoyantly rhythmic lead guitar, and the end result was a single that sounded
both like a throwback to another generation and the freshest thing on the dial
at that time. The fact that it was only a relatively modest single success (number
36) doesn't diminish it in any way, because its author has discovered that this
song had legs, something that dawned on him when he happened upon it watching television a few years back.

"It was on a show on NBC called *Ed*," Crenshaw explains. "But I was just
sitting there like, 'This is a network TV show and this is an old song now.' I
realized then that the song and the record had achieved longevity and I thought
that's an f'ing great thing. A really beautiful thing. There's like this little handful
of them from that time period that are in the air all the time."

"She Blinded Me with Science" by Thomas Dolby

THE GOLDEN AGE OF WIRELESS (1982)

There's an old show business adage that claims you should never work with children or animals. The UK electronic pop artist Thomas Dolby found out that you could add famous television scientists to that list when he enlisted Dr. Magnus Pyke to help out on "She Blinded Me with Science," a bolt-from-the-blue Top 5 pop hit in 1982.

Before discussing Dr. Pyke, however, it's important to examine the fascinating career that Dolby was already building before "Science" became such a popular subject. He was gaining renown as a session keyboardist, especially after his work was featured prominently on Foreigner's 1981 smash singles "Urgent" and "Waiting for a Girl Like You." He then put together an acclaimed 1982 debut album entitled the *Golden Age of Wireless*, which performed very well in England.

The song that would provide him his eventual US breakthrough began as nothing more than an excuse to direct a video, as Dolby was intrigued by the possibilities of this new medium. "I had a demo of it that I was asked for by my record company that would greenlight the video," Dolby explains. "I felt that it was very catchy. It seemed to be loaded with hooks. Although I didn't feel it owed very much to other music or specific songs of the time."

The lyrics to the song, for which Jo Kerr received a cowriting credit with Dolby, again came from a very specific setup for the video. "I suppose I sort of focused on the scenario of the absentminded professor and a rather beguiling, hot Japanese lab assistant," Dolby says. "I very often close my eyes and imagine things cinematically and then sort of write down the details; that's the approach I often have to my lyrics."

But Dolby felt the song and video needed something else to put it across:

> I felt that I had to have a bona-fide mad scientist character in the video in order that my own character had a foil. The frontmen of the

era were much more romantic figures like Simon LeBon on his yacht of Adam Ant in his highwayman gear or Sting with his shirt open or whatever. But I didn't want to go all-out mad scientist. I wanted to kick it back a notch. So I think having Dr. Pyke there was a good sort of end marker for me really. To my amazement, I found that he was actually listed in central casting. I could hire him by the hour or by the day.

Pyke immediately began to draw lines in the sand, however, about his participation:

> For starters, he was sort of reluctant to stretch the boundaries of his brand. For example, in the storyboard that we drew for the video, he was wearing a white lab coat. And on the day, he refused to be seen or filmed in his white lab coat because he said that his audience didn't perceive him in that way.
>
> And when I was first in the studio with him, I scrolled down the words that I wanted him to say. And when he first said his line, he sort of said, "She blinded me with science?" And I said, "It's not really a question, Dr. Pyke. It's more of a statement." And there was a pause and he said, "Well, yes, but it would be a bit surprising if the girl blinded me with science. I'm a known scientist." And I said, "Well, just trust me on this one."

Once Dr. Pyke was squared away, Dolby created something that was wholly unlike most of what was on pop radio at the time, a combination of danceable rhythms and electronic experimentation. Listening to "She Blinded Me with Science," you're never quite sure from what corner the percussion is going to come rattling, even as the snake-charmer synth riff and Pyke's wild exclamations of "Science!" keep you moving forward. Dolby holds down the center with musings about chemicals, tubes, and spheres in commotion, all while falling completely under the sway of the "tender eyes" and "poetry in motion" in front of him. It's the old heart versus head scenario—or perhaps libido versus head—played out with tongue in cheek.

Dolby modestly credits some of the song's stateside success to serendipity:

> In the US, the timing was very good, because everybody was hearing about this British New Wave invasion and everybody was hearing about MTV. And it was a product that just fit the bill at the right moment in time. It had, apart from the catchy song, a memorable video, and the image that I put forth was very easy to put your finger on. Everything sort of came together and a variety of other things went right in the business department.

> As I point out in my book [Dolby's excellent autobiography *The Speed of Sound: Breaking the Barriers between Music and Technology*], when you have a hit, you just slap each other in the back and crack the champagne. When a song is a flop that you expected to be a hit, you point fingers and heads will roll. But it's easy to forget that all ducks have to be in a row in order for a hit to happen, however much potential it has.

While that might account for the song's initial run, Dolby, who has continued his eclectic music career in addition to achieving success as a Silicon Valley entrepreneur, explains that sustaining success requires diligence:

> We've tried to manage it carefully, because it can get oversaturated. So if people want to use the song these days in different settings, some of them are very cool and don't pay very well, and some are uncool and pay a fortune. You have to do a slight balancing act in order to sort of maximize revenue and try and protect the longevity of the song. I read scripts and abstracts. Every now and then I get one about a dying chemistry professor who teams up with a meth dealer to become a drug kingpin in New Mexico. I sort of read that very carefully before I allow the song to be a ringtone. But for every *Breaking Bad*, there's a dozen or so that didn't make it or sank without a trace.

However it's been achieved, there is little doubt that "She Blinded Me with Science" has been a mainstay in the culture since its release. "I'm very grateful for that," Dolby says. "It's sort of the Holy Grail for a songwriter or a recording artist to have an evergreen song."

And if the only price to pay was dealing with a strong-willed scientist, it seems well worth it.

"Shakin'" by Eddie Money

NO CONTROL (1982)

They called him "The Man with No Control," but Eddie Money certainly had a pretty firm hold on the pop charts throughout the 1980s. Many artists during the decade did well during a two- or three-year window and then fell off due to the difficulties of trying to keep their particular styles relevant when the winds of musical change were blowing so furiously and rapidly. Yet Money practically glided from the first half of the decade to the second.

There was the Top 20 smash "Think I'm in Love" in 1982, another pair ("Take Me Home Tonight" and "I Wanna Go Back") that cracked the Top 20 in 1986, and a Top 10 killer in "Walk on Water" in 1988. Money, who is as entertaining an interview subject as he is a performer, finds the whole thing a bit incredible, including the fact that he's still out there bringing crowds to their feet with these and other well-remembered songs. "I had like sixteen songs in the Top 100," he says. "What the f***, I had a billion f***in' hits! So my voice is holding up, I still got all my hair. I just throw that sock down my pants and away we go!"

Money's jovial nature somewhat couches the fact that he is a versatile talent, adept at singing charging rockers like "Think I'm in Love" or nostalgic ballads such as "I Wanna Go Back." But the song chosen for this collection, even though it didn't even reach the Top 40, is the one that might just well be his signature song, as it sort of captures his public personality the best. "Shakin'" is soulful, bawdy, reckless, and funny as heck, putting Money in the role of lovable underdog who eventually triumphs. All that, plus it's a track that's as fierce and grabby now as it was when it was released in 1982 from the *No Control* album.

And it all started with the beat. "A guy named Gary Ferguson who was my old drummer, who was also a surfer," Money says. "Nice guy. He said, 'I'm gonna write a strip beat for you.' I said, 'What do you mean a strip beat?' What he meant was, if you go to any strip bars, you'd hear that beat. Now I'm not

58

allowed to go to strip bars; my wife would kill me. But if you think about 'Shakin',' it's a strip beat. And that's what we used."

That beat by Ferguson sets the tone right from the start, and it's accentuated by some muscular lead guitar from Jimmy Lyon. Even though Money was fond of using studio pros on his records, he always managed to coax strong, cohesive performances out of his sidemen, and such is the case with "Shakin'." Tom Dowd's production puts a fine sheen on the song, and the arrangement recedes and builds in all the right places, especially when things quiet down for the final verse before revving up thrillingly into the final chorus. Elements of rock and rhythm and blues are blended seamlessly, while Money holds it all together with a typically charismatic performance.

The tale of "Shakin'," which Money cowrote with Elizabeth Carter and Ralph Myers, is aimed at both actual teenagers and those a little older with fond memories of some of the stupid things they did back when. As Money explains it, it's an almost inevitable rite of teenage passage:

> It was just a tune about something that can happen to anybody. Driving your father's car, blowing out the speakers on the radio. I mean what kid didn't do that coming up, you know? The first car you're gonna be driving is your father's car. You're gonna have your girlfriend in the goddam car. I mean what's gonna happen? You're gonna blow the speakers out.
>
> I mean, I've talked to a million people who took their father's car and blew the speakers out. So "Shakin'" was about every guy who had a girlfriend that drove their father's car and was drinking too much. It's all about being a senior in high school.

Money makes it all sound simple, but the lyrics are constructed extremely well, managing to both tell the story and give room for a little self-reflection by the narrator. The lyrics lend the narrator just the right touches to make us root for him, such as a bit of self-doubt: "I got a little nervous/When she took her coat off." And he's self-aware enough to admit his faults: "I'm always talkin' maybe talkin' too much." The line "It takes a lonely night with nowhere to go" hints at the way youthful indiscretions can often be written off to boredom.

Meanwhile Money puts the icing on the cake with his stammering rendition of the refrain in the final moments of the song, something that hearkened back to his younger days. "I grew up singing a lot of doo-wop," he explains. "When I first started singing in high school, which was like 1963, 1964, I was singing songs with an a cappella band. That's how I learned how to sing. And there was a lot of stuff like 'Duke of Earl.' There was a lot of 'dat-dat-dat' and 'doo-doo-doo.' That was 50s, 60s kind of stuff, you know."

To top it off, the song featured a memorable video that allowed Money to act out the protagonist's adventures alongside a girl who would eventually gain much more exposure. "It became really famous because Apollonia [Kotero] did it," Money says. "She was in the video and she became very, very famous when she did *Purple Rain* with Prince. But that was the first professional thing that Apollonia ever did. At that time, she was going out with this karate teacher. And he was ready to kill me. He was really jealous."

Money was able to capitalize on the popularity of videos in part because of his manager, behind-the-scenes music legend Bill Graham. "When all those videos came out, Huey Lewis and I were really on top of the whole thing," Money says. "Bill said to me, 'We're gonna make a video because MTV is gonna be really big and I think they're gonna be putting rock-and-roll videos on it.' And I think he was one of the first ones to actually do rock-and-roll videos. All of a sudden I was like this big video star. They said in the *New York Times*, you want to get on MTV, you might as well be Eddie Money."

For whatever reason (Money claims it's because he slipped some blue language into the lyrics), "Shakin'" didn't score very big on the radio. But it has endured to the point where no Eddie Money concert is complete without it, which, because of his success in the decade, means that no discussion of the 80s is complete without it, either. And perhaps it's best to let the man himself describe its longevity as only he can:

> "Shakin'" to me is such a big song. We've been closing the show with "Shakin'" for the past thirty-five years. It's something about that strip beat.
> Everybody loves f***in' "Shakin'."

"Our House" by Madness

THE RISE & FALL (1982)

Their name promised wildness and anarchy, and, by and large, Madness delivered. But in a twist of irony the band members likely savored, their biggest worldwide hit—the one that broke them in the United States after they had already achieved sustained chart success in their native England—was a song that captured an air of sweet nostalgia that set it apart from the chart hits of the day.

Madness released "Our House" as the lead single from their 1982 album *The Rise & Fall.* By that time, they had achieved such an impressive level of recording success in the UK that they were able to release a greatest hits compilation. Starting in 1979, they released a dozen straight singles that went into the Top 20 in their native land, ten of which reached the Top 10. Yet not one of those songs was able to dent *Billboard* in the United States. The best they were able to do was a minor scrape with the Top 40 with the airy ballad "It Must Be Love." (Even after "Our House," Madness—which continued to chart in the UK all the way into the new millennium—would never again do any damage with a single in the United States.)

Perhaps the American audiences weren't ready for the band's infectious rhythms and horn-filled sound. They were labeled as a ska band by many critics, but according to guitarist Chris Foreman, also known as "Chrissy Boy" (the seven members of Madness all took on colorful nicknames), that didn't nearly cover it. "I've never thought of us as a ska band and we've never said that we were," Foreman says. "The first album (*One Step Beyond . . .*) had a rock-and-roll-type song ('Rocking in A♭') and a jazzy number ('Razorblade Alley'), to name but two totally non-ska songs."

It was that ability to leapfrog genres that made the band a British radio staple, but it took a song that recalled some of the smooth sounds of Detroit circa the early 60s for the band to achieve their biggest American success. Foreman began formulating "Our House" using some equipment that, at the time, was state of the art, before getting help from fellow Madness member Cathal Smyth, aka "Chas Smash." Foreman says,

> I wrote the song using one of the multitrack cassette players that Dave Robinson [the head of Stiff Records] had bought us. Quite an interesting device, it actually had a very basic drum machine in too. You could record at least two tracks. It wasn't a Portastudio; more like a standard cassette player, a small boom box. I think it even had a radio in it.
>
> Anyway, I had this dirgy song which I took to rehearsals. Chas had suggested we all write songs about our childhood and he wrote some lyrics along those lines to go with my music. We all started playing the song and eventually settled on a Motown type rhythm. I wrote the middle eight real quick; it was part of another song idea I had been working on. I came up with the [guitar] solo in the studio when we were recording it.

The finished product was a song that, like so many Madness hits, was instantly catchy and melodically fresh. Ace producers Clive Langer and Alan Winstanley ensured that all of the elements stood out, including the pounding piano of Mike Barson ("Barzo"), the nimble rhythmic interplay between bassist Mark Bedford ("Bedders") and drummer Daniel Woodgate ("Woody"), the peppery horns of Smash and Lee Thompson ("El Thommo"), and Foreman's piercing guitar. A subtle string arrangement brought just the right touch of lushness to a song that already boasted tunefulness and groove to spare.

Smash's lyrics, declaimed with deadpan sincerity by lead singer Suggs (real name Graham McPherson), follow in the tradition of classic songs by Paul McCartney and Ray Davies, songs that make reference to the eccentricities inherent in many English families but always stress the bonds between family members. Younger kids rumbling about, older kids fixated on romance, a harried mother, and a largely ineffectual father overseeing it all: the narrator surveys them all with an intriguing combination of anthropological distance and genuine affection.

Smash also drops some hints of sadness into the mix to match the bittersweet tug of Foreman's melody. When Mom sends the kids off to school, the narrator mentions that "She's the one they're going to miss in lots of ways." In the fast-talking run-up to the final verse, the perspective switches to the first person and strikes a tone of fond remembrance of time gone by: "And I remember how we'd play, simply waste the day away/And then we'd say that nothing would come between us, two dreamers." Those lines speak eloquently of youthful reveries that are in no way tarnished by the fact that those dreams may not be fulfilled.

While the song contained a lot of heart, the video played up some of the humor that can be mined from frantic family life and ended up looking like a wild outtake from *The Benny Hill Show*. "I usually had the video ideas, sharing with Lee," Foreman remembers. "We came up with the style, cloth caps, old geezers image. We got two very contrasting houses to film in. One was Victor Lownes's mansion. He was a UK executive for *Playboy*. The other location was this old guy's house. I felt sorry for him but I found out his house was always being used in films."

"Our House" might have gone the way of Madness's other singles, which fell on deaf ears in America, were it not for a forward-thinking executive. "A guy from Geffen Records called John Kalodner heard the song on the radio and thought it would be a hit in America," Foreman says. "Geffen released an album based on our *Rise & Fall* album, plus some older tracks. 'Our House' became our biggest hit in America [number 5 on the pop charts], a country we hadn't toured for two years. 'It Must Be Love' was the follow up and didn't do well [reaching number 33 in the United States]. We didn't write it with America in mind, we never write songs like that. We just write them."

And as for the idea that the song was intentionally aimed as a kind of homey counterpoint to what pop radio had to offer at the time? Foreman laughs that off, too: "Nothing was planned that much with Madness." That may have been the case, but "Our House" has proven nonetheless to be a musical residence worth revisiting year after year.

"Eye of the Tiger" by Survivor
EYE OF THE TIGER (1982)

Imagine you're Jim Peterik. The year is 1982. Your band, Survivor, has released two albums to middling success, with just one minor Top 40 hit between the pair. You come home and hear this message on your answering machine: "Yo, Jim, give me a call." The voice leaving that message belongs to none other than Sylvester Stallone, one of the biggest movie stars on the planet.

What would your reaction be? Peterik's reaction: "I just about dropped dead. At first I thought it was a joke, because our road manager, Sal, he was Italian and he kind of did a decent imitation."

It wasn't a joke, but before we get to that fateful call and its role in the writing and recording of "Eye of the Tiger," one of the decade's most explosive hits, a little backstory first: Peterik, who knew pop success at a young age when he penned and sang "Vehicle," a number 2 smash for the Chicago-based band the Ides of March in 1970, was an original member of Survivor until 1996. In between the making of their first and second records, the rhythm section completely changed, leaving a quintet of Peterik, Frankie Sullivan, Dave Bickler, Stephan Ellis, and Marc Droubay.

The rhythm section of Ellis and Droubay, in particular, brought a street charge to the band's 1981 release *Premonition* that intrigued Stallone. According to Peterik, Stallone said, "You know I got this movie, *Rocky III*, and I heard 'Poor Man's Son' from *Premonition*. That's the sound I want for *Rocky III*. I want something for the kids, with a pulse. Can you help me out?"

Stallone sent Peterik a preview of the movie, and he and Sullivan sat down to watch and compose. Peterik remembers,

> He sent us the rough cut of the first three minutes of the movie. That was the montage. We popped the thing in and we see Mr. T rising up looking fierce. Stallone kinda getting soft doing MasterCard com-

mercials. And during this whole montage, there was a song playing called "Another One Bites the Dust" by Queen. And it sounded fantastic. I called Stallone and I said, "Hey Sly, you already got a song." And he said, "Oh man, couldn't use it. We couldn't get the publishing." And I thought, "There is a God." I went back in the kitchen, turned down the sound and Frankie and I just went at it.

First up: The song's iconic intro. "It started with that sixteenth-note pulse," Peterik says. "I had my Les Paul around my neck and I started that really tele-pathic thing. And we were watching the punches being thrown and Frankie and I were trying to coordinate the chords with that, which in essence became as iconic as the song."

The *Rocky* franchise had certainly enjoyed success with instrumentals in the past ("Gonna Fly Now," anyone?), but this song was meant to articulate the boxer's arc in the movie, which required some lyrics. And for that, Peterik and Sullivan needed more info. "Unfortunately, we only had three minutes in the movie," Peterik says,

> So we called Sly and said, "Sly, you gotta send us the whole movie." I kept at him and said, "Look, if you want your song, we gotta know what this movie is about."
>
> He sent us the whole movie and that's when it all started to kick in. That's when we heard Mickey, his trainer [played by Burgess Mer-edith] telling him, "Rocky, you're losing the eye of the tiger." That was the essence of the Rocky story. He was getting soft. He had to get the eye of the tiger back. Frankie and I looked at each other and went, "Ok. Got it." Over the next three days, we just fine-tuned that lyric. I gotta say the lyric came really quick once we knew the story.

The band hustled into the studio to do a demo, and the timing was so tight that the unpolished recording is what you hear in the film. Yet its raw power proved difficult to re-create for the actual single and album. "It must have taken us a month," Peterik recalls. "We finally got it. My father had passed away in between. It was such a tragic thing. I had to fly back to Chicago for the funeral. And when I came back, Frankie was cranking up the final playback of Dave's vocal on 'Eye of the Tiger.' And I said, 'Man this is the greatest gift that I could ever get, coming back from this tragedy.'"

When the movie was released, Survivor enjoyed first-class treatment—but found it wasn't all it was cracked up to be. Peterik explains,

> We flew out to Hollywood to see the premiere at some very presti-gious theater. There was the red carpet and flashbulbs and the whole bit. We were parading with all the celebrities. We sat down, and,

you know, Hollywood audiences have seen it all. They're very jaded. When "Eye of the Tiger" hit in the beginning of the movie, there was a kind of "Oh, that's nice." And afterwards everyone was shaking our hands politely, "That was very good," you know.

Two weeks later, it hit my local cinema, the La Grange Theater [in La Grange, Illinois]. I snuck in the back row all alone and the place was packed. And as soon as that song hit, the place went up for grabs. There was screaming, people standing and yelling. I said, "OK, we got it."

The visceral nature of the song is obvious, not just the jab-hook-uppercut combos thrown by the opening, but also the vicious body blows thrown all song long by drummer Droubay. Peterik and Sullivan also managed to accomplish that rarest of feats for movie songs in that their lyrics don't need the context of the film to work. It is a song about "Just a man and his will to survive," but it can be any man—or woman—who needs to be reminded of what's worth fighting for. Trading "passion for glory" is a trap into which anyone can fall, and the advice "Don't lose your grip on the dreams of the past" is as wise today as when Bickler first belted it out in 1982.

A number 1 song for five weeks running is usually a good thing, but Survivor had to—you guessed it—fight to make it work for them. "In the industry, there was the idea of okay, well, they had the big movie to go along with it, of course it's gonna be number 1," Peterik explains. "So we kind of had to prove ourselves that we could do it without the aid of the Rocky franchise. Along about that time, we lost our original lead singer [Bickler], who left the band. And we were very fortunate enough to get Jimi Jamison. With the *Vital Signs* album [in 1984], that was our proving ground. As much as we cherished the Rocky franchise, we wanted to show the people that we could do it without it. That album went double-platinum and we proved ourselves."

Survivor would even crank out another training montage classic for Rocky IV in 1986 with "Burning Heart" as part of an impressive stretch of 80s hits. But "Eye of the Tiger" looms large over their catalog, as it does over an entire decade's worth of movie hits. "I didn't have a crystal ball to say in the year 2017 that song would still be relevant and still making a difference," Peterik marvels. "Still motivating people. I hear the stories every day of people fighting cancer to that song. Crossing the finish line first. Corporate ladder stories. Just on and on. And I will say, man, that's the greatest reward that any songwriter can have."

"The Safety Dance" by Men without Hats

RHYTHM OF YOUTH (1982)

If you are new to the music of the 80s and see the title above—both of the song and the band—you are forgiven if you think it was produced by artificial intelligence that was given the name of every artist and song from the decade and then instructed to randomly come up with ones of its own. But "The Safety Dance" did exist. Or does exist, because people all over the world are still captivated by this wackily catchy anthem.

Men without Hats is largely the brainchild of Canadian Ivan Doroschuk. (Other members at the time of the *Rhythm of Youth* album, which included "The Safety Dance," included Ivan's brother Stefan and Allan McCarthy.) Doroschuk originally conceived the band as a punk outfit in the waning stages of the 70s. But, as the music world changed, so did the band's focus.

"I just realized that pop music was one of the biggest platforms for getting a message across," Doroschuk says. "I just decided that if I wanted to get my message across to the most people possible, I should surround it with music that was more friendly to the ear. So I made the switch from punk guitars to New Wave synthesizers for that reason."

Many of the songs you'll find in this volume came from very specific inspirations, yet, through the skill of the songwriters and performers involved and some occasional happenstance, they resonated far beyond their initial source. Such was the case with "The Safety Dance," which Doroschuk wrote to avenge a slight against him and his like-minded friends.

"It was the late 70s and disco was dying," Doroschuk explains to set the scene. "And the DJs were just starting to mix in a little New Wave music to their disco sets. Whenever we'd hear Blondie's 'Heart Of Glass' or the B-52s' 'Rock Lobster' or something like that, we'd jump up onto the dance floor and start pogoing, jumping up and down. And we'd get kicked out by the bouncers for basically inventing slam dancing. So I went home and basically the song just kind of came out by itself. It was a direct reaction to being kicked out of bars for not being allowed to dance the way I wanted to."

Doroschuk set the song to a crackling dance beat and warm synthesizers, intoning "You can dance if you want to" right off the bat as his personal manifesto. The song was a solid hit in his native Canada, but it was only when it was released in the United States that "The Safety Dance" craze really took off. "We were in the studio halfway through recording our second record when 'Safety Dance' got released in the States and went to number 1 on the dance charts," Doroschuk explains. "We had to sort of put everything on hold and go back on the road and promote it."

"The Safety Dance" is also one of the rare songs from the 80s whose remix is more popular than its original single version. The remix includes a kind of Morse Code–like melody, the word "safety" spelled out in dramatic fashion, and Doroschuk doing a proto-rap of the song's first verse. It's all sort of quirky and a little dark, but it's the perfect setup for when the main keyboard riff triumphantly enters the picture.

In modern times, such a remix would likely be taken out of the hands of the original artist and entrusted to a DJ or producer. Yet Doroschuk handled the duties on "The Safety Dance" and sort of stumbled his way to excellence. "We were put into the studio and we were told to make a 12-inch extended remix," he says. "And we really didn't know too much about it. So on the 12-inch we just basically stretched out the song. With the spelling of the letters and the rap part, I was trying to emulate Grandmaster Flash, actually. I was channeling 'The Message,' and that was basically what came out. And the blips at the beginning, I wanted to put something in there that would announce to people that 'The Safety Dance' was coming up, kind of warning signal or something like that."

Doroschuk also credits the video, an only-in-the-80s clip where whimsicality flirts with insanity, for the song spreading so wide. "What surprised a lot of people when they saw the video is that they thought I was going to be a spike-haired, zippered-pants, pointy-shoed kind of guy," Doroschuk laughs. "It turned out it was Peter Pan running around with a midget. It throws people for a loop, but it permitted the song to cross all kinds of boundaries."

It's easy to scoff at "The Safety Dance" as naive, but you could also conceivably say that "All You Need Is Love" is naive too, if you're that sort. What Doroschuk was doing, perhaps unwittingly, was making a case that any type of behavior is acceptable as long as it's not hurting anybody. It's a song that certainly marches to its own beat, but it does so benevolently. And the way that it presages our current era—where all voices, no matter how different they might be from the supposed "norm," simply demand to be heard—is downright eerie. The song is very much of its time and niftily ahead of it all at once.

Doroschuk couldn't have imagined all that when he wrote the song and then watched it sail to number 3 on the pop charts. But he has come to accept that it has a life of its own. "I feel like the song is so much bigger than me," he says. "I realized a while ago that people didn't even know who I was. People don't even know who Men without Hats were. A lot of people don't even know what the song is called. They say, 'It's that "You can dance if you want to" song.' The song being bigger than me; I'm kind of an ambassador for the song. I'm going around the world presenting 'The Safety Dance' to people. I'm sort of the custodian for 'Safety Dance,' going around showing people how to do it properly."

A song so unique was always going to be tricky to follow up, but give Men without Hats credit for once again denting the public consciousness with the similarly sui generis Top 20 single "Pop Goes the World" in 1987. Doroschuk still tours and records under the Men without Hats banner, and he still marvels at the strange power of his biggest hit.

"That message needs to be heard still, I guess," he says. "People want to hear that they can dance if they want to. It's been cross-generational, it's been cross-everything. One of the things that was good for us is that there is no 'Safety Dance.' There's the 'S' movement with the arms, but people can move like they want. There's no uniform, there's no dress code, there's no hairstyle."

To make the "S" move, put your right hand over your head pointing left and your left hand at your waist pointing right. The genius of "The Safety Dance" is that it dares you to imagine a world where your life, like the rest of the dance, is up to you.

"Billie Jean" by Michael Jackson

THRILLER (1982)

This book is filled with recollections of some of the most brilliant songs from the 1980s. Take any one of them away, imagine it had never existed, and the decade, while a little bit lesser for the loss, would still have maintained its unique musical identity, its same aura of specialness. "Billie Jean" is indispensable, the sine qua non, that single song that, had Michael Jackson never unleashed it on an unsuspecting world, would have somehow left a void on the decade by its absence in much the same way that a person can miss someone he or she has never met.

It's impossible to overstate the import of the song. This book isn't about rankings, so the argument about whether it's the decade's best is for another time. But it is without a doubt on the short list, and it is definitely the most impactful. It melded rhythm and blues with pop music in ways never before imagined; it made music videos must-see television (and opened up the doors for black artists to succeed in that milieu); it was the peak moment in the career of the era's most famous artist; it is a song that, like some wonderful triumph or horrific tragedy, indelibly plants the moment you first heard it in your memory forever.

But for all that commemorating and mythologizing, it is crucial to remember that "Billie Jean" couldn't have become what it eventually did without the contributions of the people simply doing their jobs in the recording studio when it was laid down. Ndugu Chancler, the man whose drumbeat is the first thing that you hear when the song comes on, puts it all in perspective:

> At the time, you're recording with some good people, it's a good session, and that's that. "You don't separate it and say, "This is going to be great," blah, blah, blah.
>
> It's kind of like the luck of the draw. I just happened to be one of the ones that got that call. It's like the guys that played with Elvis

Presley. At the time, you're just doing the best you can do on that job. It's later on that it becomes a piece of history.

Chancler had no previous history working with Jackson, but he worked on many sessions with *Thriller* producer Quincy Jones, supporting artists ranging from Miles Davis to Frank Sinatra. And Chancler modestly explains that his part was readied for him by the principals behind the song: Jackson, who wrote it; Jones, the producer; and Bruce Swedien, the mixer. "They had the demo and everything all laid out," Chancler remembers. "They had the vocals and everything on the track. They basically knew what they wanted. They had a drum machine there and everything so it was all laid out. Conceptually, they already kind of knew what they wanted to do and they just described it to me. We went at it from that standpoint."

One of the most striking things about "Billie Jean" is how all the individual parts create hooks of their own but interlock to form unstoppable sonic momentum. In addition to Chancler's precisely funky beat, there's Louis Johnson's prancing bass line, David Williams's flickering guitar, and Greg Phillinganes's insinuating keyboards, all setting the table for Jackson's mesmerizing lead vocal and his various wordless exclamations. Jones achieved this effect, with Swedien's mixing help, by having each player create his part in a vacuum of sorts. "I did my part by myself," Chancler says. "That's the way we were recording back in those days. This was pre–Pro Tools and all of that. So it was nothing for session guys to go in by themselves and make parts. A lot of that was happening. We were fixing parts or creating parts. That was the brink of that concept of recording."

If the music was innovative, Jackson's concept for the lyric was shocking, so much so that Jones doubted whether it even belonged on the *Thriller* album, let alone whether it belonged as a single. The narrator of "Billie Jean" explains how a simple dance floor rendezvous escalates into a nightmarish scenario where the title character claims that he fathered her child. It's a testament to Jackson's bravery that he wrote those lyrics—with the chorus line of "But the kid is not my son" and the final verse's admission that the baby resembles the narrator making him look guilty—considering that people would immediately assume that it was a true story. But the song leaves behind those specifics and says something larger instead about the dangers of rumor and hearsay, about that terrible moment "when the lie becomes the truth."

Chancler says that Jackson wrote from experience. "We had talked about the story, about what used to happen with girls being after him and accusing him and all of that. This was subject matter that was reality that no one had ever talked about." And Jones eventually saw the song in context of the bigger picture of *Thriller* as a statement of where Jackson was at that point in his life and career. "Quincy was trying to find the best fits for all of the conceptual things that he had on the album," Chancler remembers. "Everything had to stand on its own. Once he recorded 'Billie Jean' and checked it out, he understood that was something in terms of subject matter and feel that Michael had never done. So they settled on that."

Even after all his success with the Jackson 5 and his mutliplatinum 1979 collaboration with Jones as a solo artist with *Off the Wall*, "Billie Jean" was the snowball that began the avalanche of Michael Jackson's stardom, which would help usher in the era of the mega-80s artists like Prince, Madonna, and Bruce Springsteen. The video, still as riveting today as it was when it first appeared because of Jackson's singular presence and dance moves, didn't hurt, either. The *Thriller* album kept churning out hits, one seemingly bigger than the next, so that all of the wonderful music released in the 1982–1983 era had to struggle just to escape its shadow.

But as Ndugu Chancler, who still is a performing session musician and songwriter as well as a professor of music at the University of Southern California, explains so simply and eloquently, "All of that was after the fact." And the fact remains that "Billie Jean" occurred only because of a one-of-a-kind confluence of people, skills, strategies, circumstance, luck, and the musical force of nature that Michael Jackson embodied. Yes, we would have still had 80s music without it, but it just wouldn't have been the same.

"Shame on the Moon" by Bob Seger & the Silver Bullet Band

THE DISTANCE (1982)

Throughout this book, there have plenty of songs profiled that had "hit single" written all over them from the moment they were composed. "Shame on the Moon" is not of them. Not that there is anything wrong with the quality of the song; it's a low-key stunner of a ballad. And the performance by Bob Seger is both contemplative and fiery in all the right places, while his trusted Silver Bullet Band delivers typically intuitive backing.

Considering it enjoyed its success in 1983 (after its release in the last week of 1982), at the very heart of the MTV era, you might think then that there was a flashy or groundbreaking video to support it. In actuality, Seger, who rode the song to number 2, didn't even bother to make a video clip for it.

So how then to explain the success of "Shame on the Moon," which remains one of the most beloved slow burns in Seger's massively impressive catalog of hits? Well, the man who wrote it might not be the one to answer this question, as he has since rewritten what he thought were flaws in the lyrics, but Rodney Crowell will give it a shot anyway:

> Something about the chorus, the narrator is sort of hinting that he's the one who's crossed the line, the one who's shaming himself, the one who's to blame. Maybe that kind of self-indictment was interesting for the times.
>
> I always look at these things in another way. I was lucky a few times that my songs hooked up with artists other than myself when they were reaching a commercial peak. Without a video and all of the things that were so big about 1983, it was just a time in his career where the stars were aligned for Bob and, because of that, also for me. Maybe programmers were fascinated by the ambiguity of the song. We can all say why "She loves you, yeah, yeah" was so big, 'cause

you'd never heard anything like it before. But in the case of that kind of post-Dylan impressionist language, this wasn't that new.

Crowell, who had already been building a reputation as a country song-writer whose tunes, with their insight and self-awareness, strayed fascinatingly outside of the typical Nashville formula, penned "Shame on the Moon" for his third, self-titled solo album in 1981. "I was tinkering on the guitar and the television was on," Crowell remembers about the song's origins:

> And those first news reports from Jonestown came in. I really got distracted by the news reports because it was so horrendous. It was the last time I ever wrote a song with the television on. Because I think I would have gotten the song better if I hadn't been distracted by the news report.
>
> I had the chorus, and I wasn't even sure what it was, but the words sounded good. The melody was kind of ethereal, kind of moonlit. So from there I was just thinking about how I would go with the verses. I must say that at that particular time, I was really fascinated by impressionist painters. I kind of came late into really dialing them in. So I was consciously trying to write in an impressionistic way. Which is to blur and round off the edges. You don't make it a portrait. You make it an impression.

Crowell cut a fine version of the song with his band, featuring an interesting drum pattern by Larry London that sounded like an old nag staggering into town with a weary rider on top. Not too long after that, the songwriter received a surprising message. "Billy Paine, who played piano on Seger's version of it, called me after they recorded it," Crowell remembers. "And he said, 'I think we just cut a hit on your song.' I said, 'Okay, good. I'll wait and see.'"

Paine's piano work is one of the distinguishing musical characteristics of Seger's take, especially the soulful solo. Glenn Frey added silky-smooth backing vocals, and Seger gets to the perilous bottom of Crowell's lyrics. "Shame on the Moon" suggests a lot more than it comes right out and says, allowing listeners to find their own interpretation, perhaps colored by their own experiences. Songs like that tend to have a long shelf life.

But more than that, "Shame on the Moon" delivers, with striking economy, a clear-eyed treatise on the unseen burden of every man. The narrator constantly warns listeners that there's no way for them to know the inner life of the people with whom they interact without actually stepping inside, an obvious impossibility. The lines are simple and piercing: "Some men go crazy, some men go slow/Some men go just where they want, some men never go." And the chorus, which on its surface looks up to the moon for a reason, actually lays the blame in the only place it can be fairly laid, which is right back on the man in question.

The ethereal quality that Crowell references is something that lingers long after its last notes are heard.

Crowell, however, wasn't ever quite satisfied with how he wrapped the song up:

> I talked to Bob Seger about it a long time ago and I said, "You know, Bob, I just never liked that last verse." And he said, "I thought it worked really well."
>
> I also once ran into a songwriter who will remain nameless but who also recorded it. He said, "Man, I sure like your song. I sure wish I'd been there to help you with that last verse." I said, "Thanks, man, I've been trying to tell everybody." And he said, "Well why did you record it in the first place?" And I said, "Really good question."

The songwriter also gives great credit to the interpreter:

> I said to Seger when we talked about it, "Man, that song belongs to you now." As far as I'm concerned, his performance of it far outdistances mine. His performance of it is more impassioned than mine. Which was a good lesson for me, because I played it and sang it and that was it. But he really nailed it. And I don't perform the song and I haven't, because I had to bow to his performance because it was far superior at the time.
>
> Now that you mention it, maybe I should bring that song back out and see if I can't find some of that passion that Seger had. See if I could make more out of it.

Crowell's modesty aside, it's clear that the words, as much as how they were sung, are responsible the song's ride to very near the top of the charts ("It sat right there behind 'Billie Jean,' Michael Jackson keeping me from number 1," Crowell laughs). "If asked what is it I strive for, and I can't say I was doing this when I was a younger artist; I was just painting by numbers, just trying to get to the next street corner," Crowell sums up. "But now I strive for timelessness. Whatever the average, it's probably less than baseball, less than 30 percent of what you do is timeless. Maybe if 20 percent of what you do is timeless, that will get you into the Nashville Songwriters Hall of Fame. I really want my work to be timeless at best."

Timelessness is certainly a hallmark of the oeuvres of both Bob Seger and Rodney Crowell. How could "Shame on the Moon" be anything but?

"Sexual Healing" by Marvin Gaye

MIDNIGHT LOVE (1982)

Marvin Gaye was in a creative and personal lull circa 1982. Tax issues and drug addiction problems forced him to hole up in Ostend, Belgium, to regroup. He had separated from Motown, the only label he had ever known. And his last significant hit, "Got to Give It Up," was a half decade in his rearview mirror, which, considering the drastic changes taking place in music at the time, might as well have been a millennium ago.

But he had a musical track written by Odell Brown, a relaxed and grooving thing and seemed perfect for the brand of laid-back, smoldering heat that Gaye had slathered over so many classic singles. The only thing he needed was an idea of what to sing over it. Which is when one of the unlikeliest songwriting team-ups in musical history took place to create "Sexual Healing," a runaway R&B smash and Top 5 pop hit.

David Ritz is an acclaimed writer whose bibliography reads like a Who's Who of rhythm and blues history, having written books about or with legends like Ray Charles, B. B. King, and Buddy Guy. He came to Belgium to continue work on a potential ghostwritten autobiography of Gaye when serendipity interrupted:

> It happened by accident. We'd get together in the evenings and we'd talk and he had a track. Lots of R&B songs begin with a track and it's basically a drum, a bass line, often a keyboard, but it's basically a groove without a melody or without lyrics. On the table, there was an arty book of what was really porn, I thought, from a French cartoon-ist. I kind of looked at the book and we were just talking and I said, "Man, this is weird. What you really need is 'Sexual Healing.'" And he asked, "What's that?" I said, "You've got to fall in love with a girl who's gonna love you and it doesn't involve pain." Because the book was kind of S&M-ish.

And he said, "Well, that's an interesting concept." As we were talking, the track was playing over and over again on the boom box. So he said, "Well, why don't you write a poem about that?" I said, "All right." I had never written a song before then, but I had written a lot of poems, I had written a lot of books and I thought, "No big deal." So I just started to scribble, "Whenever blue teardrops are falling," blah, blah, on a paper. He took the words and they seemed to have musical notes attached to them. And that was it. He had another boom box and ping-ponged his vocal on top of the track. And, basically, the song was written.

"Sexual Healing" is quintessential Gaye. He floats on top of the nonintrusive yet seductive rhythms. Never does it seem like he's exerting too much effort, and yet he conveys the song's deeper emotions better than any overemoter ever could. The lyrics contain the kind of clever wordplay and nimble rhyming that's a classic Motown staple ("Baby, I think I'm capsizing/The waves are rising and rising" or "You're my medicine, open up and let me in/Darling, you're so great/I can't wait for you to operate"). But there is also something deeper at play in lines like "And my emotional stability is leaving me" and "The love you give to me will free me" that, when coupled with the subtle anguish in his vocal, suggest Gaye's personal struggle for redemption.

Ritz says that his literary background counterintuitively prepared him for this job:

> I think it was more than my knowing him well, which of course helped because I was a biographer. But what really helped me is I'm basically a ghostwriter. That's what I do for a living. And when you're a ghostwriter, your main job is to put yourself in the head of the star. So it was almost like it was part of that same process, like, "Okay, I am now Marvin Gaye. What's going on in my life? What do I need?" And so I was into his head and I wrote a script that was true to him. I was just interested in helping him express what was in his heart and his head.

"Sexual Healing" struck it big worldwide and, unfortunately, stirred up a rift between Gaye and Ritz, who had been friends for five years at that point. On the album cover for *Midnight Love*, which contains the song, Gaye thanked Ritz for contributing the song's title, but "Sexual Healing" was only credited to Gaye and Brown. When Ritz persisted on the matter of credit, Gaye bristled. "I saw him at a party and he looked at me and said, 'Man, you gotta stop bothering me about this,'" Ritz remembers. "And it was the only time he had ever really been short with me because we had such a cordial relationship." Upon the advice of music industry legend Jerry Wexler, Ritz reluctantly sued Gaye for credit. "That was hell because it was a guy I adored, who had been a huge influence on my life. From a musical point of view, there isn't anybody's music that I've listened to more, studied more, or has given me more joy."

Before the suit was settled, tragedy struck. "['Sexual Healing'] was a hit, and also the hit that kind of brought him back to the United States and took him out of this long European exile, which was both good and bad," Ritz explains. "Good, in that he was able to tour behind it and go home in sort of a triumphant return, but bad in that he kind of fell back into the kind of temptations that would ultimately sort of kill him." Even as the public bathed him with adoration for *Midnight Love* and his unforgettable reimagining of the National Anthem at the 1983 NBA All-Star Game, Gaye's depression and drug habits led him to attempt suicide just four days before he was shot to death by his father on April 1, 1984. (For a closer examination of these and all the details of Gaye's life, check out Ritz's biography *Divided Soul: The Life of Marvin Gaye*.)

Ritz, boosted by the recordings he had made of his fateful songwriting session with Gaye, eventually settled out of court for songwriting credit on "Sexual Healing." (It should be noted that a few close Gaye confidants have disputed that Ritz's contributions went beyond providing the song's title.) And he also has found a way to forget the rough times at the end.

"It's kind of a story with a tragic ending in that he was never healed," Ritz confides. "But its creation happened during a glorious time together. He's always on my mind. I always feel blessed that I got to hang out with him for a long, long time. He was an extraordinarily beautiful man, a deeply spiritual guy, with all kinds of problems, but also with all kinds of incredibly positive qualities. He was an extremely compassionate person and taught me a lot about compassion. I certainly was happy to extend that compassion to him."

"Bad to the Bone" by George Thorogood and the Destroyers

BAD TO THE BONE (1982)

It wasn't a hit single, oddly enough, but "Bad to the Bone" outstrips all other 80s songs in terms of the way it has essentially become cultural shorthand. When you hear it—actually, when you hear just the opening riff, in a movie or television show or wherever—you immediately have a mental picture of the character about to show up on the screen. It has sound-tracked the exploits of everyone from the Terminator to Al Bundy. Aside from that, it is a blistering blues-rock performance by George Thorogood and the Destroyers, with Thorogood taking center stage with his gritty vocals and his motorcycle-ride-into-the-sunset lead guitar work.

You might think that the guy responsible for writing and performing this thing would be the boastful sort, but Thorogood isn't buying into the image. "Let's face it, 'Bad to the Bone' is common," Thorogood explains. "If I hadn't done it, somebody else would. It's as easy as that. And I thought about that and I kind of put a rush job on it. You know, if I don't grab this thing, somebody else is gonna do it and they'll probably do a better job of it."

Refreshing modesty aside, Thorogood is hinting at the notion that he composed "Bad to the Bone" to fall in line with other bombastic blues and rock songs he admired. He had always inhabited those genres with authenticity and verve since he and the Destroyers (which included bassist Billy Blough, drummer Jeff Simon, and saxophonist Hank Carter) had busted onto the scene from Delaware with their 1977 debut. But as he moved to a new label (EMI) for the band's 1982 release, Thorogood felt that he needed something special that his previous albums had lacked.

"I was checking out the originals of J. Geils, in particular 'Love Stinks,' with that intro," Thorogood says. "I thought that we needed a song to take us to another level. It was also the birth of MTV. You gotta play this hand while it's hot. If you come up with one tune, you can work. If you come up with three tunes, that's a career. You got more than three, you got a monster career."

Thorogood proved canny at combing the culture for what worked and incorporating that into his new composition:

> I was very intrigued with prepositional phrases in titles, like *Gone with the Wind*, "Born to Be Wild," "Blowin' in the Wind." They all seemed to work. I said, "Hmm. Those are catchy things." Then, in our neighborhood, "bad" meant "cool." There was a guy in our neighborhood who used to say, "Bad to Death." I said, "Well, that's not my style."
>
> Johnny Cash once said that when you're starting to write songs, write down a bunch of words that rhyme. How many words can you rhyme if you have a certain word? So I thought of "bone." How many words does it rhyme with? And I thought, don't make it too fancy. Make it something funny, because it's a tongue-in-cheek song.

From those initial considerations, Thorogood had a title. Meanwhile, his stammering style in each refrain was an idea he thought was ripe for reintroduction. "I remember hearing Roger Daltrey doing 'My Generation,'" he says. "He supposedly picked that up off an album called *Stuttering Blues* by John Lee Hooker. Then about ten years after that there was 'B-b-baby you ain't seen nothing yet' [by Bachman-Turner Overdrive]. I figured after about every ten years, old things are up for grabs."

He then went about penning a series of one-liners, each of which separately carries its own bluesy potency while adding up to an overwhelming whole. Prime example: "When I walk the streets, kings and queens step aside/Every woman I meet, they all stay satisfied." Even the nurses at the hospital where the narrator is born are hip to his badness. The character is larger than life and utterly compelling.

Again, Thorogood shrugs off the credit, pointing to his musical predecessors:

> If you really want to go back and do some research in blues and rock and roll, the lyrics are straight Bo Diddley. Bo Diddley's whole thing is he's the baddest man in the world. Think of the lyrics to "Who Do You Love?," the lyrics to "Jumpin' Jack Flash." There's not that many of them that are that tongue-in-cheek, over-the-top, macho thing that I was trying to do there. But if it's recorded well, sung right, and taken in the right spirit, you'll have something that people enjoy.
>
> People say, "I don't like that Thorogood guy talking about this, that, and the other." You're missing the point. It's a regular guy from a regular place, Wilmington, Delaware, who wants to be Steve McQueen. We all do.

Thorogood also saw the song in terms of humor and listener wish fulfillment. "Well, if you can make people laugh and dance at the same time, you might have something," he says. "That's been my MO since I got into the thing, actually. It's a song where a lot of guys will say, 'I want to be that guy.' It's like watching a James Bond movie. And there might be a few girls who might say, 'Well, I'd like to be with a guy like that.' Well, maybe for only an hour. So that was the whole idea of the fantasy of it."

On top of all that came a staggering performance by the Destroyers, with a little assistance from longtime Rolling Stones collaborator Ian Stewart on piano, that captures every last ounce of their live energy in the recording. In addition to Thorogood's burning up the place with his lead licks, Carter's saxophone work is pretty incendiary as well, while Blough, Simon, and Stewart keep the rhythm chugging along. And, to center the whole thing, there is the indelible riff, slightly altered from the blues classic "Mannish Boy."

Thorogood was okay with the fact that the song didn't do much on the singles charts. "The album did well and the song fit right into our live show. People liked it. I never wanted anything more than that. We needed new material; everybody needs new material. That's why you go into the studio. Some people say they're going into the studio because they want to make hits. That's their choice. With this band, it was what can we put into the show that our fans will like that's new that they haven't heard. And something we can play really good. 'Bad to the Bone' fell under all those categories."

The song's cultural ubiquity was still to come. "I just think it's a catchy phrase that people can use for anything," Thorogood muses. "Guy is gonna go play in the Super Bowl, or guy is gonna go propose. He's gonna say, 'I'm bad to the bone.' If you have something like that, it just sticks and people use it for all sorts of reasons. Usually to pump themselves up or to give themselves a little bit of self-confidence."

George Thorogood and the Destroyers are still out there living up to their name, playing their blend of rock and blues with a fun intensity that young bands can't hope to approach. In his typically self-deprecating fashion, the band's leader doesn't think deep examination of his most famous song is all that necessary. "If you take George Thorogood seriously, you're taking yourself too seriously," he claims. "Especially my songwriting."

Still, "Bad to the Bone" doesn't work unless you've got a singer who can inhabit that character convincingly. He may be an unfailingly modest, nice guy, but to us 80s music fans, George Thorogood will always be the glorious embodiment of Badness.

"Mr. Roboto" by Styx

KILROY WAS HERE (1983)

It became one of the most iconic songs of the entire decade, yet it wasn't even really supposed to be a song.

According to Dennis DeYoung, former keyboardist, lead singer, and chief songwriter of Styx, "Mr. Roboto" was supposed to be a connecting piece between a video explaining the backstory of Styx's 1983 album *Kilroy Was Here* and the band's live performances of the material. "'Mr. Roboto' was never meant to be a pop single, a hit record," DeYoung says. "It was simply expository, to go from one point to another. That's it."

Yet, when all was said and done, the song ended up at number 3 on the *Billboard* charts in 1983. More than that, its weirdness, its go-for-broke attitude, its sense of fun in spite of what was meant to be heavy subject matter, has kept it around, when it easily could have been a forgotten novelty. And the man who created it is all right with that:

> My expectations for that song were zero. If I had sat down and said, "You know what I need to do? I need to write a song that millions of people will sing for forty years," it wouldn't have been that. I wish I had ten more just like it. And I mean it from the bottom of my heart.
>
> And here's the joke of it. I know my obituary, despite the fact that I wrote "Babe" and "Lady" and "Come Sail Away" and everything else, will say, "Dennis DeYoung, writer of 'Mr. Roboto.'"

The story of "Mr. Roboto" is inextricable from the concept album that birthed it. Styx was on top of the rock-and-roll world at the start of the 80s, with their previous album, *Paradise Theatre*, hitting number 1 and spawning two Top 10 singles in "Too Much Time on My Hands" and "The Best of Times." Yet DeYoung was feeling artistically stifled. "I had made eight records that were of a particular kind and thought in my own mind that I didn't know what else to say in that particular genre," he says. "I didn't know what else to do."

Even though *Paradise Theatre* was tied to a loose theme, *Kilroy Was Here* was DeYoung's attempt to write an album along the lines of the Who's *Tommy* or Pink Floyd's *The Wall* by strictly tying all the songs to an overarching concept. Around the time of *Paradise Theatre*, Styx was accused by fundamentalists as having placed Satanic messages in their song "Snowblind" that could be heard when the record was spun backward. ("This from the band who did 'Babe,'" DeYoung deadpans, referring to Styx's lovey-dovey hit ballad.)

More inspiration came in the form of a documentary DeYoung saw around that same time. "It was on the coming technological advances in manufacturing and how it could affect the jobs of millions of people," he remembers. "In this documentary, you see what looks to be about a ten-thousand-square-foot factory floor filled with machines with robotic arms doing some sort of task. They're all working away. There's one guy in there and he goes to the door to leave, shuts off all the lights, and walks out. The camera stays on the factory floor in the dark, but all the machines, they keep going."

From those seeds sprang a story set in a future in which America has fallen on hard times and a charismatic fundamentalist TV show host convinces the population that things started going downhill with the advent of rock and roll. The powers that be thus ban the music and imprison any who would dare to play it. Would-be rock and rollers are guarded by robots, but one, named Kilroy, escapes to fan the flames of rebellion.

As for "Mr. Roboto" itself, DeYoung came up with the refrain accidentally during a tour of Japan. "I realized that getting *konichiwa* and *domo arigato* right will at least not get you arrested in Japan," he remembers. "Then I hear in a conversation, apropos to nothing, that *roboto* is the Japanese word for robot. So right away, since I really wanted to be Jerry Lewis first before I wanted to be a rock star, my mind went directly to 'domo arigato, roboto.'"

The music for the song emanated from DeYoung's acquisition of a new Roland synthesizer and the sequencing effects he was able to coax from it. When he played the finished product for friends, they were struck by its commercial potential. Not only was "Mr. Roboto" going on the album, it was suddenly in contention for the first single spot.

Styx—which at that time included DeYoung, Tommy Shaw, James Young, John Panozzo, and Chuck Panozzo—initially considered the ballad "Don't Let It End" as the song that would introduce the album. The logic, according to DeYoung: "It's not gonna scare our audience. It's not gonna upset radio. It's not gonna make anybody crazy, because they'll say, 'Oh, we know that side of Styx. We've been listening to these assholes for over eleven years. We know what that is.'"

But the strange power of "Mr. Roboto" won them over. "So we took a chance," DeYoung recalls. "And we just rolled the bones. It was a collective decision. Not my decision. But when we were making it, we had the time of our life doing it. Everybody was responsible in the band in some way for the actual arrangement and production of the song. And we mixed it. We were used to making our records, but this was crazy different."

Different indeed. Even though fans may not have initially had any clue about the backstory (DeYoung: "At the end I'm yelling, 'Kilroy!' What the hell does that mean?"), they somehow tapped into the pathos behind it. They also grooved to a song that sounded amazing, regardless of any exposition, and it still does today. And then, of course, there was the refrain. "Somehow 'Domo arigato/Mr. Roboto' got into the culture," DeYoung says. "And I think to myself, 'How did that happen?'"

DeYoung feels that some of the backlash the band received for the song came partly because they had, in a way, become imprisoned by their own massive success:

> Here's your dilemma: You have to work your nuts off to develop an audience, to get them loyal to you to essentially keep your habit going. Keep the needle in your arm, which is the ability to make the next record. You must show some financial success.
>
> The first thing you have to do is earn the right to make the next record. That doesn't mean that you're trying to be commercial. You just know that in order to get the next one, you gotta do okay on this one, because people are investing money on you. An artist wants to develop this audience. They do everything in their power to hone their style to make people like them. And then they get a huge audience and the challenge is this: How do you as the musician take your audience with you if you want to do something new? It's a dilemma.

One thing DeYoung laments is that his story for *Kilroy Was Here* didn't get fleshed out quite the way he wanted. "The original idea that I had for this concept was so much more than it turned out to be because it became apparent that I was in a band, not that I didn't know it, and people were justifiably concerned with its complexity," he said. "And so it did get, dare I say, simplified. All these highfalutin thoughts I had in my little pea brain turned out to be, in essence, 'Domo arigato/Mr. Roboto.'"

And yet, somehow, that couplet has always been more than enough.

"Suddenly Last Summer" by the Motels

LITTLE ROBBERS (1983)

If most 80s music felt infused with extremely bright colors, the music of the Motels was more like film noir. And nobody played the tortured heroine better than lead singer and chief songwriter Martha Davis, her sultry yet wounded voice just perfect for expressing the conflicted emotions on the band's 80s hits "Only the Lonely" and "Suddenly Last Summer."

Very few of the artists in this book endured a journey to their peak success quite so involved as Davis's. She started the original version of the Motels back in 1971, then went through various incarnations of the group in the decade or so before they found commercial success, hopping around California in the process. If you check out the band's Wikipedia page, you'll find a list of former members as long as your arm.

But Davis remained stubbornly pointed toward success, even when it might not have been in her best interests. "You kind of have to just be hard-headed and just have the vision that's going to guide you on," Davis says. "Luckily, when you're young and you're first starting out doing anything, your ego and your drive are so strong that it's just like, 'Obviously this is going to happen.' You just have to convince yourself all the time. But especially in my case with two children, it was very scary. Probably not even the smartest thing to do, because, after all, who makes it in the music business? It was kind of a boneheaded move on my part, actually."

The 1980s incarnation of the Motels found the mainstream success that had eluded all of their predecessors when the torch song "Only the Lonely," with producer Val Garay (of "Bette Davis Eyes") at the helm, broke through in the United States in 1982. Yet after all of the hard work it took to get there, Davis was ambivalent about the success. "I never wanted to be an MOR [middle-of-the-road], top-of-the-charts person," she says. "I wanted to be an interesting writer, somebody who sort of pushed the envelope. It was definitely the double-edged sword. Here I was, I had my first success in the States. Val Garay was a very polished producer; I like crazy and edgy. But you can't argue with success. So it was a very confusing thing."

The track that would return the Motels to the Top 10 in 1983 demonstrates how some songs are worth the wait. "'Suddenly Last Summer,' I think, is pretty much the weirdest song I've ever written in the sense that it spanned a decade," Davis explains:

> I vividly remember sitting in Berkeley, California. I may or may not have been in a band at that point, but I'd been writing songs since I was fifteen and I was definitely making music. I was just sitting in the backyard and it was a beautiful sunny day at the end of summer. All of a sudden this ice-cold wind comes out of nowhere and you know winter is right around the corner. And you feel that chill. Even though the sun is shining, there's still a coldness to it.
>
> And then I heard the ice cream truck. And I was like, well, that's probably the last time I'm going to hear that ice cream truck this year. That weird metaphor probably symbolized me being a very, very young girl, and summer came along, and my entire life changed because of a boy. I didn't even write the song then. It was just these different emotions that were washing over me. Now obviously I had already had my kids. I had already moved to Berkeley. So that part of my life was done. But I think it was the beginning of the retelling of that story.

The emotions must have lingered with Davis, because they were there ready to fill in the blanks when inspiration struck again much further down the road. "Years later, I'm down in LA," she remembers. "At around 3am, I get woken by this 'da-da-da-da-da' [sings opening riff from 'Suddenly Last Summer'], this melody starts running through my head. And I got up and I wrote the song. And all of the pieces that I had experienced ten years earlier at Berkeley were just manifesting themselves. I've never had that happen before. It just goes to show that all of the song fodder are all of these experiences in your life, stowed away in memory nooks and various places. When they decide it's time, they will make themselves imminent."

Davis also had a knack for choosing evocative, literary titles; in the case of "Suddenly Last Summer," it was one she borrowed from Tennessee Williams's play. "I'd never seen the movie or read the play," she says. "But the sound of it, the lyricism of it, is beautiful. It would drive all the sound engineers insane because it's all sibilance, so I had to learn to swallow my *s*'s. Titles are fun because, first of all, you can't copyright a title, so anything out there is open ground. And I like little phrases and words. Sometimes they will bloom into a song if I'm not careful."

"Suddenly Last Summer" certainly bloomed, in part due to the melancholy pull of the music, evoked by Steve Goldstein's softly descending keyboards. Davis's lyrics are beautiful in their simplicity, heartbroken as they are by impermanence: of a season, of a dream, of a love affair. "Sometimes I stay too long," she sings, realizing that it's dangerous to get too lost in a memory. And time can be a deceiver: "One summer never ends/One summer never begins." Plus, she possesses such a mesmerizing natural timbre to her voice that she can underplay the lyrics and still deliver a walloping impact.

Davis believes that great songs like this one are out there if you know how to bring them in. "Half the time, I don't even know what they're doing," she says. "That's part of the gift that I've been given is the ability to get the hell out of my own way and let whatever this is just come through me. You'll hear a lot of artists describe it that way. And it's an interesting thing because you have to leave your ego by the door. I still have a rule with the band that the only ego allowed in the room is the songs' ego. I am a slave to them. They tell me what to do."

Davis still writes and performs with a version of the Motels that has, believe it or not, been in place for fifteen solid years. And she is extremely grateful that she stuck with it through the lean years. "I'm so humbled by the whole experience," she muses. "We're still doing shows, and still when we come to these songs, seeing the looks on people's faces. Because that's the beauty of music. It is a time machine; it does take you back. It will take you and place you right in the back seat of that car or wherever you were at that time. It's a tremendously powerful medium. Doing it always makes me happy. The joy of making music, of playing music, of seeing people's reactions to it, there's nothing like it in the world."

"Sister Christian" by Night Ranger

MIDNIGHT MADNESS (1983)

Power ballads were in their prime in the early 1980s. As a matter of fact, some of the artists profiled in this book were experts at them. As the decade progressed, power ballads became de rigueur for the so-called hair metal bands, with songs that were too often cynical, uninspired exercises undertaken solely to pull in the teenage girls.

The era of the power ballad undoubtedly peaked with Night Ranger's "Sister Christian" from their 1983 album *Midnight Madness*, although the song wasn't released as a single until the following year, when it skied to number 5 amid some pretty heady pop chart company. It is a thrilling example of just what can happen when a song to which you can slow dance erupts into something that blows you right off the floor.

Night Ranger, formed in San Francisco at the turn of the decade, might have seemed an unlikely source for such an anthemic song. Their debut album, 1982's *Dawn Patrol*, featured a couple of songs that scraped the Top 40, but both were cut from the same hard-rocking cloth and didn't give any indication of the sentimental side that their biggest hit would eventually show.

Still, as the band's drummer Kelly Keagy, who wrote and sang "Sister Christian," explains, the song was in their repertoire for a while before they decided to record it. "When we got in there with 'Sister Christian,' we had already been playing that song in clubs before we had ever got signed," Keagy says. "So we went back to that one and re-looked at it and it was like it made sense. We had some ballads on *Dawn Patrol*, so we needed one for the new album."

What made "Sister Christian" stand out from the tortured testaments of love and devotion that usually signify slow rock songs was its subject matter. "It wasn't a love song," Keagy says. "I think that's the reason why we liked it. It wasn't lovey-dovey. It had some sort of edge to it. And it had a connection with people about growing up or moving ahead in life. That's what I wanted it to be."

The "Sister Christian" in question was not a love interest but rather Keagy's actual sister Christy; the name was changed when Keagy performed it for the band for the first time and bassist Jack Blades misheard "Christy" as "Christian." It appealed to the band's desire to produce well-rounded albums. "The idea was we wanted to have different hills and valleys on a record," Keagy explains. "And not just have it be up-tempo rock songs. We used to hear that on Beatles records all the time, that up and down of how you arrange the songs on an album and make it make sense between each one. So that was the idea, in that this one wasn't like a love ballad."

Keagy's lyrics tell the story of a girl "growing up so fast," as her brother warns her that "the boys don't want to play no more with you," hinting that they had other things on their minds when they saw her looking so mature. These warnings build up to the striking yet somewhat mysterious refrain "Motoring." "The whole thing people would ask is 'What's motoring?'" Keagy says. "'Motoring' is when you're moving through life. Okay, this is your life, you're starting to grow up. Momentum through life is everything."

Had Night Ranger released the song as just a simple ballad, it likely would have been an effective album change of pace but nothing more. But all that time playing it in the clubs had helped them hone an arrangement that Keagy held in his head when he first composed it. "When I was playing it on acoustic guitar, I had all those 'bom-bom-bom' parts," he says, referencing the musical escalation to the song's chorus. "So it made sense to keep it in there and make it this bombastic drum build."

To add a somewhat sorrowful flavor to this song about one family member watching another pull away, keyboardist Alan Fitzgerald came up with a chill-inducing piano introduction. "Fitz came up with that later, the way to intro the song," Keagy recalls. "He stuck with the chords but he brought a little bit of melodic sense in there. It became the thing that you grab onto when you hear the song."

When you put it all together, the arrangement for "Sister Christian" is such that it demonstrates the full potential of a power ballad. Everything works just right: from the stillness of Fitzgerald's beginning, to the soft heart of Keagy's melody, to the crunching buildup, to the string-bender of a guitar solo by Brad Gillis, to the final return to piano and vocal for a symmetric wrap-up. With Keagy's genuine concern and love for his sister as the sweet and the knowledge that he couldn't hope to protect her any longer as the bitter, "Sister Christian" hits every emotion you could want to experience in four minutes or so.

Even with all the song clearly had going for it, Night Ranger wasn't exactly sure whether "Sister Christian" was hit song material. Keagy remembers,

We were mixed on that, but the record company [MCA] did like it and they attached to it. They got it. But we released two other songs before that. When we got to that third single, that became a pattern with the record company. "Well, the third single has got to be a ballad." "Well, why?" "That's just the way it is."

That was the thing; they had that ["Sister Christian"] in their hip pocket. In the band, you're thinking in terms of we gotta go tour. Touring isn't about playing slow songs. But that one isn't really considered a slow song. It's just a big rock ballad.

Big enough to put Night Ranger into the Top 5. And big enough to make the song a constant presence in the culture. Perhaps no use of it was more memorable than when Paul Thomas Anderson included it in a memorable scene near the end of Dirk Diggler's fall from grace in *Boogie Nights*. The band couldn't believe the familiarity of it all.

"We were laughing in the theater," says Keagy. "Jack and I were sitting next to each other. And we were saying, 'Yeah, remember that guy in North Hollywood? This could have been filmed in his house.' We totally connected with that scene. Other than the firecrackers, it all happened to us. I mean somebody could have been following us around."

Night Ranger's "Sister Christian," the ultimate power ballad, continues to capture new audiences. And, as Keagy explains, the old audiences have reserved a place in their heart for it as well. "I don't think about it until we get in front of the audience and play it," he muses. "That's when you really realize the extent of that song and the thread that goes through all of those people. When we get to it, it's like a huge crescendo. That's when we realize, 'Oh my God. This is still so big in everybody's minds.' And thank goodness. It's a great blessing."

"Overkill" by Men at Work

CARGO (1983)

In the early 80s pop music was dominated for the most part by the British New Wave, bands that embraced synthesizers, danceable beats, and the potential of the music video as a marketing tool. Yet even the most successful of these bands and artists—including but not limited to Duran Duran, Human League, and Adam Ant—couldn't boast of the one-two punch delivered by the Australian band Men at Work in 1982, when their first two singles hit number 1 on the *Billboard* charts.

The songs in question—"Who Can It Be Now?" and "Down Under"—had actually been released in 1981 in the band's home country, but their worldwide success spurred on their eventual release in the United States. Most people originally considered Men at Work to be an almost comical band, reacting as they were to the bright pop sounds of the two smash singles and the humorous videos featuring lead singer Colin Hay's bug-eyed reactions to various nuisances.

But those tracks actually hid shadowy cores in the midst of their bubbly exteriors. "Who Can It Be Now?" traded in paranoia, while the second hit single was actually about the commercialization and overdevelopment of the band's native nation, even if it was cloaked in that reggae rhythm and sing-along chorus. "'Down Under' is really a dark song, although people don't really understand that song," Hay says. "It's not really my place to go around and correct people's views on it. To me, it's not at all light; it's quite a heavy song about the plundering of a country which is quite sacred."

Even still, Men at Work easily could have followed that album up with more of the same humorous approach, but 1983's *Cargo* felt like a conscious reaction by Hay, the band's primary songwriter, to their runaway success. "It was the undertow to the wave," is how Hay describes it now. And its first single, "Overkill," advertised this ambivalence and reticence pretty clearly this time around; even the title seems like self-aware commentary. Although it veered from the band's previous image, it succeeded (number 3 on the charts as the kickoff to another monster album) because it was such an airtight combination of piercing songwriting and scintillating performance.

For Hay, the song was a direct reflection of where he stood at that point in his life, the thrilling yet perilous precipice where circumstances force you to leave the familiar and comforting behind for the unknown, for all its potential good and bad. He explains,

> "Overkill" was more introspective in the sense that it was kind of realizing how much things were changing really quickly. And I was dealing with realizing that I had addictive problems and that I was going to be diving in the deep end, with me having a lot of success and all the things that brings. I was kind of realizing in a sense the possible pitfalls of that. You've gotta be up for it.
>
> It was realizing, walking around the same neighborhoods, that everything that you had done previous to that, everything was going to change, everything was going to be different. No anonymity anymore. It's like that situation of standing up on the high board and thinking, "Okay, am I going to take the plunge?" And you know you are, but you just gotta pick your moment.

The lyrics to "Overkill" articulate how daunting such an experience can be with the very first line: "I can't get to sleep." In the second verse, the narrator seems to be at war with himself over his old haunts, how they can seem alternately like a safe haven or a prison: "It's time to walk the streets/Smell the desperation/At least there's pretty lights/And though there's little variation." Meanwhile he is plagued by apparitions that vanish before he can confront them, as evidenced by the haunting refrain of "Ghosts appear and fade away."

There could be no mistaking the lyrics of "Overkill," as happened with Men at Work's previous smashes. But that doesn't mean that the song wallows; the churn of the rhythm is far too relentless for that. Meanwhile Greg Ham, the band's multi-instrumentalist, gives the song the feel of film noir with his lonely saxophone. "He had a great unique tone and he was my friend," Hay says of Ham, who passed away in 2012. Hay also credits the chemistry of the band (which at the time also included guitarist Ron Strykert, bassist John Rees, and drummer Jerry Speiser) for the song's success: "There was no real talking about what people were gonna play. They played their personality."

Hay adds a fierce guitar solo in the break that leads to more dreamy sax from Ham, and then the modulation into perhaps the most striking quirk of "Overkill:" the vocal octave jump taken by Hay in the final verse. The idea to do that came as a happy accident. "You write it and you start in a certain key," Hay muses about the process. "Because E is a great key for guitar, you start singing it like that. And then as you're rolling along, you think about the higher octave and you say, 'Oh, I can get there. F***, that's good!' You kind of surprise yourself when you sing it. You think, 'Well, I can actually do that.' You do it and don't really think that much about it. But then people comment on it and you think that actually it's not that usual for that to happen where you jump the octave in the last verse without it being falsetto."

The shifting sands of pop music, along with intraband tensions, eventually proved too stern an obstacle for Men at Work, who would release just one more album, 1985's *Two Hearts*, which carried little of the magic of the first two LPs. Hay has maintained an impressive solo career as a singer-songwriter, however, and he has come to realize that the meaning of a song like "Overkill" can sometimes be elusive to even the author. "There's some things you don't even realize you're writing from a personal standpoint," he says today. "Sometimes you don't really realize what a song means till years later. It's a strange thing. You're just kind of writing these things down and the resonance of them or the greater meaning of them sometimes is lost on you. And sometimes you even try to shroud things in humor or shroud things because you aren't really quite sure what you're trying to say. Sometimes it becomes obvious later and sometimes it doesn't."

What is obvious, from the opening saxophone notes to the hauntingly unresolved ending, is that "Overkill" proved that Men at Work could be downright brilliant without being the least bit funny.

"I Want a New Drug" by Huey Lewis and the News

SPORTS (1983)

When a band has as many hits as Huey Lewis and the News racked up in a decade, it can be difficult to pick a definitive one. "I Want a New Drug" is an ideal showcase for the kind of instrumental talent that the News (consisting of Chris Hayes, Mario Cipollina, Johnny Colla, Sean Hopper, and Bill Gibson at the time of the song's recording) artfully displayed, and it is also one of the finest examples of both Lewis's song-crafting expertise and his ability to deliver material with abundant gusto and heart.

It also might be argued that it is the most important song in the band's career, as it helped to springboard an album that became one of the biggest of the 80s. The third album is often when a band ascends to a new level. Lewis and company did that with 1983's *Sports*, but at the time they were thinking more in terms of fighting for their musical lives.

"Our first record [1980's self-titled debut] did nothing," Lewis explains. "The second album, *Picture This* [in 1982], had 'Do You Believe in Love?' which was a big hit. But the second single was a ballad, 'Hope You Love Me Like You Say You Do,' and it didn't work. Our third album—and what a sign of the times that we actually got three chances at it—our third album had to be a hit."

Lewis sussed out that it would take more than the band's enchanting live audiences with their seamless blend of rock, pop, and soul:

> We had to have radio hits. The album came out in '83, and by then, all radio was programmed. Everything was CHR, Contemporary Hit Radio. FM radio, which was anything and everything in the 60s, was now programmed to CHR. So was AM radio. There was no internet, and there were no jam bands. It was all about you having a hit single.
>
> That was our hardest task, to craft a single that we could get a Top 40 hit with. So we aimed *Sports* right at that. We weren't feeling

confident at all. We were struggling to make sure every single one of those tunes was kind of aimed at radio, but we didn't want to repeat ourselves. That's why the album is so disparate. When I listen back to the *Sports* album now, I realize it was an album of its time, a collection of singles.

"I Want a New Drug," which would become the second of a staggering run of four Top 10s and five Top 20s for the band from the *Sports* album, was created while Lewis was suffering some early-morning sluggishness. "I had a long night, shall we say," Lewis laughs. "I woke up and I had an early appointment with Bob Gordon, my then-publishing attorney, at like nine in the morning. I got up and I remember I had a headache. I drove to his place and I had the idea on the way. I walked in and I said, 'Bob, do you have a pen and paper?' I wrote down most of the song. And that's all I had was the lyric at first."

The music, on the other hand, didn't come so easily:

> I shared it with some of the guys. We made a couple false starts with the song, to be honest with you. People thought it was gonna be okay, but I didn't. I remember really believing in the lyric, and thinking this song wasn't good enough. So I finally got up the nerve to tell the guys that I didn't think that we were going in the right direction.
>
> Finally, I remember I was at home and Chris Hayes [the News' lead guitarist at the time] called me up on the phone and he said, "I got it. 'I Want a New Drug,' I got it. I got a great riff." I said, "Come on over." So he came over and we had a little cassette player, he played it and I sang it and that was it.

"I Want a New Drug" boasts some impressive playing by the band, both in terms of conjuring a relentlessly funky groove and shining when individually spotlighted. Lewis, meanwhile, manages to tell a story about infatuation that doesn't sound like it's been told in song a million times before. His lines are unshowy but clever and flow with the smoothness of Motown's classic hits.

The narrator goes on an endless search for a narcotic, accompanied by a long list of demands about what it should and shouldn't do. But Lewis saves its real purpose for the chorus, the music briefly dropping away so that it's clear: "One that won't make me nervous, wondering what to do/One that makes me feel like I feel when I'm with you/When I'm alone with you." The song is funny and sexy while seeming like it simply rolled right off the songwriter's tongue, which it essentially did.

Lewis and the band loved it, but others weren't quite on board with the song's potential. "They were afraid of it, the record company, because it had the word 'drug' in it," Lewis says. "I remember we played Roseland Ballroom in New York City and the label came out and everybody went crazy to that song.

Because of that, I convinced them to make it the second single. But they insisted on the record, on the little 45, and I still have one, that it's called 'I Want a New Drug (Called Love).'"

Luckily, that title didn't stick. "I Want a New Drug" played a big role in sustaining momentum that would soon be unstoppable, and Lewis was glad that was the song that did it. "It was a band song," he explains:

> It's all about the band. There's no way a bunch of LA songwriters write a song like that for somebody. Whoever sings that song, wrote it. That's what was so good about it for us. It didn't fit a hit single formula.
>
> When the record came out, the first single was "Heart and Soul." And that just sounded like a hit. We didn't even write it, but it sounded like a smash to me. So we cut it, sure enough, it's the first single, it goes and it's a hit. The second single was "I Want a New Drug." And I always touted that one. That's the song that will be massive, because it's about us, it sounds like us. It's a band thing. It's very personal, that song.

The longevity of *Sports* proved something of mixed blessing to the band. "We had to eventually forbid them to release any more singles, because it was silly already," Lewis says. "It beats you up finally. Too many videos, and too much MTV. It kills you for a long time."

But Lewis and the band nonetheless put together a record as impressive as any group in the decade. Meanwhile, "I Want a New Drug" and the band's numerous other hits still thrill audiences while showing remarkably little wear and tear. Lewis says that longevity is

> really the thing you end up being proudest of. Did you know it all along? Of course not. But were you kind of aspiring to it? Yeah! I came from older school. We don't have any tattoos. If it had been four years later, I would have been tattooed head to foot if I thought it would have helped. It was an audio thing in our day. So we didn't have the style thing together, or the fashion thing together or any of that stuff.
>
> We were anachronistic then. And with our songs, I was always try-ing to write stuff that would be timeless, rather than time-sensitive. And now, at this ripe old age, it's actually served us well.

"Cruel Summer" by Bananarama

BANANARAMA (1983)

Girl groups are a rich part of pop and R&B history; it's impossible to imagine the charts in the early 60s without stalwarts like the Supremes, the Shirelles, and many other trailblazers. As rock and roll started to dominate the landscape with the British Invasion, psychedelia, and eventually arena rock into the 70s, bands populated by just women began to fade from the scene. Only in the 80s, where everything seemed possible again, did girl groups once again start to assert themselves in the pop world with authority.

The US charge was led largely by the Go-Go's, a West Coast–based quintet who combined punky energy with unerring songwriting smarts on hits like "We Got the Beat" and "Our Lips Are Sealed." In the UK, however, the premier girl group of their time was Bananarama. They shared with the Go-Go's a sense of songcraft and hooks that upheld the girl group tradition, but the trio of Sara Dallin, Keren Woodward, and Siobhan Fahey built their sound with the dance floor in mind, teaming up with savvy producers Steven Jolley and Tony Swain and layering their sultry harmonies amid peppery beats.

In Great Britain, they proved immediate successes, churning out five Top 10 hits in a two-year-stretch. "Cruel Summer" was the last in that run, but it was the first to break through in the United States with any potency. Many European artists yearned for American success at that time, but according to Dallin, Bananarama didn't sweat any part of the business side of things too much. "We were very young when we put the group together, Keren and myself eighteen, Siobhan twenty-one. We never looked at it as a business and did what came naturally."

While many young artists are at the mercy of managers or record company executives who call all the shots, from the beginning this trio dictated their musical direction. "We'd always written and cowritten our songs and Bananarama was absolutely our own creation," Dallin says. "We would hear tracks in clubs that we liked and seek out the producer. We were very much in control of the direction and sound."

The songwriting part of the equation was something that the three women learned fast, after the bulk of their early singles covered other material. "When we started out we rehearsed a couple of covers, 'Aie a Mwana' [their first single] being one of them, which Terry Hall [from the Specials and then Fun Boy 3] bought," Dallin says. "Our collaboration with them catapulted us into the limelight. 'Really Saying Something' became our second single, and from that success we started a songwriting partnership with Jolley and Swain. We were learning everything at this point, in the public eye, not least how to write and arrange songs, hook lines, melodies, harmonies, all while expressing yourself. It's still my favorite part of the business."

When it came to "Cruel Summer," the band found a way to create a summer anthem that's torrid and steamy but yet, in its lyrics, actually dismissive of the heat. "Jolley and Swaine gave us a rough backing track and we then worked on the top line and lyrics," Dallin recalls. "There was a rare UK heat wave and a heat wave in the city, in London, is always unbearable, as we are so ill equipped to deal with it, zero AC. We were really busy with work at this point in our career and all our friends were booking holidays. And we couldn't go with them."

"Cruel Summer" differs from many of the early Bananarama hits in that it's a shade darker, seemingly carrying more at stake. Some of that is a by-product of the minor keys, but it's also in the trio's harmonies, usually warm and inviting but here bringing a cold sting, bemoaning a faded romance as they try to will the sweltering heat away. The track manages to capture both the flair of the tropics, with the marimbas, and the sweat of the city, via the slick guitars and percussion crash. "It sounded so different to anything else around at the time," Dallin muses. "Having worked with the Fun Boy 3 where we all took a different instrument in the studio and built up these rhythms, I think that inspired us with 'Cruel Summer.'"

Even with everything it had going for it, "Cruel Summer" still needed a boost in the United States, and it came courtesy of Ralph Macchio. The song wasn't even released in the United States until 1984, a year after it came out in Europe, to coincide with its inclusion in the movie *The Karate Kid*. When that movie took off, the song followed. "I recall being told that the film producer was driving down the freeway and Rodney on the Rock [a famed LA DJ] was playing the song," Dallin explains about the *Karate* connection. "And he just loved it and wanted it in the film. We went to see the film in LA and seeing our names come up on the credits at the end was brilliant. We made it! Hollywood!"

"Cruel Summer" rolled to number 9 on the *Billboard* charts, and Dallin admits that, although it wasn't an original goal, the US success suited the band well. "We were in the US when 'Cruel Summer' was breaking," she says. "And we were on the beach at Santa Monica and the song was being played on every radio station all day long, which was so exciting. Once it was a hit, we couldn't believe just how big it was. We even had Mike Tyson serenade us with it at the Sunset Marquis."

Bananarama continued their run of hits into the early 90s in the UK and added a couple more smashes in the United States, including their number 1 cover of Shocking Blue's "Venus" in 1986. Fahey left late in 1988 to pursue other musical avenues but returned to the fold in 2017 for fresh Bananarama performances, lending hopes that there might be more music from the original lineup still to come.

In any case, they achieved the kind of success that didn't happen very often for the so-called girl groups of the era—and come to think of it, groups of any makeup would certainly take Bananarama's track record in a heartbeat. In the meantime, their anti-summer summer anthem continues to captivate, although when Dallin is asked if the band consciously tried to subvert seasonal expectations with "Cruel Summer," she laughs it off: "Not really. We were just stuck in the oppressive heat of London when we wanted to be lying on a beach in the South of France."

"Sunglasses at Night" by Corey Hart

FIRST OFFENSE (1983)

Only twenty-one years old when he delivered "Sunglasses at Night," a debut smash single and source of some of the most memorably iconographic lyrics from that period in pop music, Corey Hart seemed like an overnight sensation at the time. After all, how could he possibly have been a grizzled veteran at such a tender age?

But that's sort of what he was, as he had been performing publicly for about a decade by the time he released the album *First Offense* in 1983. And during that time, he had experienced the kinds of highs and lows you would expect for an up-and-comer. But his persistence and belief in himself carried him through. "Yeah, of course when things didn't pan out as I had hoped, those insecure shadows loomed over me," Hart says. "But deep down I was convinced by working assiduously hard and keeping at it, I would eventually catch a break. I was focused from a very young age to develop my craft as a singer-songwriter. So despite my early rejections to secure a record deal, I remained undaunted in its pursuit."

Uncommonly young artists are often subject to record company executives and other higher-ups dictating the source and the tone of their material. But the Montreal-born Hart wisely insisted otherwise. "When I finally signed my record deal at nineteen [with Aquarius Records] I was euphoric," he remembers.

> The only contractual clause I cared about was the one securing me complete artistic and creative control. Royalty percentages, management terms, publishing splits all meant absolutely nothing to me. In retrospect it wasn't a very savvy business model to follow, but that's life. Much like in the mold of a Billy Joel or Bruce Springsteen, I always wanted to write all of my own words and music. Had any of the interested labels insisted I record outside original material, even

100

at the risk of losing the long-coveted record deal, I was prepared to keep my personal songwriting covenant inviolate.

Once he had the deal in place, Hart churned out an album's worth of material, but he still had the nagging feeling something was missing. The phrase "My cigarette is wet" lodged in his brain and inspired a new demo with an intriguingly dark melody line, but he still thought it lacked the right lyrics.

During his time in London recording the album, Hart had picked up his first pair of Wayfarer sunglasses, which he never got to wear there because of the constant rain. When he returned home to Montreal, the phrase "I wear my sunglasses at night" popped into his head; it fit neatly onto the "My Cigarette Is Wet" demo, and a hit was born. Even though the album was technically complete and Hart's recording budget had been exhausted, he convinced his label the song was a necessary addition. (For a more thorough examination of this story and of his fascinating career, Hart's illuminating autobiography *Chasing the Sun: My Life in Music* is highly recommended.)

Although he was in charge of writing the songs, Hart did have excellent support that helped push "Sunglasses at Night" to another level. The penetrating synths that open up the song and pulsate through its entirety were recorded beautifully by producers Phil Chapman and Jon Astley, while Andy Barnett's brawny guitar part lends the music guts and heart that bust through the synthetic shell.

Hart's vocal is a crucial element as well: pouting and teasing in the verses, fierce and defiant in the refrains. It's a good match for a lyrical style that concerns itself more with fascinating imagery than any linear story. "Sunglasses at Night" seems to detail a relationship where deceit and power plays pass for communication. The vivid wordplay and the urgency with which Hart delivers those words create a world within the song where the stakes are crucially high for all involved.

For Hart, this style of writing lyrics that courted idiosyncrasy and shunned simplicity was second nature even at the earliest stages of his career. "I always wanted to be an honest storyteller even if at times I was elliptical, arcane, or missing the mark altogether," he laughs. "I just relistened to a song from my debut album called *Araby*, which was inspired by a James Joyce short story I read when I was seventeen. In retrospect, it wasn't too shabby an effort for a teenager."

Unlike some artists who are ambivalent about the potential success of their creations, Hart immediately understood just how big "Sunglasses at Night" could be. "I intuitively felt the song was going to be a hit and I wholeheartedly believed," he explains. "I was also very young, naive, and idealistic. I suppose this part of the formula actually played in my favor because I never factored in failure as a viable option. RFK wrote, 'Only those who dared to fail greatly can ever achieve greatly.' During my teens, I would write those words in my journal at the start of each calendar year, along with Churchill's inspirational 'Never Surrender.'" (The latter phrase would inspire a Top 5 hit from Hart in 1985.)

"Sunglasses at Night" didn't take very long to touch a nerve with the listening public, hitting number 7 in the United States. The instant success combined with Hart's good looks courted the kind of intense fandom that can be intimidating. "There is no 'on-the-job' training for pop stardom," he says:

> It was often quite terrifying with the frenzied, surreal, pandemonium fervor of my younger female fans. I'm not moaning about it, just answering truthfully.
>
> Stardom also made my nascent, predisposed, loner personality traits even more pronounced. But thankfully I never allowed the rock star mythology, with all its absurd hedonistic entitlements, ever [to] enter into my inner consciousness. I knew if I ever normalized this altered state of reality it would quickly unravel my core foundation.

So it was that Hart was able to sustain a successful recording and performing career that still continues to this day, even as his music stays relevant in the culture; the Hulu show *Future Man* featured his music prominently in 2017, and he even made a cameo appearance. Hart's talent and work ethic likely would have earned him a significant place in pop music anyway, but those quotable lyrics and striking music right off the bat from "Sunglasses at Night" certainly didn't hurt.

"I'm extremely humbled by the eclectic array of artists who have covered 'Sunglasses At Night' over the years from all over the world," Hart muses:

> Jazz, country, heavy metal, hard core, hip-hop to big band orchestra: You name the genre and it's been interpreted to "Sunglasses at Night." Lyrically, I was trying to capture a cool rebellious spirit a la James Dean when I originally wrote the lyrics. And yeah, here we are three decades later still talking about their relevance in today's cultural landscape. That's pretty awesome.
>
> I suppose writing, "Don't switch the blade on a guy in shades" wasn't such a foolish notion after all.

"She's a Beauty" by the Tubes

OUTSIDE INSIDE (1983)

"Step right up, and don't be shy," beckoned Fee Waybill of the Tubes, and audiences certainly heeded his call, making the band's "She's a Beauty" a Top 10 US single in 1983. Considering the somewhat circuitous path the band took to get to that point and the slightly risqué subject matter of the lyrics, it might not have seemed like a sure thing at the time. But dynamism, charisma, and humor proved too enticing a combination for listeners to resist.

The Tubes formed in San Francisco in 1975, immediately gaining a kind of underground following for the wild antics they perpetrated in their stage show and the subversive nature of singles like "White Punks on Dope." Yet they seemed for a while to be destined to forever linger outside the mainstream, something that Waybill wanted desperately to change. "Regardless of what they might say, nobody wants to be a cult band and be obscure and not sell any records and not make any money," Waybill explains. "We always wanted success. After five records with A&M, they released us because we didn't have any success. They kind of got tired of having some cutesy cult band on their label that weren't making them any money. So they released us. We had a great stage show. A great reputation. But we didn't sell any records."

At the beginning of the 80s, the Tubes' management floundered in finding a new deal for the band until they met with Bobby Colomby, an original member of Blood, Sweat & Tears who became an A&R executive at Capitol Records. Capitol signed the band, and, as Waybill remembers, Colomby hooked them up with a crucial collaborator. "He said, 'I got a guy who can change it all for you and give you commercial success.' And that was David Foster."

Foster's fingerprints can be found on a whole slew of 80s hits, and he clicked with Waybill and fellow studio ace Steve Lukather (also of Toto) as the trio wrote "Talk to Ya Later" for the Tubes' 1981 debut with Capitol, *The Completion Backwards Principle*. The song was a worldwide hit, but was passed over for release in the States. "At the time, everybody was doing big monster ballads," Waybill recalls of the decision. "And 'Don't Want to Wait Anymore' was the single they released." "Don't Want to Wait Anymore," sung by guitarist Bill Spooner, crawled into the Top 40, a modest success that seemed to be only setting the band up for the next step.

"She's a Beauty" came together quickly, thanks to the virtuosity of Lukather and Foster. "It probably took two hours to write it," Waybill says. "Lukather is just so unbelievably quick. We dicked around a while and he came up with a lick and we went, 'Wow, that's it! That's the lick.'" Meanwhile, Foster went to work putting all of the song's elements together, from the dynamic opening with synths and guitar through the mysterious breakdown in the middle of the song to the triumphant return of the sure-shot chorus. "Foster is a genius," Waybill marvels. "He arranged a lot of it. Working with Foster was unbelievable. He pulled together the whole bridge and the modulation. It was an amazing time working with him."

As for the lyrics, Waybill conceived the idea from a trip he took to a red-light district in the San Francisco area known as the Tenderloin. "I don't know why I was there, looking for costumes at some pimp store or something," he laughs:

> They used to have a thing called "Pay a Dollar, Talk to a Naked Girl." It was like an outdoor phone booth in front of a massage parlor, only the phone booth, it was all enclosed, except for the front. And you put in a dollar, and this screen would come down and there's a semi-clad woman kind of teasing you and pretending to take off clothes. Only she didn't really take off much. She'd take off a little bit, and then you gotta put in another dollar. She actually never did get naked. But all the time, talking about "Come on into the massage parlor, and we'll take care of you," that kind of thing.
>
> Instead of reacting to her come-on, I just went, "What are you doing here? You're gorgeous. This is really lame. You shouldn't be doing this." But she never broke. She just kept saying, "Come on in, I'll meet you inside." So that's kind of what the song is about. The song is about this girl, told with kind of a sarcastic, flippant attitude, like I always am.

Still lacking a chorus, Waybill borrowed from Humberto Gatica, the engineer who worked with Foster, who hailed from Chile and had a way with catchphrases. He had similarly inspired "Talk to Ya Later," and in this case, his common exclamation of "Beauty" to hearing something on the playback that he liked was the impetus.

"She's a Beauty" goes a long way on the cleverness of Waybill's lyrics and his ability to deliver them in the vocal with tongue-in-cheek salesmanship. The carnival barker narrator doesn't hide the fact that there won't be much outside of teasing emanating from this transaction: "You can say anything you like/ But you can't touch the merchandise." And, his sarcasm aside ("You're gonna like her 'cause she's got class"), there is an alluring nature about his pitch to the humdrum passers-by looking for a taste of the tawdry: "You can step outside your little world."

It didn't take much contemplation for Waybill to realize that the Tubes had their breakout hit. "We came home late from the studio and we had just done 'She's a Beauty,'" he says. "I woke up the manager at like three o'clock in the morning: 'You gotta check this out, this is f'in' awesome.' We seemed to know right away. It's one of those songs that just hits you."

The Tubes still use "She's a Beauty" as either a showstopping closer or an attention-grabbing opener in their live sets. And Waybill still inhabits his deranged carnival barker role with glee. "I still wear the barker hat and the jacket from the video. It's still the biggest response we get. We've kind of upgraded the arrangement a little bit. It definitely still works. When we start to play it, everybody stands up and comes to the front."

You can check them out for yourself, or you can just take Fee Waybill at his word. After all, as "She's a Beauty" says, why would he lie?

"Every Breath You Take" by the Police

SYNCHRONICITY (1983)

It is very rare that a band bows out when they are still on top of their game. More often than not they hit their peak early on in their career and then produce diminishing returns, for the most part, the rest of the time the members are together. When people attempt to list those bands that do call it a day at their highest point, most mention the Police, who sailed off into the proverbial sunset of their massive 1983 album *Synchronicity*, which included "Every Breath You Take," their most successful single and one of the biggest hits of the decade.

While the idea of leaving while the getting was still good might have been in the back of the minds of singer/bassist Sting, guitarist Andy Summers, and drummer Stewart Copeland, the actual reason for the Police's dissolution following that album came down to the fact that the trio, particularly Sting and Copeland, could no longer work together in anything resembling harmony. And producer Hugh Padgham, who worked on three albums with the band, had a front-row seat for the theatrics.

"We mustn't forget that was their fifth and last album," Padgham says today. "On the first album, it was Stewart's band. Stewart got the pieces together. He found Sting playing in a support band in Newcastle. And he saw that Sting was good and plucked him out of that environment and put him into a band. Pretty soon they had hits, but Stewart, from his point of view, still thought that it was his band. But Sting said, 'Well I'm the one who's written all the hits.' So he had become the de facto leader of the band and that was where all these tensions came from."

The good news heading into the album was that Sting had once again penned some killer songs for the project, including "Every Breath You Take." "Before we went out to Montserrat to record it, I went to Utopia Studios in London where Sting was making some demos for that album," Padgham says. "And I remember going down there and listening one evening; Miles Copeland, the manager, was there as well. And we listened to this song and Miles said, 'My God, that's a goddamn hit!' And I think that Sting had more or less written that guitar part that Andy Summers plays. I think it was reinterpreted by Andy. But I'm pretty sure that chord structure and kind of riff was how it was."

Yet when the band got into the studio, their old surliness with each other quickly surfaced, with the producer caught amid it all. "It was really destructive sometimes," Padgham remembers. "If I tried to be Mr. Producer or whatever, they'd just tell me, 'F*** off, it's none of your business, if we want to fight, we'll fight,' that sort of thing. In some ways, it was quite pathetic and childlike. But at the end of the day, I think those tensions probably lent massive excitement to the record. If everybody's so relaxed and laid-back and happy and stuff, I'm not sure that's necessarily the best environment."

Still, the atmosphere was so toxic that the breakup almost occurred prematurely. "When we went out to Montserrat to record this album, we were there for two weeks before we had anything on the tape that we could call a song," Padgham recalls. "It was that bad. And Miles Copeland flew over, even though he hated coming to Montserrat because it was in the middle of nowhere. He came over and I distinctly remember the band and him, while I was privy but on the periphery, having a meeting about whether we were going to carry on recording this album or give it up there and then. The consensus was that we would carry on."

When it came to recording "Every Breath You Take," Sting and Stewart Copeland again locked horns due to the drummer's wish to complicate what he saw as a basic song. "One of the problems with 'Every Breath You Take' was that Sting and I wanted a very basic drum pattern to go through the song," Padgham says. "And Stewart always wanted to show off with his drums. Twenty years later, when they were inducted into the Rock and Roll Hall of Fame, Stewart did not want to play 'Every Breath You Take' because he thought that it was too basic and that it wouldn't show off his drumming."

The songwriter prevailed. "It came down to Sting sort of saying, 'It's my song. You'll play it how I want it,'" is how Padgham remembers it. And it's hard to argue with the end result. Yes, the chord changes are familiar, but there is an inevitability to them that mirrors the unavoidable fracture of the relationship that the lyrics detail. Sting and Summers play their parts dutifully and with little fanfare so as not to provide distraction from the tune, but Copeland snaps that left-hand snare with a vengeance, calling the listener to attention each time and providing stark contrast to the more sedate instruments alongside him. It's like the Police's interpersonal relationships are playing out in a musical microcosm.

As for the lyrics, many people want to be soothed by them, to hear some sort of affirmation in the narrator's insistence that he will be by the girl's side perhaps even when she's unaware. But the moodiness of the music and the cool detachment in Sting's vocal suggest otherwise, that instead this is when the line between love and obsession gets trampled. Things heat up in the bridge, as the unyielding rhyme scheme hints at the kind of laser focus the narrator utilizes in his tireless—some would say creepy—pursuit. Hear it how you want, but this is a pitch-black song hiding in plain sight.

That didn't stop it from being catchy and perching atop the US charts for the better part of two months. More hits followed from *Synchronicty*; the Police toured it dutifully. And that was that for the band, at least in terms of studio albums. Even now as the song has easily ascended into classic status, Padgham has a hard time separating that success from the tumult that surrounded its making. "I feel very proud and privileged that I was a part of it," he admits. "It came together in the end, but there were moments where it was extremely stressful from my point of view because I'm the producer and I'm responsible for making 'Every Breath You Take' a hit, because everybody knew that it was a hit song. You could hear it just from the demo. So if I hadn't made a good job of it or whatever, that would have been really terrible for me."

Thus, with "Every Breath You Take" and *Synchronicity*, the Police saved their best for last. And that's okay, even if we now know that their conflicting personalities ensured that it would be their last, one way or the other.

"Talking in Your Sleep" by the Romantics

IN HEAT (1983)

Being an artist in the 80s often meant that if you wanted to stay popular, you had to be able to adapt to the often rapidly shifting musical tastes of the time. The Romantics, who hailed from Detroit, Michigan, possessed that kind of malleability. They also had the resiliency to overcome a serious swale in their career and some intraband drama, eventually getting it together in time to triumph with the 1983 Top 5 hit "Talking in Your Sleep."

At that point, the group had already released one bona fide classic, although it hadn't yet been discovered by the type of audience that would eventually embrace it. "What I Like about You," written by band members Wally Palmar, Mike Skill, and Jimmy Marinos and included on the band's self-titled 1980 debut album, didn't make too much of a dent on the charts, reaching only number 49 despite finding an irresistible middle ground between power pop and punk. A video did well on MTV, though, and the song eventually took off in popularity once it was used in television ads at the end of the decade.

While "What I Like about You" took a long path to the top, "Talking in Your Sleep" rocketed into the public consciousness upon its release as the first single from the the Romantics' 1983 album *In Heat*. Yet the band's trajectory from their debut to that point would have looked like Death Valley had it been put on a graph. Neither of their albums between the debut and *In Heat* did much business, and the band also lost one of its founding members, if only temporarily.

Mike Skill, who formed the band with grade school buddy Jimmy Marinos and was the lead guitarist, left the band and didn't perform on their 1981 release *Strictly Personal*. "We had creative difficulties," Skill says of the reason for his departure. "I was out because I couldn't get with the look of the band. I really had a punkish attitude. That kind of blew up and we split ways."

Although Skill's absence did no favors for *Strictly Personal*, it proved to be a crucial factor in the band's success once he returned, this time taking over as the group's bassist while Coz Canler held down lead guitar. "I came back to the band with a fresh outlook," he remembers. "I had been out for a year and a half. A lot of the bands coming out of England at that time were the New Romantics. I was off the road at home and settled, and I was kind of hearing what was going on. I think I came back in with a 'What's happening now' kind of thing, in a lot of ways, while still coming from a 50s, 60s writing angle."

That blend of throwback and modern is what makes "Talking in Your Sleep" such an intriguing single. Yet it almost didn't see the light of day, as the album was pretty much considered complete without it. "I had the basic bass line for 'Talking in Your Sleep,'" says Skill. "We had finished up ten songs but we needed another one. And the producer [Peter Solley] said, 'What about that one idea you had in preproduction, the bass thing?' So we started jamming with it. We thought it might work. We got in the control room and pulled out a keyboard and started working on a turnaround and some lyrics to get to the chorus."

That bass line was inspired by the most famous music ever to emanate from Skill's hometown. "That Motown bass just stood out for me, and the melodies," he explains. "I loved James Jamerson [bassist for the Motown house band]. The level of writing at that time, the bar was so high."

Canler's guitar, which was influenced in part by the 12-string parts made famous by the Beatles and the Byrds, provided a bit of a classic sound as well, while also adding counterpoint to the bass. Yet Solley's production was apropos for the pop charts at the time, with Marinos's drums miked for maximum, crashing impact and Palmar's vocals echoing through the proceedings. Hooks are everywhere.

The song also cultivates an air of mystery, and that is played up further by the lyrics. "Talking in Your Sleep" captures a relationship in which suspicion runs rampant over trust, perhaps because it's been given reason to do so by the girl in the song, perhaps because the guy's past experiences are coloring his new ones. "Don't you know you're sleeping in the spotlight?" Palmar asks, an image which proves there is nowhere this girl can turn for privacy. The words are as efficient as Motown, as insinuating as film noir.

If the Romantics were at all doubting the poppier direction that the song took them, they quickly received reassurance from an unlikely source. "We hadn't yet played it live," Skill says. "The only indication that we ever got was a guy who was working sweeping up the studio [Criterion] said, 'Man, I've heard a lot of people. But that's a number 1 hit.' He had been there for Eric Clapton, Aretha Franklin, the Allman Brothers, all these people who had been in this studio. So we walked out of there with a good feeling. And it took off."

Although that studio worker's prediction fell just short, at least on the pop charts (where it hit number 3), the band had created a multigenre smash. "Talking in Your Sleep" reached number 2 on the rock charts and topped the dance list at *Billboard*. That meant the Romantics were headed for whole new levels of popularity, and they adjusted their appearance accordingly. "The shows were getting bigger, the stages were getting bigger," Skill remembers. "The sound got louder too. So we were more animated in our look. The show jumped off the stage more."

In Heat spawned another Top 40 hit in "One in a Million" and proved to be the best-selling album of the Romantics' career. It's a career that got a further boost when "What I Like about You" enjoyed its belated resurgence, and one that still finds the band bringing their mélange of styles and eras to a wide variety of fans.

"No one had any idea that people would still be listening to it and hearing it," Skill says of "Talking in Your Sleep." "I'll be at home with friends and family, and I'll walk to the store and it's on. It's constantly happening. I don't know what it is. It's either 'Talking in Your Sleep,' 'One in a Million,' or 'What I Like about You.' Those three and a couple others, we can go on the road with them."

For the Romantics, that road has been occasionally bumpy, but it's one that 80s fans are glad they traveled to leave us with two unmistakable classics. That those two songs sound like they come from two distinctly different bands says something about this group's ability to roll with the changes.

"Cherish" by Kool & the Gang

EMERGENCY (1984)

Rhythm-and-blues artists did not have an easy time finding their footing at times in the 80s. Part of that can be blamed on the initial reluctance by MTV to play black artists on the channel, putting them severely behind the curve in terms of exposure. It was also difficult for that era's R&B to establish an identity; considering that disco, which had been a brief but explosive cultural force, was still lingering at the start of the decade and rap absolutely blew up by the end of the decade, those who were playing a more traditional version of rhythm and blues could easily get lost in the shuffle.

Kool & the Gang had no problems finding their footing. As a matter of fact, the band that first began way back in 1964 in Jersey City, New Jersey, with brothers Ronald and Robert "Kool" Bell stomped on much of their competition throughout the decade. You can tell it in the numbers: of the seven albums they released in the decade, three went platinum and another three went gold. Of course they dominated the R&B charts, with sixteen Top 20 singles, but eleven of those tracks also rose to the Top 20 on the pop charts as well, including a number 1 ("Celebration") and a pair of number 2's ("Joanna" and "Cherish"), demonstrating their unmatched crossover appeal.

The run of success stemmed from a decision the band made at the tail end of the 70s to move away from the fusion that had marked their previous work. "From the 70s, we wanted to make pop music," Ronald Bell explains. "So we left our funk/jazz roots and went into this whole pop thing. I wanted to make a big record. I remember this country-and-western record that was out long ago that went, 'All I need is one hit record.' I always wanted to make a record like 'The Twist.' So I focused on taking the jazz chords out of the music and turning it into pop music. We came up with 'Celebration.' From there on, we were on a roll, searching for the next hit."

The move in a more pop-oriented direction coincided with James "J.T." Taylor coming aboard as the lead singer; you couldn't find a much silkier vocalist in any genre. By the time the band came in to record 1984's *Emergency*, it didn't matter much that they were in their third decade of existence, a time when most acts are relegated to the nostalgia circuit. Kool & the Gang were just getting warmed up.

According to Ronald Bell, there wasn't any great scheme in place to make *Emergency* any grander than the rest of their work. They were simply getting the job done like they always had. "We had no clue," Bell claims. "We just kept going. It was like, 'Let's write some more music.' I love music, so I keep writing it. You never know with these things. I guess we were on a roll. I know we were focused; that's one thing we were."

The *Emergency* release cycle kicked off with a pair of scorching-hot up-tempo numbers—"Fresh" and "Misled"—guaranteed to fill up any dance floor. The third single, and what would prove to be the biggest hit of all the killers on the album, would keep those people out on that floor, only this time they'd be pairing up and holding each other close.

Ronald Bell got the ball rolling on "Cherish" by composing the basic music track. The tinkling synth part he conjured was inspired by the keyboards from the Irene Cara hit "Flashdance (What a Feeling)," but slowed down and with an altered melody. Bell then handed it off to his lead singer to see what he could do. "When James heard it, he liked it, so he started writing lyrics to it," Bell recalls. "We were in the Bahamas at the time and we were on the beach, with the scenery. He was there with his wife-to-be at the time and I guess that's what came out."

Many people know the single version of "Cherish" through radio airplay and the beach-themed video. But the album version might be even more luscious, as it holds off on kicking in the rhythm until the first verse is complete. It also includes stellar saxophone work from Curtis Williams. "It was just a different approach to it, experimenting with the song," is how Bell explains the competing takes available.

No matter which one you prefer, the romantic appeal of "Cherish" is nigh-impossible to resist, in part because it doesn't succumb to the fairy tale, preferring instead to honestly confront love's realities. Taylor's lyrics certainly play up the positives in a loving relationship, walking on the shore hand in hand and the like. But there are more questions than answers in the song, the most vexing being how to reconcile the notion that love is supposed to be forever with the fact that life is not. "The next life that we live in remains to be seen," Taylor sings querulously. The only thing you can do, as the band's lush vocals in chorus reaffirm, is "Cherish the love we have/We should cherish the life we live."

The run-up to the chorus takes an even darker turn, a part which Ronald Bell eventually took in stride after first being surprised when Taylor presented it to him. "That lyric was a little weird for me," Bell laughs. "It's like, would you make it through the night if she died? I don't know, man. You figure it out. You can't say would 'you' make it through the night, 'cause you're already gone. Would I make it through the night, too? What, I'm just gonna die with you?"

Semantic questions aside, "Cherish" slow-danced its way to everyone's hearts, solidifying *Emergency* as the biggest-selling album in the band's illustrious career. Ronald Bell doesn't try to overanalyze why such songs strike a chord:

> Most of the time when you write a song, you never know. You write it and you think it's great but you never know how the audience is going to embrace these kinds of things. Sometimes you think, "Oh man, this is gonna be a smash!" It smashed all right. It smashed and burned. It didn't go nowhere.
>
> But people like what they like. And I guess with the spirit of love, what God puts in people's hearts, songs about relationships are what works.

On that front, "Cherish" certainly sets an imposing standard. But then again, this is a band that has a catalog with versatility and quality to spare, something Ronald Bell surely appreciates, even if it does create some uptown problems. "It's very humbling," he says:

> Listen, if one person likes my song, I'm good. You want people to always accept what you do. And collectively, we have done well. Today, we still travel all around the world. The songs have transcended the personalities, and it's just the music from the beginning to the end.
>
> Of course, we have to play "Celebration" last. What are you gonna play after that? That and "Jungle Boogie," they really take it over the top. People will say, "You didn't play so-and-so." We only got an hour and a half here. We can't play all those songs but they want to hear all those songs. It's a blessing, man. It truly is.

"Valotte" by Julian Lennon
VALOTTE (1984)

Most debut singles intend to make a bold statement, perhaps with aggressive instrumentation, in-your-face hooks, or even, in some cases, self-mythologizing lyrics that are meant to define the artist for quite some time after the fact. In the case of Julian Lennon, his introduction to the US listening public came via a languid, dreamy ballad in which no action really takes place, unless you consider sitting an action. Whatever momentum there is to propel the song emanates from the thoughts of ambivalence and self-doubt that roil inside of the narrator's brain and the messy emotions troubling his heart.

This counterintuitive single proved to be the right call, because, after all, a great song is a great song. "Valotte" casts such a mesmeric spell that most listeners probably never even noticed that the song title is not mentioned in the lyrics. It haunted its way all the way up into the Top 10 back in 1984, the first of two Lennon singles (the peppier musically if still bittersweet lyrically "Too Late for Goodbyes" followed it up) to do so for an album (also named *Valotte*) whose restrained prettiness was an antidote to the look-at-me tenor of the pop charts at that time.

For Lennon, the choice of first single surprised even him. "It was a record company and management choice," he explains today. "I, we, the lads thought it a little unusual, but what did we know? We were just kids, so we went with the flow."

Unlike many of the songs in this book, which came from a burst of initial inspiration, "Valotte" required more of a gradual process, one that encompassed several months of work and even a couple of locations, one of which even underwent a reconstruction for art's sake. Lennon says,

> I recall it initially started in London at the first house I ever rented there, on St. Luke's Road, Westbourne Grove. This lovely French

woman rented her house to me, and I did promise to try to look after
it. But I was a slight tearaway at that time and decided to turn her
large bedroom, with vanity room, into an open live studio as such,
the vanity room becoming my bedroom during this time.

My dear friend Justin Clayton and I had set up the room like a
rehearsal space, beaten up upright piano, drum kit, couple of synths,
etc., and a few cabinets for guitar and bass. I believe Justin came to
me with the initial arpeggiated guitar line for the verse first, and then
I played around, until I came up with the chorus.

From there, Lennon, Clayton, and Carlton Morales, the trio who were
listed as cowriters on the song, decamped to a location whose grandeur started to
weave its way into the track as they molded their initial efforts into shape. "We
had some lyrical content at that point, like the first line and verse and possibly
parts of the chorus," Lennon says. "But that would have all come together when
we actually went down to Nevers in the middle of France, where [Château] Le
Manoir de Valotte was. Which was where we finished all of our demos, without
distraction, apart from great food and wine."

Lennon and Clayton worked together, intertwining ideas and motifs until
the finished product started to become clear. "I think once Justin and I had the
theme, things rolled out relatively easily," Lennon recalls. "I think Justin came
to me with the verse initially and I pulled the chorus together. Then I mostly
wrote the lyrics, as I normally do, with a few ideas and lyrics here and there
from Justin."

Once the song reached the recording studio, it received a lovely polish from
ace producer Phil Ramone, who was chosen by Lennon to helm the album. The
end product is an ideally matched combination of elements uniting to project a
nether region common to young people just beginning their adult lives, one full
of heavy responsibilities and romantic entanglements, caught halfway between
hope and doubt.

That kind of delicate balance is something Lennon strove to strike with
all of his work. "I certainly think Phil and the string arrangements added to it,
but it was always there from the get-go," he says. "That's something I've always
tried to achieve: the marriage between lyric/music and melody. All have to be
saying, or singing, the same tune or theme. Otherwise for me, none of it works.
All elements must complement each other. That's when I get goosebumps and
the emotions pour out."

Those emotions, in the case of "Valotte," were also inspired by Lennon's
odd situation at the time, a musician writing songs that hadn't yet found a home
and weren't guaranteed to be heard by anyone other than those who were playing them. Hence, the memorable first line: "Sitting on the doorstep of the house
I can't afford." When asked about it, Lennon doesn't have to dig very deep to

remember its origin: "Literally considering the reality of the situation I/we were in, and thinking, 'Well, lets be honest here. What are we really thinking and hoping for and where are we now?'"

"Valotte" is a song that expertly captures a moment in time when your whole life is ahead of you, a thought that can cause as much angst as excitement. That angst extends to the relationship that haunts the song's narrator, who is self-aware enough to understand that love is not always forever, promises to the contrary notwithstanding. "I can see your face in the mirrors of my mind/Will you still be there?" Lennon sings, his voice betraying the tumult that unanswered question engenders.

That self-awareness also manifests itself in the way he sees his limitations with clear eyes at a time when others might think they know it all. "We're not so clever as we seem to think we are/We've always got our troubles so we solve them in the bar." In other parts of the song, however, the directness of the lyrics is bracing: "Do you know there's something wrong?/'Cause I've felt it all along," the narrator asks, and it sounds like we're eavesdropping on something intimate and tender. That kind of ability to cut through the minutiae and ephemera and get to the heart of the matter, well, let's just say that songwriting trait clearly runs in the Lennon family.

"Valotte" is all of the things that a hit single in 1984 generally wasn't, so the fact that we're spotlighting it in this volume as one of the most iconic songs of the decade really says a lot about its ability to overcome those preconceived notions. The narrator sings in the chorus about "Sitting on a pebble by the river playing guitar," and this song perfectly catches the cathartic beauty of what such an act must feel like to those who have the ability to do so. And when you can do it while capturing a time, a place, and a set of emotions that most us have felt at one time or another—all the things that Julian Lennon manages to do with this song—you'll pass the test of time with flying colors.

"Smuggler's Blues" by Glenn Frey

THE ALLNIGHTER (1984)

We are here to sing the praises of the music of the 80s, yet one drawback must be admitted. For the most part, the songs that made it into the mainstream did not address or question current events with any degree of thoroughness. Rap music, which started to gather widespread popularity as the decade wore on after staying underground in the early part of the 80s, deserves commendation for its part in bringing inner-city issues to the fore. Yet even in that case, the hip-hop-flavored songs that tended to break through to the pop charts usually were of the lighthearted variety. In the 80s, the radio was where you went to ignore the world's issues, not be confronted by them.

That's what made the success of Glenn Frey's "Smuggler's Blues," both in terms of its ability to court a wide audience (it made its way to number 12 in 1985) and its willingness to take a stand on a social concern, all the more striking. That the stand it took was far from the common knee-jerk reaction at the time made it even noteworthy.

As was the case for just about all of Frey's career outside the Eagles, he utilized the songwriting assistance of Jack Tempchin to bring "Smuggler's Blues" to life. According to Tempchin,

> When the Eagles broke up [following *The Long Run* in 1979], I hadn't yet written a song with Glenn, although he had made two of my songs ["Peaceful Easy Feeling" and "Already Gone"] famous with the Eagles. Pretty much right away, as soon as they broke up, he called me and said, "Let's try writing some songs." And I went over [to] his house and we wrote a couple of songs the first night. We were already great friends. We'd been friends for ten years, but we'd never written together before. So for fourteen years, till the Eagles got back together, I was his songwriting partner. I think I wrote everything but a couple of songs on his albums with him.

The pair were in the process of writing the songs for 1984's *The Allnighter,* Frey's second album, when Frey came to Tempchin with some interesting new subject matter for a song. "Glenn came down to San Diego, where I live," Tempchin says. "I'd just built a studio in my backyard; I took a double garage and soundproofed it. Glenn and Irving Azoff, his manager, had purchased the rights to a book about the cocaine trade called *Snowblind* [written by Robert Sabbag and subtitled *A Brief Career in the Cocaine Trade*]. Glenn and Irving were going to make a movie from the book, so they wanted some songs. And then Glenn had the idea to do 'Smuggler's Blues.' We would look at it from the point of view from the criminal."

Although Frey and Tempchin had all of this text from which to draw for the song, the two didn't really need to do much research to put the song together. "Glenn and I may have had past acquaintance with fellows who did that for a living," Tempchin laughs. "Our lives had research enough in it, so we pretty much knew a lot about it already. I didn't even read the book. Basically, we just got into it and said, 'Here's what we think about this whole thing.'"

The two set about assembling the basic ideas for the music right there in Tempchin's makeshift studio. "To Glenn, 'Smuggler's Blues' meant it would be a blues with slide guitar and some cool groove," Tempchin says of Frey's idea. "That was his concept and we started from there. I had an 8-track tape recorder and we did the demo right there. I had a Linn-9000 drum machine, which I operated and used for sequencing. Because of that, Glenn started calling me Jack 9000. That name stuck, but he shortened it to 9K. And Glenn played some monster slide guitar."

Tempchin recalls that the pair were really excited to sink their teeth into a subject that usually wasn't the stuff of radio fare. "The writing was real interesting," Tempchin says. "We were in the throes, which we still are, of the war on drugs. Which is a very poor concept. It hasn't worked at all anywhere it's ever been tried. The drug laws are blue laws. It's like everybody's doing the drug, like with booze in prohibition. But they can throw you in jail if they want to, because everyone's breaking the law. And they don't throw everyone in jail."

Tempchin praises his songwriting partner's ability to distill the complex topic into lyrics that stick with you. "Glenn was an all-star with one-liners," he says. "He was an extremely funny guy, and he had a great ability to encapsulate giant thoughts in tiny phrases." Tempchin got in his share as well, and you can hear these witty and cutting remarks from this expert songwriting duo all through "Smuggler's Blues": "You be cool for twenty hours and I'll pay you twenty grand"; "It's the politics of contraband"; "From the office of the president right down to me and you."

But it's the complete story that Frey and Tempchin concoct that really separates the song. Frey's idea to utilize the perspective of the smuggler was a brilliant one, because it allows him to make points about the subject that he never could have made otherwise. "Smuggler's Blues" works as a crime thriller (and the movielike video plays up that aspect of it), but it's also a subtle denunciation of a system that creates a booming industry out of the crime itself. "It's propping up the governments of Colombia and Peru," Frey sings, but he also notes that drugs, the money needed to buy them, and the weapons needed to protect them make their way through America. Everyday people get caught up in "the lure of easy money," leading to a kind of Wild West scenario where violence runs rampant. The street jargon rolls off Frey's lips like poetry, leading to the inevitable conclusion where "someone had to lose." What they lose is unspoken but isn't hard to fathom.

A chance meeting between Frey and *Miami Vice* mastermind Michael Mann even led to an episode of the show centered on the song, with the singer doing a nice acting job as a world-weary pilot for drug runners. Although the movie of *Snowblind* never did get made, the fact that it provided the impetus for "Smuggler's Blues" made the optioning of it more than worthwhile. It turned out to be one of Frey's biggest solo hits, one that had a lot more on its mind than your average *Billboard* gate-crasher.

Tempchin recorded his own version of the song at one point, and he laughs to think of his old buddy's laid-back advice. "He was saying, 'You just want to say that more casually. You don't want to lock it into the rhythm. You just want to make it conversational.'" The songwriting partnership between the two continued through all of Frey's records until his death in 2017. Tempchin is proud of all their work together, although "Smuggler's Blues" holds a special place in his heart: "We really stepped out and said something that everybody knows, but you're not supposed to say."

"Rock Me Amadeus" by Falco

FALCO 3 (1985)

If you flipped on your radio at any point during the summer of 1985, you were likely to hear the life story of Mozart recited to you over hip-hop drums and crackling guitars. If you turned on MTV around that same point, you were bound to see Falco, wearing a poofy Amadeus wig and rapping in German about the rock-star qualities of the classical composer. Strange though that description may seem, the phenomenon that was "Rock Me Amadeus" (and "phenomenon" is a better term for it than "song" due to its numerous remixes) transcended novelty status to became a worthy pop sensation.

Falco, born and raised in Vienna, emerged from the punk scene there to enjoy his first flashes of stardom when his German rap-pop hit "Der Kommissar" crossed over to England and America via a translated version by the group After the Fire. When his next project failed to hit those heights, Falco went looking for new collaborators, which is where the Dutch brothers Ferdi and Rob Bolland entered the picture.

Having been successful pop artists as teenagers in their own country, the brothers gravitated toward working with international artists as writers and producers. "We realized that, by working with international acts, we could get our music to a much broader range of audiences and markets," Ferdi Bolland says. "I'm glad we made the switch because we went on to score many hits, and worldwide sales of our songs and productions have surpassed 65 million. The challenge and fun part was coming up with new songs and production styles to exactly fit all these totally different artists and bands."

In this case of Falco, finding that fit took some convincing, as the three songs the Bollands worked up for him—the most famous of which played off the recent popularity of the movie *Amadeus* and all of which would become hit singles—were all rejected. "Falco did not respond to us at all but only through Horst [Bork, his manager], saying that he didn't like the tracks because he

121

would never, being from Vienna, do a song about Mozart," Bolland recalls. "He compared it to the Bolland brothers singing a song about wooden shoes from Holland."

Falco was eventually convinced, and an arrangement was reached by which the Bolland brothers would write and record the tracks and Falco could contribute lyrical ideas to those essentially finished products. But the initial meeting between performer and producers did not go well:

> As Hans Hölzel [Falco's birth name], he was an introvert, almost to the point of being shy, noncommunicative. When he transformed into his Falco alter ego, he was the proverbial 80s rock star, doing all the things he saw as being part of that image, like drinking heavily, doing drugs, trashing hotel rooms, etc. We had never met him or spoken to him until he flew to Holland and arrived at our studios to do the rap parts on our first three songs. Horst had already warned us, prior to arriving at the studio, that Hans was a bit nervous about meeting us and had indulged in a substantial "liquid breakfast" that morning. They came in at 10am and Hans was totally pissed. Not a bit but completely. He struggled through his first line, "Hi, so you're the famous Bolland brothers, g-g-g-great to meet you," and could barely stand upright. We sat down to chat and get to know each other but it was obvious to us and Horst that Falco was in no state to do any recording that day.
>
> We politely suggested that he go back to his hotel and we saw him again the next morning. That's when we started the rap recording. This was to become the fixed model for many future recordings and evolved to the point where I would sit in the studio control room recording the vocals, and Rob would stand next to Falco in the recording booth, holding him upright and miming the next rap parts to him. Always with his "good friend Johnny Walker" by his side.

Yet even in the midst of this chaos, Ferdi Bolland knew they were on to something:

> The combination of the old-school Juno synths, Linn drum, the Roland 808 drum machine, and our live rock band with the huge live drum sound worked great. Also Falco's cool Viennese-dialect rap and our English backing vocals were a new touch, which set the track apart from all other stuff on the market at that time. As the song, production, and lyrics of "Amadeus" were pretty much all done before we even first sent the song to him, Falco's contribution consisted of adding some words and lines in the two main verses of the song. The unique and over-the-top crazy way in which he performed the

rap and lead vocal in the track, especially in the fade-out of the song, really added a great extra element to the production.

In America, the single version backgrounded Falco somewhat in favor of the Mozart "biography," which was interesting in its own right. But the best version is the one that accompanies the memorable video, as it's the take where Falco combines the suave elocution of his rapping with unhinged screams, bouncing all that off the Bollands' production techniques in crazily endearing ways. And the chorus remains a thrillingly effective sing-along, no matter what your native tongue.

Yet even the song's creators didn't expect the utter world domination "Rock Me Amadeus" would enjoy. "After the final mix was finished and we did all the remixes, we really had the feeling that it could be a hit worldwide but never thought it would be number 1 in the USA," Ferdi Bolland recalls. "That was a total shocker and a lifelong dream come true. Also the fact that it simultaneously hit number 1 in the UK *and* USA was way beyond our expectations."

The Bollands and Falco continued their association for years, churning out a string of albums and singles that enjoyed European success, if not the worldwide notoriety of "Rock Me Amadeus." Alas, as Ferdi Bolland explains, when Falco's success waned, the Hans Hölzel side of his persona fell on hard times as well. "A couple of years before he died we lost contact," Bolland says:

> He wanted to get away from it all and was in a dark period in his personal life. I got the call on a Sunday morning. I was in my kitchen when a journalist called me to say Falco had died in a car crash in the Dominican Republic [at the age of 41 on February 6, 1998] under suspect circumstances, because he drove head-on into a bus at noon in broad daylight after drinking heavily at a local bar. I believe, as many of his inner circle still do, that it was a planned suicide. I couldn't believe the news when I heard it, but somehow I always knew deep down inside that Hans would never live to be seventy. He lived and died as a true pop icon.

And like all pop icons worth their salt—and thanks to Ferdi and Rob Bolland's expert stewardship—he left an undeniable calling card. "Rock Me Amadeus" may have been celebrating Mozart's work and life, but it painted an indelible portrait of Falco in the process. Old Wolfgang might not have understood the context of the tribute, but he surely would have enjoyed the eccentric charisma of the man paying it.

"St. Elmo's Fire (Man in Motion)" by John Parr

ST. ELMO'S FIRE (ORIGINAL MOTION PICTURE SOUND TRACK; 1985)

Songs that were meant to inspire were relatively common in the 80s. Some were good, but many more crossed over into the realm of treacle. John Parr's "St. Elmo's Fire (Man in Motion)" proved to be one of the most high-quality and successful examples of this quasi-genre, hitting number 1 in the United States in 1985 and crossing over worldwide. Perhaps the reason it turned out so well is that Parr found some potent inspiration of his own—only that inspiration didn't come from the motion picture that caused the song to be written in the first place.

Parr was an interesting combination of journeyman and overnight success circa 1985. He had been playing in front of audiences since his teenage years, but his recording career never got much further than supporting and writing songs with well-known names throughout the 70s and early 80s. Yet once he finally secured his recording deal, he was ready for it: his first solo single, the sultry "Naughty Naughty," immediately hit the Top 25.

"Naughty Naughty" caught the attention of mega-successful producer David Foster, who was then assembling the music for *St. Elmo's Fire*, a movie featuring many of the young actors who would come to be known as the Brat Pack. He invited Parr to participate, and Parr was flattered enough by the invitation to set aside his misgivings about the state of movie music at the time. "For me, I thought at that time that soundtrack songs were a dirty word," Parr says. "I really thought people shoved in their tenth, eleventh track off the album into the movie, with no respect for the story or whatever. I was frustrated by the corporate stuff that I was hearing in movies."

He intended to change that by writing a song with Foster, but, to his chagrin, the producer was so wiped out by the sound track assemblage that he asked if Parr would be okay singing a prewritten track. Parr pleaded with Foster until the producer agreed to give him an hour in which they would try to compose a song. "We went in the control room, and there was just a Linn drum and a keyboard in there," Parr remembers. "And we wrote a song in fifteen minutes, and I said, 'Wow, this is great.' And he said, 'No, we can do better.' So we wrote another song in fifteen minutes and I said, 'Wow, this is even better.' And he said, 'No, we can do better.' And the third one was 'St. Elmo's.' We did it all within an hour. David had done the chords and I kind of came up with the melody. But I was struggling with the lyrics."

The reason for his temporary writer's block: Parr had been given a plot synopsis of *St. Elmo's Fire*, and he wasn't impressed. "David told me what the movie was about," he explains. "I was a kid from Yorkshire that left school at sixteen and this movie was about rich college grads who didn't know what to do with their lives. So I had no empathy with them at all."

Luckily, Foster tried to jolt Parr's creative juices with another idea. Parr remembers,

> So [Foster] said, "Look this has nothing to do with the movie, but I'm gonna show you a videocassette of this guy that came in the studio last week. He's from my hometown in Vancouver." So he put the video on. It was a little local news item. And there's this beautiful-looking guy named Rick Hansen, looked like young Kennedy on the screen. He was just talking about what his dreams and ambitions were. And then the camera pulled back and I could see he was in the wheelchair. He said that he was able-bodied two years ago and that he had all these dreams and aspirations. He said he had a car crash and it changed his life. He was paralyzed, while his friend walked away from the crash without a scratch. Rick had his spine severed.
>
> He said that he was gonna get in his wheelchair and he was gonna wheel twenty thousand miles around the world to raise money and awareness for spinal research. And the hairs are going up on the back of my neck and I'm starting to feel things. The video comes to a close and it shows that he's got this really beat-up camper van. His friend who walked away from the crash is driving it, and he's gonna follow him around the world in this camper van. And on this side of the camper it says, "Rick Hansen World Tour—Man in Motion."

Parr had exactly the impetus he needed to write the words that would match the stirring tenor of the music, all while sneakily connecting everything to the film. "I went back to the hotel that night," he says. "And with hotel notepaper I wrote 'Man in Motion,' just about what I imagined this man's journey was going to be. I wrote it as if I was him. But I was mindful that the film company weren't going to swallow it. So I made every line ambiguous. When I talk about 'pair of wheels,' they think it's Demi Moore's jeep. When I say, 'Just once in his life, a man has his time,' they think it's when Emilio Estevez gets the girl. Of course it's not, but they think it is."

When he stepped to the mike to sing the song, Parr went for the gusto. "It is an over-the-top vocal, but it is about a guy wheeling fifty miles in a chair for two years. And that's who I was being," he says. He also knew instantly that the song was something special. "When I came off my vocal mike, I walked away and went down on my knees and thanked whoever it was for giving it to me. I take no credit for it."

Somehow, Parr's lyrics manage to transcend any hokey goings-on from the film and even Hansen's specific story to evoke the kind of stubborn obstacles that face every one of us. Over Foster's rafter-rattling keyboard riffs, he steps up with a combination of self-awareness ("You know in some ways you're a lot like me/You're just a prisoner and you're trying to break free") and defiance ("You broke the boy in me/But you won't break the man"). In this song, the notion "St. Elmo's Fire" leaves any tie-in to the film behind and becomes nothing less than the unquenchable flame of the human spirit.

For Parr, the side effects of the song were as important as its chart position. "This was pre-internet," he says. "Rick Hanson had no notoriety or anything, and by the time he was in China, everybody was lining the streets singing 'St. Elmo's Fire.'"

Nor has the song's inspirational potency lessened over the years. "I do a lot of shows where afterwards I come out and meet people and talk, and the stories you hear about the song," Parr muses:

> One girl told me she was dyslexic, and she said that she taught herself not to be dyslexic through that song. Now her life is devoted to teaching people how to get over dyslexia using music. Things like that, it's bigger than hit records. It's just life-sustaining.
>
> It's funny how it survives outside of its context, like people training in the gym to it. Rick once sent me a telegram and said, "Some days, I get out of the camper and I don't think I can do it. If I'm ever tired, I just put the song on and I can do another twenty miles." The power of music never ceases to amaze.

"Separate Lives" by Phil Collins and Marilyn Martin

WHITE NIGHTS (ORIGINAL MOTION PICTURE SOUND TRACK; 1985)

For the most part, the duets that did the most damage in the 1980s were the big, florid ballads, many of which were tied to motion pictures and used as the so-called love theme. Think of "Endless Love," by Lionel Richie and Diana Ross, from the movie of the same name, or "Up Where We Belong," by Joe Cocker and Jennifer Warnes, from *An Officer and a Gentleman*. These songs were so filled with inherent drama and import that one voice simply wasn't enough to convey it, but when a man and a woman were cast to sing such a song, viewers and listeners could imagine it as the internal dialogue of the hero and heroine on the screen.

What you'll notice about the aforementioned songs is that the artists chosen were all pretty much established in their careers either as hitmakers or at least vocalists of impressive renown. Which is why it seemed such an odd choice in 1985 to pair up Phil Collins, perhaps the era's most ubiquitously successful artist on his own and as a member of Genesis, with Marilyn Martin, who was a complete unknown to the public at large. Yet the end result was "Separate Lives," and it's hard to argue with a number 1 song and a ballad that still sounds convincingly like two people coming apart in the most painful way possible.

We know all about Phil Collins, but who was Marilyn Martin? Martin was all of twenty-one when she was handed the costarring role in "Separate Lives." Prior to the song, she was content as a supporting singer to some pretty impressive artists. "I had been singing for several years in Top 40 bands playing six nights a week, five sets a night, when an opportunity to sing background vocals on a Joe Walsh tour in 1983 came my way," Martin remembers. "The headliner on that tour was Stevie Nicks, and after a few weeks Stevie invited me to sing with her as well. Needless to say, I was thrilled."

Her connection to Nicks led to the next step in her unlikely journey to the top of the charts. "After that tour, she invited me to be a part of the recording

of her *Rock a Little* album, and it was during that process that I met the head of
Atlantic Records, Doug Morris," Martin says. "Doug would come to the sessions
to hear Stevie, and one evening he asked if I had any demos he could hear. To
my utter amazement, he eventually offered me a solo recording deal."

This is usually the part of the story where the young singer goes through
the process of finding songs for her debut release, a process that occurs in fits
and starts, with no guarantee that the end product will ever see the light of day.
But Martin's career took a different trajectory. "The timing of events was pretty
miraculous," she muses:

> Around that time Phil Collins turned in his *No Jacket Required* album
> and pointed out a song to Doug that he had recorded but didn't seem
> to fit the flow of the rest of his album, and that song was "Separate
> Lives." I think Phil brought it to Doug's attention because he be-
> lieved in the song and thought Doug could find a good home for it.
>
> It was about that same time that songs were being sought for
> the upcoming movie *White Nights*. Doug thought "Separate Lives"
> would be great in the film as a duet and somehow convinced Phil to
> allow me to add my voice to his already recorded track. I was filming
> a music video with Kenny Loggins for *Vox Humana* when I got the
> news. And I remember telling Kenny that I was going to sing a duet
> with Phil Collins and him looking at me like I had lost my mind.
> It just seemed so beyond the realm of possibility. I had come from
> Top 40 bar band singer to touring background singer to duet partner
> with one of the most amazing artists of our time in a relatively short
> period of time.

The song was written by Stephen Bishop, known for his singer-songwriter
work in the 70s and 80s, with hits including "On and On" and "It Might Be
You." Many songs detail the breakup, but "Separate Lives" is about the aftermath, that weird limbo area where feelings still linger for that other person even
when you're attempting to move on. Hence the girl in the song calling the guy
to tell him that she has found somebody new yet still misses him.

What's impressive about Bishop's composition is how honest it is about the
difficulties of rising above in a situation like that. "You have no right to ask me
how I feel/You no right to speak to me so kind," goes the chorus, detailing
that point where forgiveness seems far off. The production on the song, done by
Collins, Arif Mardin, and Hugh Padgham, is clever, starting out with just Collins and some lonely guitar chords before the chorus comes thundering in and
Martin joins him in full voice.

Even though "Separate Lives" was made without the two artists being in the
same room, the chemistry they forge is palpable. Collins was a known quantity
in the ballad department, but the song doesn't work without Martin's ability to

get inside her character and the way that the anguish in her voice demonstrates that there is no winner in this post relationship game.

That she was able to rise to the occasion is impressive considering her newcomer status at the time. "The first time I heard 'Separate Lives' it took my breath away," Martin says. "It's not often that you hear such a beautifully crafted, lyrically heartfelt song. Phil's vocal was completely mesmerizing, and the thought of replacing even a word with my voice to create a duet was incredibly intimidating. But I think that if you're going to use your voice effectively, the most important quality you need is honest emotion, putting yourself in the moment of whatever information the song is evoking."

The nature of her debut was so striking that it made it difficult for Martin to follow up; after a Top 40 hit with her solo debut single "Night Moves," she never again dented the charts. "The truth is, I didn't really know what I wanted to do as a solo artist," she explains. "I didn't have a favorite music genre that might have dictated my direction, which is why I recorded a variety of styles of songs. At the time I was having so much fun recording all kinds of fun music, like a kid in a candy shop. But that wasn't a wise career move, because I probably confused a lot of people and never really created a unique sound for myself."

Marilyn Martin's career has come full circle, as she is once again a much-in-demand backup singer. But nobody can take away her brilliant turn in the spotlight on "Separate Lives." "Phil's amazing voice and the caliber of the songwriting made the success understandable," Martin says. "I was just stunned to have been a part of such a musical event." Gracious words indeed, but her contribution as the perfect foil for Collins is integral to the success of one of the decade's finest duets.

"Life in a Northern Town" by the Dream Academy

THE DREAM ACADEMY (1985)

Nick Laird-Clowes had a choice to make. He could either stick around with Gilbert Gabriel, his bandmate in the London-based band the Dream Academy, and try to keep alive a group that seemed to be going nowhere, or he could go on a vacation to India with his girlfriend. "I told Gilbert that I was going to India," Laird-Clowes remembers. "I had to have a break from it. And he said, 'If you're going to India, the band is over.' So I said I wouldn't go."

At the time, Laird-Clowes was second-guessing his decision. But in just a few hours' time, he and Gabriel would begin composing "Life in a Northern Town," one of the most evocative singles of the mid-80s. It stood out boldly from its rhythmically aggressive brethren on the pop charts with its restrained arrangement and retro instrumentation. Letting India wait for a bit seems to have turned out all right.

Laird-Clowes had already been a member of two bands that had pretty strong connections in the music industry, yet both had gone under. The singer felt like he wasn't happy with the music he was making, and his association with Gabriel helped him understand why.

"I realized I was copying other people," Laird-Clowes says:

> That was the only way I knew how to learn. I learned by copying my favorite records and writers. The trouble was if they were contemporary and you were any good at copying them, you ended up sounding just like them. And by the time you came out, they'd already moved on because they were originals.
>
> Gilbert played me Ravel and other composers and he got me thinking about how to take a different angle with it. And I started playing the acoustic guitar. I can't tell you how "out" the acoustic guitar was. Everything was synths. I just thought I was going back to

130

what was not fashionable. I thought we've gotta do what we like and what we believe. He and I both strategized and talked about that.

The pair simply stopped listening to current music and went their own way, honing their sound for about a year based on the psychedelic experimentation of the late 60s and the intricately arranged records they loved by the Beach Boys and the Beatles. Yet there wasn't much interest for what they were doing, which is why things came to a head that fateful day in Gabriel's bedsit apartment on the outskirts of London.

As Laird-Clowes explains, a bolt of inspiration came from the deepest of doldrums. "And I felt so depressed that that day I went to rehearse with him while my girlfriend was getting on the plane," he remembers. "I went to his little place and we sat in the kitchen, drank tea, and felt really gloomy about life. I was getting too old and it was never gonna happen. I had my chances. We started talking about what we were gonna do and we said, 'Why don't we write a song with an African chorus?'"

The two began working out some parts on acoustic guitar; Gabriel's had just three strings, while Laird-Clowes was playing the guitar featured on the cover of British folk legend Nick Drake's album *Bryter Later*, which seemed to mystically steer the song's direction. "We started singing these melodies and these melodies seemed to be taking me to Nick Drake," Laird-Clowes says. "I couldn't work out why, but it felt like that."

That night, Laird-Clowes took the tape home to work on it. As he was writing some lyrics, he found that he couldn't remember the African-style chorus the pair had worked up earlier that day. Instead of looking for it on the tape, he started improvising and came up with the memorable "Hey-ma-ma" refrain that would adorn the final song.

As for the lyrics, a recent experience as a television presenter in the northern English city of Newcastle suddenly came to the fore for Laird-Clowes. "It was such a gloomy experience down there," he remembers. "The north of England was not like London or the rest of England. It was really suffering under unemployment, and people were standing in line outside the pubs at 11 in the morning. The northerners were brilliant though. There was a resilience in them that was completely different to what I'd been experiencing."

Around that same time, Laird-Clowes also came across multi-instrumentalist Kate St. John, and she added some lovely woodwinds to the song in her first sessions as a member of the band. The arrangement is not unlike the so-called baroque pop that briefly flourished in the 60s, when Lennon/McCartney and Brian Wilson's songwriting wanderlust also inspired bands like the Left Banke and Procol Harum to add classical instrumentation to their pop song structures.

Laird-Clowes tells a story in the lyrics about a mysterious visitor who enthralls the residents of a small town before moving on and vanishing into the night. While the song was dedicated to Drake, the stranger in question could be anyone who briefly brings sunshine into dreary lives. The song's brief flashes of poverty ("All of the work shut down") are contrasted by the ebullience of the chorus. Strange, beautiful, and sweetly sad, "Life in a Northern Town" is a song out of time, and all the better for it.

In terms of production, the song got a boost from the involvement of David Gilmour, the famed Pink Floyd guitarist and singer who was a longtime acquaintance of Laird-Clowes. For the Dream Academy frontman, Gilmour's sage advice meant as much to him as his knob-twiddling on the track. "He would say, 'You make the tracks yourself,'" Laird-Clowes says. "'Your record will be good or bad dependent on you getting what you want. If you allow people to tell you what you want, you will be unhappy, you won't learn it, and it won't be good.' He gave me the belief that I must follow my own course in what I was listening to and stop at nothing to get it right."

The odd thing about "Life in a Northern Town" was how it succeeded despite receiving little support. The Dream Academy's British label (Blanco y Negro) felt it was too weird, while their American label (Warner Bros.) bemoaned the lack of a bass guitar on it. Yet it found its way to the charts (hitting number 7 in the United States), much to the band's surprise. "We were getting our picture taken on a Thursday night," Laird-Clowes remembers, "and we said to the photographer, 'You gotta stop because we gotta watch *Top of the Pops*.' We'd all watched it since 1964 when it started. On it comes and the presenter says, 'In at number 40, the Dream Academy with 'Life in a Northern Town.' We said, 'What? No one even f***ing told us.' I thought if you went into the charts you were at least told by some manager or someone that it had happened. We virtually fell off the chair."

Although the Dream Academy released three critically acclaimed albums, there were no more hits of the magnitude of their biggest smash. "Life in a Northern Town," on the other hand, has maintained impact, much to the amazement of Nick Laird-Clowes:

> Who knew that sampling would come up, and it would be sampled and become a dance hit? Who again thought that Little Big Town, Sugarland, and Jake Owen, Southerners, would want to do it as an encore on their tour? They placed it as an extra track on a live album and it went in the country charts.
>
> It's unbelievable. Particularly when you think of what it came out of, it's extraordinary.

"Broken Wings" by Mr. Mister

WELCOME TO THE REAL WORLD (1985)

Many movements in the history of pop music begin with ebullience and joy, only to evolve into contemplation and moodiness. For example, think of how the simple pleasures of the early stages of the British Invasion in the 1960s eventually transformed into music that spoke truth to the tumult of the times.

A similar pattern emerged in the 80s. The so-called New Romantic boom started off the decade with synthesizer-driven music that was often clever and cheeky, but the songs were more about escaping the world's problems than confronting them. A kind of reaction against that began to build up by the middle of the decade. The synthesizers and drum machines were still there, but the melodies were more downcast and the lyrics tended toward ambivalence instead of outright glee.

Mr. Mister found a foothold at the height of this countermovement with their surprising number 1 single "Broken Wings" in 1985. They weren't newcomers by any stretch; not only had the band members been key cogs in other outfits dating back to the previous decade as well as studio hired guns for other artists, but they had already recorded and released an album a year before their breakthrough hits. Yet they seemed new when their album *Welcome to the Real World* showed up on the scene gushing hit singles and demonstrating that brooding music could indeed be commercially viable in that time period.

Two of the group's members, Richard Page and Steve George, had also been together in the band Pages, formed in Phoenix, Arizona, in the late 70s. Pages had focused on a style that was a bit too fusion based for the pop charts. "Since we had exhausted the ideas we had for Pages and hadn't had any real success, there was a desire to change things up and try something different," Page explains.

Page and George took on studio work with other acts, all while plotting a new band whose music might be more palatable for the masses. They teamed up

133

with guitarist Steve Farris and drummer Pat Mastelotto to form Mr. Mister, but their 1984 debut, *I Wear the Face*, didn't do much better than Pages had done.

There easily could have been an implosion at that point, especially since Page was contacted by popular bands Chicago and Toto as a possible replacement for departing frontmen. Yet he held fast to his vision of what Mr. Mister could be, banking on the songwriting talents of George, lyricist John Lang, and himself to produce something that could break through.

"There was no panic," Page explains. "Every album is a learning experience and we just decided to go forward with what we really liked ourselves. We figured if we liked it, others would, too. Steve, John, and I knew we could write songs in many genres. Since we appreciated so many kinds of music, it made sense to push for a more relatable sound."

"Broken Wings," with Page's bass and George's synthesizers as the impetus, turned out to be the breakthrough moment for that relatable sound. "The song was written around the bass line with the sustained chords on top. John Lang had the lyric idea and the song happened very quickly," Page remembers. "Everything about that song came really fast."

With just the two instrumental elements, Page's four-note bass riff and George's stretched-out synths, the pair effortlessly established a sumptuous musical setting. From there, other touches were laid on top, but more as atmosphere than as center-stage material. That refusal to show off allows the mood to persist for the almost six minutes running time of the song (in the album version) and to linger even beyond that. As a matter of fact, even without words "Broken Wings" would have been a successful piece.

That musical bed is contrived in such a way that, if there were going to be lyrics, they needed to be thoughtful. Lang provided that while demonstrating the same kind of restraint as the music. Instead of taking on specific issues, he reduces matters to a one-on-one level. In fact, the opening lines, when read on the page, sound like they could come from a 50s blues-rocker ("Baby, don't understand/Why we can't just hold on to each other's hand"). When they're hooked up with the meditative music, they sound like the beginning of some ancient parable.

As the song progresses, the Book of Love makes an appearance, and the start of the refrain ("Take these broken wings/And learn to fly again") paraphrases the Beatles' "Blackbird." But those referential underpinnings intermingle with the philosophical bent of the rest of the words (which were partially inspired by the poet Khalil Gibran's "The Broken Wings") to create a song that can work on many levels. You can hear it as a simple song about a lovers' reconciliation, or you can hear it as a universal plea for the unification of all hearts and souls.

Page's vocalizing works with either of those interpretations, as he tears at the lyrics with desperate fervor as the song progresses. Looking back at "Broken

Wings," he doesn't remember it as the by-product of any conscious plan mapped out by the songwriters or performers within the band. "Songs just rise out of inspiration," he says. "There wasn't a lot of awareness about trying to make something happen. It just happened, in spite of all the normal consciousness we had going at the time. The song was there floating around in the ether and we somehow got to hear it and bring it to life."

Page also sees it as a culmination of everything Mr. Mister had going for them. "I think the combination of musicianship and production made the track what it is." That said, it's understandable—considering that none of the fine work the band's members had done prior to the song had found a large audience—that there weren't high hopes for the potential of "Broken Wings" as a world-beater. "I thought it was a really good song but didn't think it had 'hit song' written all over it," Page explains. "I was surprised at how quickly it caught on."

"Broken Wings" caught on to the tune of an eventual spot on top of the pop charts in 1985 and made Mr. Mister radio and video stars. The serious feel of the song certainly didn't scare away pop audiences who were used to music that didn't carry that same kind of metaphorical weight. Besides, the band's double-talk name proved that they didn't take themselves too seriously. That they were able to follow up the song with the uplifting "Kyrie" (another number 1), and the rocking "Is It Love" demonstrated that Mr. Mister possessed some versatility.

Mr. Mister couldn't sustain the momentum of those monster singles. When they returned in 1987 with *Go On . . .*, the public had moved on; a fourth album was shelved and the band broke up. Yet they will always be remembered as one of the artists that were ready when the tastes of the public turned toward somber reflection. And Richard Page is fine with that legacy.

"I'm always amazed at how our music had touched people over the years," Page says. "Had success never come, I probably would've been an old bitter bastard wishing things were different. Now, I'm just an old bitter bastard with a little success!"

"And We Danced" by the Hooters

NERVOUS NIGHT (1985)

Like many so-called overnight success stories from the 80s, the Hooters actually had to scratch and claw their way to the point where they seemingly arrived from nowhere in 1985, churning out three Top 30 hits and opening the show at the fabled Live Aid concert in that same year. The fact that they were able to perform that day in their home city of Philadelphia was sweet vindication.

Eric Bazilian and Rob Hyman founded the band at the beginning of the decade, eventually sharing singing and songwriting duties on the vast majority of the band's songs. As Bazilian explains, the indifference to the band was frustrating in the beginning. "Philadelphia was sort of a black hole for artists," he says. "We were so close to New York. But we couldn't get New York to come to Philadelphia. So we'd go to New York and we'd play for ten people. And they'd tell us that we weren't electric, whatever that means. So we had to just make ourselves undeniable."

The Hooters managed that feat with a 1983 debut album (*Amore*) that sold in great numbers in Philly. To top it off, Hyman and Bazilian helped Cyndi Lauper with her mega-smash debut album *She's So Unusual* that same year, making them hard to ignore and eventually helping them secure a deal with Columbia Records. "By selling the numbers of records that we did regionally and by the live following that we had, and then having the little extra cachet of the Cyndi Lauper record, we were able to finally convince them," Bazilian says. "But it was not an easy road for Philadelphia artists. It's never been."

Since the band was still a bit of an unknown entity to the nation as a whole, they rerecorded three of the *Amore* songs ("Two of them weren't broke and we broke 'em," Bazilian jokes) for their Columbia debut titled *Nervous Night*. Still, new material was needed, so Bazilian and Hyman headed out for a songwriting retreat, which is where "And We Danced" was born.

"We went to this resort in the Poconos," Bazilian recalls:

136

It was mostly people with walkers, which actually worked out pretty good because there were no distractions. I had my 4-track cassette setup. We just threw down a whole bunch of ideas. And the very last idea we had was this chorus. I remember we had gone to see the lounge band, who were very entertaining, to say the most. And we were walking back and we just started having this conversation about melody, kind of a very theoretical conversation about what kind of melodies we liked and why. We stumbled on the melody as we were walking. By the time we got back to the apartment we were staying in, we had a chorus. The words to the chorus came quickly. And we did a quick little demo, which was kind of a calypso thing with completely different verses.

We came back with fifteen, twenty different song ideas. And we played them all for Rick Chertoff, who was producing the record. That was the last one we played him, and he was like, "That paid for your trip."

Even with that promising beginning, "And We Danced" still needed an arrangement and a melody for the vocals in the verses. Chertoff helped by encouraging them to cut loose in a more rocking fashion. "We went through quite a process in finding the arrangement, because at that point we hadn't really rediscovered our rock roots," Bazilian says. "We were still kind of a ska/reggae-rock band. And we were trying to play everything with some element of the islands in it. But Rick really pushed us to rock out. He was the one who really told us, 'Hey can you turn that guitar of yours back up to where it used to be when I first met you and you were a rock God?' And I reluctantly agreed."

The melody in the verses came about when Bazilian altered the tune of Robert Palmer's "Johnny and Mary." To play off Bazilian's arpeggiated guitars, Hyman's bright keyboards, and drummer David Uosikkinen's pulsating beat, the band added a gentle combination of mandolin and melodica (the "hooter" instrument that gave the band its name) that would be used for the bridge and the intro.

Meanwhile, the lyrics, sung with gusto by Hyman and Bazilian, do an excellent job of throwing a bunch of rock-and-roll archetypes—such as the local dance, the irresistible girl, and the guy making his play for her—into a blender and then subtly undercutting them. Notice the band playing "out of tune" and the phrase "We were liars in love" in the refrain. Listeners could either enjoy it at innocent face value or find the wistful tinges underneath if it suited them.

Even though it was chosen to be the second single after the more experimental "All You Zombies," "And We Danced" was the song that roared to the Top 20 and opened the doors for the elongated success of *Nervous Night*. It also led to their experience at Live Aid, which Bazilian claims was as surreal as it was brief. "We got there at like six-thirty in the morning and it was total chaos," he says.

"And we never got to sound check. We walked up there totally cold. And we did two songs. People ask me what do I remember. I don't remember anything. We walked up. And we walked off. One hundred twenty thousand people saw us there and apparently a billion were watching on TV."

Although they might have seemed like a long shot for success in the 80s, with no gimmick other than being a hardworking band of talented writers and performers, Bazilian claims that he and Hyman expected at some point they would find their way to the audience they eventually reached. "I don't think we were really surprised because we knew that we had done the work," he says. "We knew that we had been good soldiers and good students, gone to school, done our homework."

That homework is still paying off: the Hooters still play to appreciative audiences, and they make sure to make frequent stops in or very near their hometown. As a matter of fact, the producers of the ABC sitcom *The Goldbergs*, which is set in the 80s in the City of Brotherly Love, asked the band to appear on an episode as themselves in 2018 playing—what else?—"And We Danced." It turns out that Philly connection finally started working in the Hooters' favor after all.

"Cry" by Godley & Creme
THE HISTORY MIX VOLUME 1 (1985)

The uninitiated might have assumed that Kevin Godley and Lol Creme were upstarts when they released their hauntingly original 1985 single "Cry," which sobbed its way into the Top 20 in the United States and the UK. In actuality, the two had been an instrumental part of the band 10cc, which streaked across the pond for a string of pop hits in the 70s, including "I'm Not in Love" and "The Things We Do for Love." And fans of the burgeoning music video craze in the 1980s might have recognized them in the credits of some of the era's most memorable clips, as directors of classic videos by Duran Duran, the Police, and Herbie Hancock, among many others.

As Godley explains, he and Creme had a funny way of popping in and out of the public consciousness. "We kept kind of doing stuff, and occasionally something would tickle the public's taste buds," he laughs about the pair's sporadic successes. "Cry" was one of those moments in their career when their willingness to innovate and their songwriting chops combined to find a home with a broad audience, especially when a groundbreaking video was added to the package.

Godley and Creme also possessed a secret weapon in another 80s behind-the-scenes icon, producer Trevor Horn, who saw potential in a musical piece from the pair that had been hibernating for quite a while. "We actually began to write the song fifteen years before it was completed and recorded, strangely enough," Godley says. "It wasn't one of those epiphany moments where the words come and the tune comes. We only had the first verse. That's all we had. And we always thought it was very good, but for some reason or another, we never managed to take it any further. So it just kind of sat there on ice."

When they convened with Horn in London to record in the mid-80s, they went digging in the past for material. Godley remembers,

On the second day of the sessions, we plopped out this little chestnut that we'd never managed to finish. Trevor suggested that we use a Synclavier [a combination synthesizer/sampler], which I'd just got. And J. J. Jeczalik, who was working with him at the time, started turning the music into a loop. While Lol and I went and played table tennis or something like that, they created some kind of a structure around the very basic premise of the first verse.

When we came back into the studio, I was instructed to write some more words. Just write something that felt interesting and try singing to what they'd done. So it was all very intuitive as opposed to much of a thought process going on. We were sort of experimenting until we had something that worked. Thank God we weren't medical students. It was completely different than what I thought the finished thing would ever sound like. I think what Trevor brought to it was that sense of simplicity that he saw in the initial tune. We followed his lead, just adding and responding to suggestions. And it didn't actually take that long to put together. I've found this in most of the best songs: There's less thought and more intuition involved.

The arrangement that was settled upon is strangely mesmerizing, loping along amiably until at times, out of nowhere, Creme interrupts with watery guitar chords that jar the listener out of any lull. Godley came away impressed with the unpredictability of it all. "It's hypnotic," he says. "It keeps your attention. And you're never quite sure what's coming next. It's never quite what you expect, but it kind of is. In other words, it keeps you hypnotized but it keeps you on your toes as well."

The lyrics, meanwhile, dovetail nicely with the music, as the narrator slowly builds his case against the girl that he's addressing for her neglect and mistreatment of him, eventually rising up with a torrent of emotion that he's held in for too long. There's something incredibly damning about the line "You don't even know how to say goodbye"; even as she was leaving, she couldn't grant him a scrap of consolation, instead digging the knife in farther. His final, simple summation: "You make me want to cry."

For the words, Godley followed the lead of the few lyrics he had written all those years before. "What we'd already written in that first verse was pretty much like that anyway," he says. "To take off in another direction wouldn't have really worked. We were following what already existed, so we just took it down that road and said what needed to be said. 'Cause it starts off like that: 'You don't know how to ease my pain.' There's nothing in the way. It's a very direct statement."

Godley credits the way that Horn emphasized that directness ("Simplicity is something that we'd avoided for a while," he says about he and Creme's career path around that time), while adding eclectic touches like the cartoonishly high vocal notes that end the song. "It was the 1980s version of Auto-Tuning," Godley says of the finish. "They just took it up an octave on the harmonizer. They sampled the note I sang and extended it for far longer than I could hold it."

As for the video that accompanied the song, it only came about because Godley and Creme's original idea—to film the famed British ice dancers Jayne Torvill and Christopher Dean—fell through. "We thought it sounded like the kind of song that anyone could sing," Godley says of their backup plan:

> So why not get a load of anyones to sing it? We'll just mix between the faces and see what happens. It was kind of a throwaway idea, like a B-side.
>
> We looked in a casting book, picked out a lot of faces, and sent audio cassettes to everybody. When they showed up at the studio, we sat them in a chair against a black background. As best as we could we lined their eyes up. I think we probably filmed about forty-five people. But the magic happened when we were actually in the edit suite. We tried this editing technique called a soft wipe. Before we were going from whole face to whole face; with this we were going kind of nose outwards and top of the head downwards. And what we discovered was that we would create a person that didn't exist on the way from one face to another. And it was like, "Whoa! This is interesting." It took us off in a different direction. And that to me is the magic of the video, as well as the performances that we got.

The analog technology that the pair used to make the video was soon widely copied using the digital method called morphing, but it's hard to beat the charm of the "Cry" video. It's also difficult to think of a song from the 80s quite like it, with music and lyrics that perfectly capture the waning and rising anger that accompanies the denouement of a love affair.

For Kevin Godley and Lol Creme, they knew they had something that would make an impact. "I remember when we finished the video, we had a sense that there was something special going on," Godley muses. "You do get that occasionally. The hairs on the back of our necks were standing up a bit. It was the combination of the song and the video; it was like there's something interesting going on here. You can't really second-guess these things."

"The Original *Miami Vice* Theme" by Jan Hammer

MIAMI VICE (1985)

It is hard to explain the *Miami Vice* phenomenon to people who didn't live through it, in part because much of what it introduced to television has become so widely copied that these tropes have become second nature to modern audiences. In addition, the show peaked creatively so quickly that by the time many people caught up to it, it wasn't quite as sharp as it had originally been, with the exception of a stray episode here and there. (Stick with the first two seasons if you're planning to binge so you can understand the fuss, because that's when the series hewed closest to reality-based plots and before it ran a bit off the rails.)

Most everyone who did tune in faithfully every Friday night to the show did so in part to see the latest exploits of detectives Sonny Crockett and Rico Tubbs, and in part to see how the show's maestro, Michael Mann, would weave a just-right pop song into a pivotal scene. Adding to all was the musical score of the show, a brooding, mysterious thing that conveyed the inner monologue of two cops who rarely unloaded their emotions about the bad guys who got away and the toll taken on the good guys trying to catch them.

The man responsible for that score was Jan Hammer, born in Czechoslovakia and an innovator in electronic music on his own as a composer and as a member of rock-based outfits like the Mahavishnu Orchestra. Circa 1983, Hammer was in Los Angeles finishing up work on the music for a film and was scheduled to take a red-eye out of the city to his home in New York. Since he had a little time on his hands, a friend suggested that he visit Mann, who was working on a new project. "He started talking about this show and it sounded really exciting," Hammer recalls. "He was trying to describe that he wanted the music to sound unlike anything on TV at that time. Basically we started talking about different sounds. And I had a cassette with some of my sketches. What I played him was the '*Miami Vice* Theme.'"

Without having seen a single frame of film for the show, Hammer had inadvertently composed the theme song that would eventually become a chart-topper. Both men thought that perhaps they could even improve upon it. "He liked this one very much, so he said, 'Let's try something else,'" Hammer says. "I actually wrote three different versions of something else. After all that was exhausted, he said, 'Oh, no, I like the first one.'"

The piece to which they eventually returned for the theme was composed primarily on Hammer's Fairlight synthesizer, with some grinding rhythm guitar that he played separately also included. He had also sampled some of his own drums, including the steel drums that so wonderfully evoked Miami's tropical feel. "It was sort of like a very early EDM [electronic dance music] kind of thing," Hammer says of the "*Miami Vice* Theme." "And I was just experimenting with combinations of different rhythms from left and right in stereo and how they were overlapping. It was more like an exercise. And then it really evolved into a really exciting groove and a beat."

Used in the credits over film clips of other Miami signifiers like jai alai, speedboats, and bikini-clad pedestrians, the track invited us into the world of exotic danger that the show promised each week. The machine gun percussion at the start of the song beckons instead of frightening away, while Hammer's churning rhythms and wending synth guitar hook pull us in even deeper. It set the tone for the show and, in its complete version, made for a captivating listen even with the visuals absent.

Buoyed by that success, Mann placed a kind of absolute trust in the composer that surprised even Hammer himself:

> I worked on the two-hour pilot. I would spend a lot of time in LA working with Michael and going back and forth. Once that was finished, he was very confident that we would get picked up. Although you never know. You show a pilot and it might just bomb.
>
> So he was saying, "When we go into production on the series, I want you to run with it." Meaning whatever you want and put it wherever you want it. It was just an unbelievable freedom that I've never experienced on any other project. And I'm sure that Michael doesn't work that way at all ever. He's pretty much a hands-on guy. But he just decided to let me run with it.

Hammer ran with it to the tune of another international hit in "Crockett's Theme," initially composed for a scene where Don Johnson's Detective Crockett is hiding in a safe house with his son because there's been a hit placed on him. Again, Mann trusted Hammer to capture the emotions of the scene in ways that dialogue couldn't. "It was something that I loved to do, where music advances the story," Hammer says. "The dialogue sort of disappears. But there's still a lot of stuff happening, and the music is totally propelling it forward. That was something that I loved about the show."

As for the "*Miami Vice* Theme," Hammer couldn't believe how it sailed through the pop charts, a relatively unheard-of accomplishment at the time for an instrumental. The icing on the cake came in the way he found out the song had reached the apex. "The week before, we were already in the Top 10, I was watching it," he remembers. "I remember Stevie Wonder was number 1 with 'Part-Time Lover' and I was saying, 'Am I going to knock off Stevie Wonder?' So I was at home and the phone rings, and the voice says, 'Hi, this is Henry Mancini.' And I said something along the lines of, 'Sure you are.' But it actually was him, and he was just calling to give me early congratulations because he saw *Billboard* come out and it said you are number 1."

Jan Hammer might have been humbled by hearing from such a famed composer, but his own feats have been pretty awe-inspiring as well. Part of that success, especially with his work on *Miami Vice*, comes from his willingness to venture into uncharted musical territory. When asked if he worried that Michael Mann's idea for the show might have been a little too visionary for mass public consumption at the time, he shrugs the idea off. "There's never such a thing for me as 'too ahead of its time,'" he laughs. "I was all in right there."

"Your Love" by the Outfield

PLAY DEEP (1985)

Maybe it was fitting that the Outfield, despite hailing from Great Britain, took their band name from that most American of pastimes. After all, they enjoyed excellent success in the States while being largely ignored in their home country. Why that is a mystery might be explained away by the vagaries of different countries' tastes or the band's style of music or even their timing. In any case, listening to it now, it's difficult to understand why anyone, regardless of their land of origin, should have been immune to the musical charms of this engaging trio.

The Outfield wasn't doing anything new, for sure, but they always did what they did extremely well, and without any off-putting posturing about it to boot. They were like the rock band next door. Yet their greatest hit, the 1986 Top 10 winner "Your Love," admitted a little bit of bad-boy behavior into their squeaky-clean sound, making it a surprisingly subversive offering from this smiling band.

The trio of bassist/singer Tony Lewis, guitarist/songwriter John Spinks, and drummer Alan Jackman had been working together under various names and utilizing various styles since the late 1970s. "I went to school with Alan and met John in 1977," Lewis explains. "We were in Sirius B, a prog rock band, in 1977, and we disbanded in 1978 as punk exploded onto the British scene. We were in different local bands and formed again as the Baseball Boys in 1982."

Yet even as they battled their way through different incarnations, they still held firm to their dreams of an eventual breakthrough. "We were always confident," Lewis says. "We were tunnel-visioned to succeed. So we played small gigs, pubs, and clubs to gain experience, whilst working day jobs. And we recorded evenings and weekends at Scarf Studios, which was run by our first manager."

They eventually settled on a power-pop sound that drew the attention of Columbia Records, setting them up for their 1985 debut album *Play Deep*, the title continuing the baseball tie-ins. With opening single "Say It Isn't So," the band established a formula from which they would rarely stray: churning mid-

145

tempo rhythms, bold harmonies, Spinks's knack for writing hooks, and Lewis's ability to sing them way up on the octave scale without sounding the least bit strained.

"Your Love," on the surface, sticks pretty close to that winning lineup. "'Your Love' was written in fifteen minutes in John's flat," Lewis remembers. "He shouted the lyrics down the corridor and I wrote them down." The arrangement is smart from beginning to end. The solo guitar open provides a slightly different way to hear the three chords that have made up rock music since the beginning. In the middle sections of the song, the guitars interlock and entwine, while Lewis keeps up a steady bounce on bass. Chapman announces every shift in tone with his crashing snares. The final verse comes back to the isolated guitar and vocal before the climactic return to the giant chorus. Textbook tension and release courtesy of the band and producer William Whitman.

Seemingly textbook anyway. Even at first listen, it's hard to miss that there are a bit more minor keys in there than usual. There is also a bit more anguish in Lewis's vocal than normal, and the harmonies tug at the gut with just a little bit more ardor. And the obviously audible line in the refrain of "I don't want to lose your love tonight" suggests a few clouds have entered the group's usually sunny picture.

The lyrics in the verses, which aren't always that easy to discern thanks to Lewis's unique phrasing, start to reveal the sneakiness of the story. "Your Love" is actually a tale about a guy whose girlfriend is away and who decides to assuage his loneliness with a one-night stand. Yet Spinks's lyrics and Lewis's performance, for the most part, keep you on his side.

"Josie's on a vacation far away/Come around to talk it over," the song begins. "I ain't got many friends left to talk to," he laments. "You know I'd do anything for you," he promises. When she objects, he tries semantics to make his point: "Just cause you're right, that don't mean I'm wrong." The poor guy has shaking hands and a worried mind.

You can almost look past the way he plies her by saying, "You know I like my girls a little bit older." You can maybe forgive the fact that he wants her to "keep it under cover." And you can maybe even overlook that the first line of the refrain is "I just want to use your love tonight."

Again, Lewis's naturally innocent-sounding voice makes us root for him even as engages in the deepest deceit. And Spinks's construction shows how convincing some lotharios can be. The last trick the songwriter pulls: when the girl leaves, we can't possibly be sure if it's after she has rejected him or if she has acceded to his request. Again, subversive stuff.

Lewis is still playing it straight after all these years about the meaning of "Your Love" and whether he and Spinks were consciously trying to sneak the song's true intent past the listening public. "It was a tongue-in-cheek song and

I sung it as John directed me," he says. "We were a struggling band who were trying to break through. In hindsight, I can see that the narrative is intriguing, but in all honesty, I just sung it."

Even if that's the case, it still doesn't deny the fact that "Your Love" has a lot more going on than your average pop song. It can be enjoyed as a track that just sounds pleasing. But you can also have fun with it and dig deep into its deceptively simple frame to find either honesty or larceny.

By any measure, "Your Love" enthralled listeners. It moseyed its way from rock radio into the thick of the pop chart wars and ended up nestled in the Top 10. It gave the Outfield necessary momentum that helped them to a total of five Top 40 hits in a six-year span. And, although the well of hits ran dry as the 90s dawned, the band would prove resilient enough to occasionally re-form for studio albums in the next two decades, proving that old formula still had a lot left to offer.

In 2014, John Spinks, who wrote the vast majority of the band's material, succumbed to liver cancer at age sixty. As Lewis says, that effectively ended the career of this fine group. "Without John, we are not the Outfield," he says.

Still, the gleaming sheen on their best songs holds up as well if not better than many of the other, smoother operators of the era. And "Your Love" can stand up pretty tall against any of the era's best, whether you're looking for pure ear candy or smart storytelling with a twist.

For Tony Lewis, the legacy of the Outfield and its most famous song, to extend the baseball metaphor, might not be a perfect game, but it's an impressive complete game performance nonetheless. "I'm proud of the achievement of the song," Lewis sums up. "I have a great deal of sadness that John is no longer with me, but I have long and happy memories of playing and performing. And the song is timeless. So it is extremely bittersweet."

"If You Leave" by Orchestral Manouevres in the Dark

PRETTY IN PINK (ORIGINAL MOTION PICTURE SOUND TRACK; 1986)

Throughout this book, there have been many examples of classic 80s songs that were written in a rush. But there is one song from the decade that became a hit after it was hastily written out of necessity. "If You Leave" is an eleventh-hour miracle that transformed a band that had previously been known for their synth-pop experimentation and left-of-center lyrical subject matter into the kings of high school romance.

OMD (shortened from the mouthful of Orchestral Manouevres in the Dark) was one of the most successful pop bands in Europe at the start of the 1980s; not bad for a group that shunned the traditional topics and traded in songs about airplanes and oil refineries. Yet for all their success in their native England and parts nearby, they only cultivated a small cult of American fans.

"It was very frustrating," says Andy McCluskey, who founded the band with Paul Humphries in 1978, of OMD's relative lack of popularity in America:

> With the early hits, we were in control. We didn't even have an A&R man; we did exactly what we wanted and we sold records no matter how weird and bizarre we were.
>
> Except in America. There were only a couple of alternative stations that would play us or college radio. So we were very underground in the States, whilst we were on the front cover of *Smash Hits* and selling millions of records in Europe. It was just really weird.

What changed it all was a call from John Hughes, the cool teen movie screenwriter and director of choice in the 80s and a bit of a kingmaker when it came to choosing bands for his sound tracks. "John Hughes contacts us and says, 'I'd like the band to do a track for my next movie,'" McCluskey remembers. "This was just after Simple Minds had 'Don't You (Forget about Me)' in *The Breakfast Club* and we were like, 'Oh, yes, we'll do that please!' When it came to

148

music, he was a real Anglophile. He loved his English 80s pop music. That's why he asked for Simple Minds, that's why he asked for us. So many of the tracks in his movies were from British pop artists."

The movie in question was *Pretty in Pink*, a love triangle set in high school—where else?—with a little class warfare thrown in for good measure. The band was given a script where the movie's princess-in-rags heroine, played by Molly Ringwald—who else?—chooses to be with her quirky best friend Duckie (Jon Cryer) at film's end instead of handsome rich suitor Blane (Andrew McCarthy). OMD tailored a song called "Goddess of Love" for the movie's closing scenes based on that scenario.

That's when, as McCluskey remembers, fate and focus groups intervened: "They test-screened it and all the teen girls went, 'No, no, no. He's her best friend. She needs to end up with the good-looking guy for the happy ending.' We'd gone home and written 'Goddess of Love' and when we got back to LA, armed with the 2-inch tape ready to mix it, [Hughes] said, 'Guys, I'm really sorry, but we've reshot the end of the movie and it's got a completely different storyline now. We like your song, but is there any way you can write us another that's got different lyrics that would be more appropriate now to the new ending?'"

The band was about to go on a mini-tour in less than two days and didn't even have any equipment with them. But they knew the opportunity was simply too good to pass up, even with the hassle they would now have to endure. They rented a studio and equipment and got to work:

> Just off the top of our heads, we sat down and started writing a song. Paul blocked out some chords. We laid down some drums. I wrote the lyrics, cut a guide vocal. We did the whole thing in about fourteen hours, finished it at about three in the morning. We bounced down a rough mix onto a cassette. Then we phoned for a motorcycle rider who took it to Paramount and left it for him at the gate.
>
> We left the studio and probably didn't get to sleep till about five. Finally we got a phone call at nine the next morning from our manager saying, "Yeah, John's heard the new song. He loves it. Now go back in the studio and finish it up." So we crawled back in the studio.

As usual, Hughes's musical taste was right on point. Somehow McCluskey and Humphries had hustled out a last-minute song with simple, direct pleas that sounded exactly like what you would actually say in the moment of romantic despair, rather than what you hoped you might say if you had time to think about it. The desperation of it all was perfect for the prom scene where McCarthy makes a last-ditch effort to win Ringwald back. But, movie context aside, "If You Leave" still elicits sighs of wonder, as the swooping keyboards and Martin Cooper's bluesy saxophone play off the anguished vocal harmonies. McCluskey gets the big moment at the end, unleashing the final line ("Don't look back") with the kind of force that just might pull that special someone away from the car leaving town and back onto the dance floor.

OMD got the star treatment when the film opened, but they were in for a rude awakening. "We hadn't seen anything until we went to the premiere," McCluskey recalls. "The only thing John had said to us was, 'We've filmed the dance scene at the prom using "Don't You (Forget about Me)." So can you write a song that is the same tempo, which is 120 beats per minute?'"

"And we did. So we wait and we wait and the movie's great and everybody is loving it. We finally get to the part where we said, 'Here we go, this is us.' And not one person was dancing on the beat. It didn't matter what tempo it was. The editor still couldn't get them on the beat!"

McCluskey says that if the band had any time to feel the pressure of writing such an important song so quickly, they might not have come up with something so memorable. "Because we had to do it off the top of our heads, it was like a craftsman song. It's not one of our most radical. It's not a song that's really alternative or was gonna change the world. It was just two musicians in their midtwenties who had learned their trade and could put something together. What we were lucky with was that we got a great tune."

"If You Leave" gave OMD their long-awaited US breakthrough (hitting number 5) and still sticks around in minds and hearts today, perhaps, as McCluskey offers, because it touches on a universal experience of the young and easily heartbroken:

> The idea was you'd all been through school together. And this was the end. It was goodbye to a possible romance, but it was also goodbye to all of the friends that you'd known. You were all going in your different directions. The line "Seven years went under the bridge" is for an English high school, whereas an American high school would be only four. So it was the end of friendship as well as a potential romance.
>
> The movie has a timeless quality, because all Americans have been to high school, they've been through what those kids were going through. All high schools end with a prom. And this is the prom song.

"Welcome to the Boomtown" by David + David

BOOMTOWN (1986)

In the 1980s, the pop music industry was so booming that successful artists were usually compelled to record as often as possible, milking their golden touch for everything it was worth. That makes the project known as David + David, who alit upon the rock scene for one brilliant album and the stunning single "Welcome to the Boomtown" but never followed it up, somehow even more compelling.

Then again, there was always something about this pair that was unique and more than just the sum of the impressive individual parts, David Ricketts and David Baerwald. The two were up-and-coming musicians who met, hung out at Ricketts's LA apartment with a portable studio making demos, and suddenly found themselves, however briefly, the darlings of critics and rock fans who wanted music with more intelligence and depth than the norm.

As Ricketts recalls, the fact that the two artists were coming at the project from slightly different backgrounds is what it made it so intriguing, even to them. "We didn't necessarily know the direction it was going to take," he says. "Art rock was how I saw it. Baerwald brought more of a kind of country influence to it than I could have done. So that made it pretty interesting. Then it was kind of like, okay, what are we going to do with all this? The combination of the two of us seemed to have this originality to it, which we were kind of discovering as we went. That was exciting to me."

At the time of the 1986 release of the duo's album *Boomtown*, which came about when record company execs at A&M heard and were impressed by the pair's homemade demos, heartland rock—as purveyed by megastars like Bruce Springsteen, John Mellencamp, and Tom Petty—was extremely popular. But David + David tended to create soundscapes that veered away from the chunky guitars and churning rhythms favored by those folks, all while turning the spot-

151

light on a seedier brand of character than was typical. And that had a lot to do with their West Coast location at the time the pair came together.

"Welcome to the Boomtown," after all, began as a sketch called "Welcome to LA." Ricketts's wailing, sorrowful guitar intro was in place right from the start, "calling the faithful," as he puts it. From there, Baerwald created lyrics partially based on people that the pair had encountered. Ricketts remembers,

> Kevin was a friend of mine, the inspiration for that character. He was kind of the quintessence of an LA type of guy. He wasn't a drug dealer or anything like that. He was kind of a handsome guy. So that was partially fiction and partially biography.
>
> The Miss Christina thing, I think Baerwald was driving around and saw a woman driving a Porsche that said Christina, the license plate, which was very LA in a way. That's pretty much all you had to say if she's driving a 944, which she was. So they're pretty much fictional and yet based on probably things that we intersected with, just people living in LA at that time.

In the hands of David + David, "Handsome Kevin" becomes a college drop-out selling drugs from a local Denny's. "Miss Christina" may have the fancy car and all of the material possessions one could ever hope to accrue, but she isolates herself in her room, the "cocaine in her dresser" her favorite pastime. The final verse suggests a tragic yet inevitable end to the tale: "The ambulance arrived too late/I guess she didn't want to wait." And the chorus allows for some reflection on the entire scene, providing slogans like "Pick a habit, we got plenty to go around" and "All that money makes such a succulent sound" that win points for accuracy, even if the local chamber of commerce won't be adopting them anytime soon.

The music manages to evoke both intrigue and melancholy, which Ricketts says was accomplished as much by omitting elements as it was inserting them: "I like that space, because it had a kind of elongation that allowed for you to be able to focus the vocal and the lyric in a way that was very visual. I wanted it to be cinematic and everything. At the same time, I wanted the rhythm to create this momentum that the listener gets on the ride with. By the time the first line of the verse comes in, you're already well along for the ride. You just kind of go with it. And then Baerwald had that terrific voice, which made for a great narrator for the stuff."

On the one hand, it's a minor miracle that the song and album, emanating as they did from such unusual origins, both snuck into the Top 40. ("Welcome to the Boomtown" topped out at number 37 on the pop charts, but it was an oft-played track on rock-based stations at the time.) Yet the quality of the music produced by David + David was such that it seemed more success should have been forthcoming. "If we'd have kept going, it might have maybe been a different conversation," Ricketts admits. "At the time it seemed really big and then after a while, maybe that wasn't quite enough."

Ricketts and Baerwald continued working with each other on other projects, but never again under the David + David banner. "We investigated and we've got quite a bit of stuff," Ricketts explains, but he cautions that the first project was one of a kind. "Just kind of maintaining the mojo is a little difficult. We were in that space where we couldn't help ourselves there, which is pretty fantastic."

Besides, that lone album, spurred on by the brilliance of "Welcome to the Boomtown," left enough of a mark. And it's highlighted by one of those songs from the era that, when it's played, causes a reaction with discerning fans who remember how it stood out at the time. "It had a resonance with people," Ricketts says. "And I read stuff on the internet sometimes and Baerwald and I work together intermittently, and it still seems like there's this pocket of people out there that it seemed to make a really powerful emotional connection with. And that's gratifying."

Equally gratifying to Ricketts is the knowledge that David + David proved that rock music success can come even from the humblest beginnings and unlikeliest sources. "I remember people telling us, 'You can't do it that way,'" Ricketts muses. "But if you have a point of view and you're able to convey it? Yes, you can do it that way."

"Keep Your Hands to Yourself" by the Georgia Satellites

GEORGIA SATELLITES (1986)

The term "southern rock" has always been a bit difficult to define. Nonetheless, it's safe to say that the 80s wasn't the best decade for this loosely defined genre. With the exception of ZZ Top (again, iffy if they qualify) and .38 Special, there weren't any consistent hitmakers from the genre.

The Georgia Satellites didn't have the consistency part down; they were pretty much on the road to ruin after their first and only smash. But, man, did they ever get that one hit right and really do that elusive southern rock style proud with "Keep Your Hands to Yourself." Come to think of it, forget the genres; this song rocks, no matter how you classify it.

The Georgia Satellites certainly didn't worry about how they'd be defined when they emerged from Atlanta at the start of the decade, broke up, and re-formed after an EP they made with a tiny British label enticed Elektra to sign them. According to singer, rhythm guitarist, and chief songwriter Dan Baird, they were simply concerned about how their traditional four-piece rock band structure would work in an era of synthetics.

"We just didn't have any synths, or any desire to have them," Baird says. "They wouldn't have been a very good fit. I was more worried that we'd never get to make a record. When we finished it, I hoped they would actually release it. Not because of sonics, but the fact that we were an anachronism."

With Baird's no-BS vocals and sly humor, Rick Richards's guitar thunder, and the Stones-y rhythms of bassist Rick Price and drummer Mauro Magellan, the Satellites focused on the kind of bluesy rock and roll that, while it may indeed have been a pop chart anachronism, never goes out of style with people throwing back a few in a bar. And their first single was so much raunchy fun that it was impossible for even the hypersensitive arbiters on pop radio to stop it.

"Keep Your Hands to Yourself" was born while Baird still had his day job. "A friend of mine had it said to him in a bar trying to put a move on a girl," Baird says of the title:

> I laughed and remembered. Two weeks later I was riding the bus home from work as a construction surveyor, kinda nodding off, and the first verse just came out of nowhere, most of the second too.
>
> I did know it was a song. I had no pen or paper, mumbling all I could remember all the way home. I opened front the door, went and wrote it down quick. I smoothed out verse two. I thought it needed three verses, so I wrote another.

"I got a little change in my pocket, going jing-a-ling-a-ling," begins the tale, over a grinding guitar riff. Baird goes on to deliver a timeless story about a common stumbling block between men and women, the guy lusting after the girl, the girl holding off the guy until he marries her. "That's when she told me a story 'bout free milk and a cow," the narrator says, stymied by one of the oldest clichés in the book. All his pleas and sweet-talking end in frustration, as evidenced by the refrain: "She said don't hand me no lines and keep your hands to yourself."

Richards is allowed to cut loose during several instrumental breaks, letting out all the frustration and sexual energy that the narrator is forced to bottle up. It's the kind of barreling, story-driven rocker that Chuck Berry originated and perfected at the onset of rock and roll music. "He was an influence on everything I've ever done," Baird says of Berry. "Now this tune is more obvious than some. There was some Carl Perkins in there, too, just played louder."

If that were all "Keep Your Hands to Yourself" had to offer, it still would have made an impact on attitude alone. But what separated it, giving it a quirk that anybody who has ever heard the song has likely attempted to imitate when singing along, was Baird's decision to let his vocal purposely hopscotch up the scale while singing the words "No huggee, no kissee." Not only do you have the funny phrasing, but you also have, as Baird calls it, the yodel.

"It just follows the guitars and bass in the solo," he says of the sudden octave jump. "It made us laugh, it might make someone else laugh too. Who doesn't need a laugh?"

The yodel helped separate "Keep Your Hands to Yourself" from the rock competition in 1987, as it managed to strut all the way to number 2. It was somehow telling that the song was kept out of the top spot by Bon Jovi's "Livin' on a Prayer," since that was the kind of streamlined, corporate-friendly rock to which the Satellites should have been a long-term alternative. But Bon Jovi knew how to handle their success. As Baird says, his band simply didn't have that kind of discipline once the accolades came their way.

"We weren't ready for success," he says. "No one is. They only made so many Iggy Pops, and I bet you ain't one of them. It is different in that room from your regular life. Very surreal. No handbook out there. Super-disorienting."

The Satellites released two more albums with the original lineup, with nothing approaching the success of the debut; Baird was gone before they re-formed in 1993. Baird understood the formula for success, but he understands now that the nature of their hit single made it impossible for them to follow that formula:

> Most bands back then, if they were either great, lucky or both, make record one, build a following playing dives and opening for anyone with an audience larger than theirs, and grow the fan base for eighteen months. Go make record two, repeat. Find towns that you can play twice a year. Grow audience, go to record three and hope for a breakthrough at radio. In this scenario, all the guys in the band are in the same boat, have got an oar, and need to pull in the same direction, toward "Success Island." If you all don't, you will fail or fire the guy that's not pulling.
>
> We got there in record time in an atomic speedboat. I thought, "What the hell we do now? We made it here. What's next? More of the same? I'll write some more rock-and-roll songs, but if I yodel again, I will be in a tiny, dismissible box for the rest of my life." No thanks. Would we have traded the rocket ride? Especially at the time? F*** no. Did it screw up the band? You betcha. Chasing phantoms is not what I ever wanted to do.

Baird moved on from the Georgia Satellites, who continue to perform with Richards leading the way, to become a respected performer and songwriter, both on his own and with various collectives, in the alt-country genre. And he loves the fact that his most famous song is within reach of others with big dreams like the ones his former band once harbored.

"What I'm proud of is writing a song that thirty-five years later is being played tonight somewhere on this planet by a band that needs to get some butts outta their seats on a three-set night in a bar or lounge in Anywhereville," he explains. "It's simple enough to try to play well, but you don't even have to do that. I've seen the YouTube videos of the local guys giving it a go. Believe me, you don't have to knock the ball outta the park. Just get close and rely on mass memory."

"The Way It Is" by Bruce Hornsby and the Range

THE WAY IT IS (1986)

In the category of unlikely number 1 singles, "The Way It Is" definitely maintains a special position. It was released in 1986, a time when the lyrics of the highest-charting hits tended toward the disposable and the music of those same songs skewed to the artificial. Artists also generally needed a striking or exotic look to make an impact with the video accompanying their latest opus. If you didn't have the flashy sound and vision, you most likely didn't have a hit.

How Bruce Hornsby fit into that equation is hard to figure. The lanky keyboardist looked more like a science teacher who doesn't grade too harshly or your cousin who towers over everyone in the family photo. His band, the Range, played music that wasn't rock and certainly wasn't pop, instead balancing deftly between country, blues, and even jazz. And the song that broke big for him was a lament for social ills that was reasoned and sagacious enough for an op-ed piece, but perhaps overqualified for the pop charts.

And yet "The Way It Is" rocketed to number 1 upon its release in 1986. "I'm fairly cynical about all this, and I think of 'The Way It Is' as a novelty hit, but in the best sense," Hornsby says now about the song's surprising ride. "I think it connected because it had a fresh sound that was pleasing and sort of went down easily. I say 'novelty' because it usually only works once. Then maybe people connected with the lyrical content."

Considering the song was the first music most fans had ever heard from Hornsby, many assumed that he was the new hotshot singer-songwriter on the block. But he was actually anything but an overnight success. Although he was signed to 20th Century Fox Music in 1980, nothing really came of it but a lot of Hornsby playing on demo recordings by other artists. ("They used to pay by the overdub. Consequently, those were the thickest demos ever recorded," he jokes.)

While he labored on other people's records, Hornsby strove to find what it was that he brought to the table as a songwriter. "So during that period, I was mostly working to find my own voice that seemed unique to me," he explains. "And the least 'commercial' tape, the most original-sounding one, was the one that got me signed," Hornsby says, recounting his record deal with RCA. "'The Way It Is,' 'The Red Plains,' and 'Mandolin Rain' (three songs from his debut album) were all on that demo tape."

Yet the higher-ups at RCA still were concerned about the commercial viability of "The Way It Is," with its long instrumental passages and downbeat theme. They instead cast their lot with the peppier "Every Little Kiss" for the first single. "RCA thought 'The Way It Is' was a B-side, but then it broke in the UK, then throughout Europe, and then throughout the rest of the world," Hornsby recalls. "It was obvious at that point that it would be the next single after 'Every Little Kiss,' the first American single, which got to number 72 with an anchor on the *Billboard* Hot 100."

It helped that Hornsby assembled a band in the Range (David Mansfield, George Marinelli, Joe Puerta, and John Molo were the group's members on the album *The Way It Is*) that could make just about anything sound dynamic. "The Range was not at all trying to be a hit act," Hornsby contends. "We were trying to be more of a modern version of the Band. Accordions, mandolins, fiddles, and hammer dulcimers abounded in that first record. But the sound that seemed to resonate, move people the most, was the piano-playing I was doing, and that became the sound for which we were known."

Hornsby does play a nimble solo on "The Way It Is," while the Range settle into an effortless groove that makes the midtempo music go down extremely smooth. There is also the catchy if somber piano hook that keeps bringing listeners back to a trenchant set of lyrics about people who are being persecuted for circumstances beyond their control. Those waiting in a welfare line are stymied in their search for employment; others are denied access to something simply because of the way they look. The final verse implies that the Civil Rights Act ("They passed a law in '64/To give those who ain't got a little more"), well intended as it might have been, lacked the teeth to effect true change.

Hornsby also details the way that indifference can segue so easily into cruelty: "The man in the silk suit hurries by/As he catches the poor old lady's eyes/ Just for fun he says, 'Get a job.'" He also simplifies the absurdity of racist arguments: "Said 'Hey, little boy, you can't go where the others go/'Cause you don't look like they do.'" "Did you really think about it before you made the rules?" is the retort, but even that doesn't change the ignorant opinions within the song.

"I wrote the song based on having grown up in a small southern town where certain narrow-minded attitudes were fairly common and impactful on local events," says the Virginia native. What Hornsby couldn't have anticipated at the time was that the combination of social consciousness and piano hook would make the song catnip for samplers for years to come, with Tupac Shakur and Snoop Dogg just two of the artists who would reimagine it.

The song's turning point comes in the chorus, when Hornsby fights against the shoulder shrug of the refrain with the telling line "Don't you believe them." He sings the line with matter-of-fact disgust, as if he couldn't be sure that his message would get through in a climate where stubborn minds are difficult to change. It was his way of speaking out against complacency, and it's a big part of the reason the song has stayed so relevant through the years.

Not that Hornsby, who added several more thoughtful hits in the decade, would complain if "The Way It Is" suddenly seemed dated or unnecessary. As he explains, "Just when one thinks we are making progress in race relations and tolerance, appalling incidents will occur that shock and sadden anyone who is interested in equality in American life. So sadly, the song still retains a bitter-sweet topical quality."

Bittersweet indeed. But there was victory in the fact that Hornsby had the courage to write it and perform it, especially since it was his introduction to music fans everywhere. And perhaps there will come a time when the wisdom of "The Way It Is" will seem self-evident to all and the song will become a relic of an uglier time rather than a sad depiction of the status quo.

"Shake You Down" by Gregory Abbott
SHAKE YOU DOWN (1986)

The 80s were filled with innovative music, with many examples of that innova-
tion to be found throughout this volume. Yet the path that artists trod to make
such music didn't deviate too much from the way it had been throughout music
history. The old story of artists and bands working their way up through clubs
and bars, making demos, selling themselves to every record company they could
find before getting a contract, and so on, still held pretty true.

Then there was Gregory Abbott, who was teaching English at one of the
most prestigious universities in the United States when he decided to devote
himself full-time to making music. Good decision, that: Abbott's self-written,
self-produced debut album went platinum in 1986 on the strength of its title
track. "Shake You Down" became one of the era's biggest soul smashes, crossed
over to the top of the pop charts, and managed to inscribe a brand-new term in
the romantic glossary.

It's important to note that Abbott didn't just drop his chalk and copy of
Chaucer and head for the studio all at once. He had been working in bands and
learning instruments and production as side gigs prior to his massive debut.
Abbot explains his somewhat unique career path:

> During graduate school and beyond, even when I was teaching or
> working on Wall Street, I was always in a band, writing, and keeping
> my musical skills sharp. Academia is primarily a left-brain activity
> and music is right brain, so I found the balance very comfortable. I
> studied the music industry and decided that if I approached it more
> seriously, I could make a career out of it.
>
> Up to that point it had been purely pleasure. Perhaps it surprised
> some when I got into music full-time, but for me it was an un-
> derstandable and comfortable transition. All the things that I have
> learned about human nature from my years in academia support me

in my songwriting. They help me analyze and interpret what I'm seeing and experiencing.

Blessed with the rare vocal ability to sound smooth and romantic without overplaying the lover-man antics, it made sense that Abbott's runway hit single would be an ode to seduction. "'Shake You Down' was one of those songs that came rather easily once I had made a decision on the rhythm and the chord progressions," he says. "The melody and lyrics followed fairly intuitively. I was in the throes of new love at the time, so I was in 'high inspiration' mode and eager to express what I was feeling."

Abbott got the ball rolling with a sultry melody and sharp lyrics. His narrator spends much of his time staring down a love interest and sending her vibes until she gets the picture ("I'm glad you picked up on my telepathy," he sings). He knows how to slow play it with coos and whispers, but he also knows when it's time for the hard sell: "Come on, girl, let's shock the show," Abbott suggests in this closing rap. Above all, he keeps things classy, even if we know what his intentions are.

"One of the things I learned at Berkeley and Stanford was the power of using symbolism, imagery and metaphor," Abbott explains about his lyric-writing process. "In other words, rather than graphically spelling it all out, sometimes it's more powerful and romantic to express your feelings poetically by suggestion."

To top it all off, Abbott came up with a new way to describe a come-on that has stuck stubbornly in the culture since the song dropped more than three decades ago. "Good luck with that one," Abbott laughs when asked his inspiration for the refrain "You read my mind, girl, I'm gonna shake you down": "My crazy brain is making stuff up all the time. On a serious note though, I was trying to express what a lover feels when he is planning his love attack on the object of his affection. He's going to 'shake her down.'"

As befits a former professor, however, a thought process was definitely at work. "Romance is often a combination of desire and danger, of attraction and trepidation," says Abbott. "There is something seductive yet scary about the passion we see in a lover's eyes when they are about to lay the big shakedown on you. What will happen next? That's what I wanted to express."

At a time when it was difficult for soul-based artists to break through when the charts were dominated by big-production pop songs, Abbott enjoyed mammoth success by sticking to the old-school virtues of predecessors like Sam Cooke and Al Green. "I've always held the vintage soul singers in high esteem and I've learned a lot by studying their work," Abbott muses. "At the time my record came out there was definitely space for a reappreciation of classic soul music. The important thing for me is to always attempt to sound fresh and authentic, not derivative. That often means sounding like nothing you currently hear on the radio. I know as a listener I'm always excited to hear something different and new."

Different and new while beholden to some of the greats is a good way to both describe and start to understand the success of "Shake You Down." Abbott does a great job mimicking classic soul structures, such as the way the harmony vocals take the refrain while he improvises off it with the lead, or the way he includes a brief spoken-word section to demonstrate the seriousness of his plight. Yet the novel lingo and the clever way that Abbott utilizes it keeps the song from being a mere tribute.

Still, a number 1 spot on the pop charts for a recording newcomer with no real hype behind him before the song was a striking result. "I really didn't anticipate anything one way or the other," Abbott explains. "I was just happy to have my first album out and have my music heard. We knew we had a good album, but I don't think you can predict an outcome such as 'Shake You Down.' Although there are those, of course, who claim they can. My job as a writer is simply to put forth my best effort, express myself as honestly and authentically as possible. The rest is out of my hands."

Such a levelheaded way to look at it is what you come to expect from Abbott. And it likely also helped him to put in perspective that he was never again to cross over to the pop charts, although he did manage several more charting R&B songs. His music continues to do well with his loyal following, however, which includes a strong international audience. And he's still—as he was when he broke through—a hyphenate, doing a little bit of everything professionally while still playing his music whenever he gets the chance.

"Music has always been a part of my life," Abbott says about his journey to this point:

> It's as though I've created my own personal soundtrack as I go. It is this soundtrack that I share with my fans, or "fams" as I prefer to think of them, since they have become like family. They've followed me from major label to independent. They've supported me through the transition from when folks bought vinyl albums to today where people primarily stream and download. They have been there through the ups and the downs, allowed me to grow and become strong. In other words, they've enabled me to live the beautiful life of a working musician and for that I am indebted.

"Someday" by Glass Tiger

THE THIN RED LINE (1986)

It usually isn't as easy as Glass Tiger made it look upon their arrival on the pop scene in the middle of the 1980s. They formed as the band Tokyo in Canada in 1983, signed a deal with EMI/Capitol in 1985, and then ripped two straight Top 5 singles off their debut record in 1986. That kind of whirlwind success usually didn't happen, even in the 80s, where anything seemed possible.

Lead singer Alan Frew claims that the group did have to pay their dues, however, even as he is a bit flabbergasted by how it all turned out. "We were hard-working musicians," Frew says today. "Wrote in the basement. Slugging it out in the bars. And thirty years later you're in the fabric of world music."

Based on their immediate success, one might think that the group had been culling material for a few years before they got their record deal, honing the best songs to the point where they were flawless. As a matter of fact, Glass Tiger (which included Frew, Al Connelly, Sam Reid, Wayne Parker, and Michael Hanson) wrote all but two of the songs on their 1986 debut album, *The Thin Red Line*, after being signed. The catalyst was Jim Vallance, an ace producer whose credits included fellow Canadian star Bryan Adams.

"The demo that got us signed contained other songs that never made it," Frew remembers. "The true irony is that when the record company signed us one of the first things they asked us to do was go to Vancouver and work with Jim Vallance. We flew to Vancouver and on the very first day we ever worked with him, we wrote 'Don't Forget Me (When I'm Gone)' and 'Someday.'"

The first part of that heady one-two punch, "Don't Forget Me (When I'm Gone)," was a horn-filled up-tempo groover similar to what George Michael often conjured with Wham! It also featured a guest vocal from Adams that likely helped to bust down the door with US audiences. The song went to number 2, and Frew claims it would have grabbed the top spot had the record company not erred with its initial choice of single.

"The Americans for whatever reason decided they wanted to release 'Thin Red Line' first," Frew says. "And we didn't fight it. What happened was all the border stations like Minnesota, Detroit, Buffalo, they wanted nothing to do with it, because they were listening to this three-and-a-half-minute, uptempo pop song that was taking Canada by storm. It went to number 1 to all the individual stations, but it had already peaked by the time it was just hitting the Midwest and making its way down to LA. In those days in America you had to have sales and airplay running simultaneously to hit number 1, and we got a little disjointed and peaked at number 2."

Still, number 2 is nothing to sneeze at. Some doubters might have wondered if the group could follow that up without an Adams assist, but Glass Tiger knew it had the goods in another song that would, in many ways, outstrip its predecessor. "We knew that 'Someday' was a strong song," Frew remembers. "'Someday,' in America, was in a lot of ways a more lucrative and bigger hit than 'Don't Forget Me' was. It crossed over to adult contemporary, and it charted Top 7 and Top 5 on the pop and the AC charts. I actually have an ASCAP record here at home because it was one of the ten most-played songs in America in 1987. So we knew that it was a great follow-up for 'Don't Forget Me (When I'm Gone).'"

On that heady day when they were writing these world-conquering singles, Frew and Vallance took advantage of a moment when the rest of the band took five. "What happened was we'd written 'Don't Forget Me (When I'm Gone),'" Frew explains. "The guys were smokers at the time and Vallance and I were not. So they went outside to take a break and Vallance goes on the keyboard and gets this riff happening. And I immediately started emoting a melody and then I said, 'When I come home/You telephone.' But I said, 'Nah, it sounds too formulaic.' No major thought to any of it. Just emoting thoughts and words that came in mind, and the next thing you know 'Someday' was born."

Frew believes that the best songs are the ones that come quickly. "Only a fragment of time in my writing history have I ever had a concept that I wanted to turn into a song," he says. "And I think most commercial adult contemporary and pop writers are like that. The idea of running about with pen in hand and deciding you want to write about the crumbling wall or whatever, I don't know. I may sound a little flippant about lyrics. But with all my songs, I emote and I write and then I look back on them. Two or three years later you look back and it all makes sense."

He created a song where the narrator is tortured by a somewhat ambivalent love interest, forever trying to connect with her only to be stymied. In the chorus, he imagines a day when she'll have her comeuppance and be the one struggling. "Someday" doesn't try to impress with cleverness, but it delivers its point extremely well, from the direct punch of the lyrics to the gospel-tinged release of the chorus. It lets you get in there, vicariously feel this guy's pain, and come out the other side either identifying with his torment or feeling lucky that you're not in his shoes.

Frew laughs about the idea that his tortured vocal makes it sound like he lived through the experience he related in the song. "'Someday' was definitely a boy-meets-girl song, and I used to have a cheeky habit when I was a young guy in a relationship," he says. "I was in a popular band. I knew most things with girls I met were pretty doomed. But I, for some reason, used to write the lyric as if I had been dumped. As if the tables had turned on me. Maybe I didn't want to share responsibility for the truth that it was me doing it. When I look back on 'Someday,' it was definitely one of those moments. In actual fact, he [the narrator] is probably the one that caused it."

"In Canada we set a record," Frew says of the band's incredible start. "We won the Juno award for Single of the Year back to back two years in a row off the same album." Like many 80s bands, however, Glass Tiger couldn't keep that level of success as time progressed. But also like many 80s bands, they still continue to perform to adoring fans, especially in their native Canada. That's been all the more rewarding for Frew, who has been able to recover from a serious stroke he suffered in 2015.

And Frew is eminently grateful for the Glass Tiger ballad that still causes a great crowd reaction all these years later. "It's very iconic," he says. "Sam usually does this tinkling on the piano where you don't know what's coming. And I say to the audience, 'Let's close our eyes and pretend it's 1986.' That always solicits a cheer. And then the second it kicks in and they know it's 'Someday,' it gets a huge response."

"Seasons Change" by Exposé
EXPOSURE (1987)

Everybody underestimated Exposé, even as they churned their way to seven straight Top 10 singles at the tail end of the 80s. Even Jeannette Jurado, who sang lead on many of those smash hits, didn't think much of their potential as she was joining the group.

"When I went to Florida and I signed the contract and began recording, I really thought I was gonna come home in a couple weeks," Jurado says. "I didn't see it happening. I didn't pay attention that much. The band that I had been in was really a huge R&B band. I wasn't really a fan of the whole dance thing. And I thought I was going out there just to get cool studio experience. I wasn't thinking that far in advance. Little did I know that ten years later I'd be singing in the same group under the same contract."

Exposé's run peaked with "Seasons Change," the fourth Top 10 single from their 1987 debut album and their first to hit the top spot on the *Billboard* pop charts. One of the amazing parts of the story is that Jurado, who sings lead on the track, and her bandmates Ann Curless and Gloria Bruno, represented an entirely new incarnation of the band from the one that had begun just a few years earlier under the guidance of Miami-based producer Lewis Martinee.

The first trio, which consisted of Sandee Casanas, Ale Lorenzo, and Laurie Miller, scored dance chart success with the singles "Point of No Return" and "Exposed to Love" in 1985. Yet by the time the band's debut album was released in 1987, the transformation to Jurado, Curless, and Bruno was complete. Differing reports abound as to the whether the original group members were fired or quit, but nonetheless, Jurado, who was approached after her band opened for Exposé and she impressed Martinee with a cover of "Point of No Return," says everything happened in a whirlwind. "I think I signed in the summer and our first single was released in November of that year," she remembers. "And we were already charting by February of the following year."

And did they ever chart. "Come Go with Me," a rerecorded "Point of No Return," and "Let Me Be the One" all shot up into the Top 10. Martinee was able to cast the singers for each of those high-energy songs extremely well, even if he kept them on a bit of a knife's edge to do so. "The lead vocal was never promised, like you were absolutely going to sing lead," Jurado explains. "I think what was going on is he was bringing each one of us into the studio and trying us on different songs."

When Jurado heard "Seasons Change"—written, like the majority of Exposé's songs, by Martinee—it dovetailed nicely with her personal experience, allowing her to deliver a lived-in vocal. "I just think particularly on 'Seasons Change,' it has a lot of meaning to me as far as not having someone with you today and wishing that person was there," she says. "That kind of came out emotionally in the performance. Chalk that up to the life I had growing up and the people that were close to me, losing some of them, and how it affected me in my life. On that song, the lyrics just kind of spoke to me. Going into the studio, I remember thinking about that and having a heavy heart about it. And it all came out."

There were a number of things working against the potential success of "Seasons Change." First of all, it was a ballad. The group had proven themselves on the up-tempo predecessors, but they had to overcome skepticism of their ability this time around. "I think that the record company was a little afraid to release a ballad knowing that we had the whole dance reputation," Jurado says. "But it was really important to us to get it out to the public that we could sing. And I think 'Seasons Change' was an opportunity to do that."

There was also the notion that no band in history had ever delivered four Top 10 singles from their debut album. But Exposé simply didn't know any better. "We were so caught up in the whole fever and craziness of what we were going through," Jurado says:

> By the time the three of us got together and got into the studio, the songs were pretty much waiting for us. Louis had the songs written. Arista Records was standing there, contract in hand. It was very, very quick.
>
> We were very young and very naive when it came to the record industry. We were all saying, "Well, isn't this the way it's supposed to happen?" Especially when you're young and you dream about being on the radio and you dream about making videos. It was just the perfect storm for us. And I don't think we realized what a miracle it was and what an amazing experience it all was and what the record had done professionally. I don't think we realized it until the release of the second album when we went, "Wow, how come this isn't doing as well as the first one?"

(Not that 1989's *What You Don't Know* was a slouch, as it contained three more Top 10s.)

"Seasons Change" was able to overcome these obstacles in large part due to the emotional performance Jurado delivers of a song promoting familiar but still affecting sentiment about relishing what you have before it leaves you. When she sings, "I'll sacrifice tomorrow just to have you here today," the quaver in her vocal ensures that you believe it. Jurado might have been initially concerned about Exposé's proclivity to dance music, but the band delivers movingly authentic soul on this track.

The wild ride Exposé enjoyed while the band members were still so young (ranging from twenty to twenty-three at the time of the release of *Exposure*) was occasionally a bumpy one. "I think emotionally we were prepared," Jurado says. "And I think as far as our ability to go out there and perform and carry it out for the public, represent the group, yes, we were prepared. Because we had all been singing in our different bands and things up until that time. But professionally and contractually, business-wise, I don't think we were prepared. We were all a little bit naive. Had we been a little bit smarter about that stuff, we could have handled it better."

Still, the trio was able to re-form in 2006 after a long hiatus, and Exposé continues to perform for an appreciative group of fans. That's pretty impressive longevity and a formidable legacy for three women who were hastily thrown together and forced to deliver. Says Jurado,

> There's a part of the show where we tell people we'll be in the back and we'll be signing autographs. And the stories they tell us are wonderful. We have a huge gay following, and so many people say that our music was the background in their life as they were feeling comfortable coming out to their parents or family. One guy told us, when he got divorced, he and his wife fought over who got the Exposé records. And so many people say, "We named our daughter after you, because when we were going together and we were alone, 'Seasons Change' would be playing . . ."
>
> And it's like, Oh, my. That makes me the godmother.

"Don't Mean Nothing" by Richard Marx

RICHARD MARX (1987)

This book celebrates artists who achieved great success in the 1980s, but it goes without saying that there were many in that era whose work was never recognized and whose hopes of stardom were dashed. Richard Marx had tasted that bitter cocktail of heartbreak and frustration, but he was able to channel it into "Don't Mean Nothing," a single that launched one of the most massive careers of any of the decade's singer-songwriters.

Marx hailed from Chicago and was something of a songwriting prodigy, writing a pair of big hits for Kenny Rogers before he was twenty-one. Yet when he started to make the rounds to pitch himself as a performer, he met with serious resistance:

> I get it, because almost every artist I can think of, especially the most successful artists, experienced some level of rejection for a period of time. In my case, what was interesting to me was that I got rejected by every label based upon songs that became number 1 songs. I got "Endless Summer Nights" rejected, "Should Have Known Better" rejected.
>
> But I experienced very few periods of discouragement. I've always had this relentlessness and an "I'll show you" mentality. I put out my first record at twenty-three, so I wasn't some old, jaded guy at that point. But I experienced my share of being told I sucked.

Once Marx did sign his deal, he made the savvy decision to write new stuff, even though he possessed a lot of excellent songs in his hip pocket. "I look back at that as a really important decision because I was always trying to think big picture and long-term," Marx explains:

> And I think that if I had ten songs and recorded all of those ten songs that were written prior to me having a record deal, and then

169

that album was successful, I would have faced the typical sophomore slump. You know, you have your whole life to write your first album, six months to write the second one.

But I wrote more than half the first album after I got my record deal. Number one, I remember wanting to feel that pressure a little bit and get used to it. But also, I felt like, once I'd gotten signed, I was really more inspired than ever. I thought, "People are gonna f***in' hear this." I felt really strongly about "Endless Summer Nights," "Should Have Known Better," "Have Mercy." I wrote "Don't Mean Nothing" a few days after I shook hands with Bruce Lundvall and he said, "Welcome to Manhattan Records"—never thinking that would be the first single or the breakthrough song. I just wanted to write a really great, fun rock song.

Marx initially came up with the riff that drives "Don't Mean Nothing," then called Bruce Gaitsch, a friend and collaborator from his time in Chicago, to help him flesh out the music. They based the groove on Joe Cocker's version of the Randy Newman striptease classic "You Can Leave Your Hat On." Gaitsch left and Marx was then left to work out the lyrics, which evolved from his specific experiences to a more universal lament.

"It began as my personal diatribe," Marx remembers:

I remember coming up with "Welcome to the big time." To this day, if I'm doing a gig somewhere, and we get off the elevator and have to go through the kitchen, through the garage to get to the stage, I'll still say, "Welcome to the big time!" It was a phrase that we used to kid around about. The first verse I wrote was the whole thing about the producer, and I had already experienced that thing that happens when you haven't made a name for yourself yet and you're doing all the work, and the big-time producer decides that he's gonna take cowriter. And you either say, "F*** you," and you get nothing out of it, or you suck it up. I used to say, "100 percent of nothing is nothing." So I played some of those games, but I was resentful of it.

And then I felt I don't know if there are two more verses to write about this. That's when I thought it shouldn't be all about me anyway. It should be about the guy in the cubicle that's just fed up.

Marx was dedicated to find the best talent he could to bring his artistic vision to life. "I always wanted to make an organic band-oriented record," he says. "I had this wish list of musicians that I always wanted to work with, all these guys that I saw in the credits of all the records that I loved. The records were always made very organically with men and women in the room playing instruments. In '87, the majority of what you heard on the radio was machine-oriented, synthetic stuff. A lot of which I loved, but I didn't really relate to it as an artist. I wanted people to talk about the songs and the performances of the musicians on my records."

Yet little did he know that his debut single would feature three members of one of the most successful bands of all time. "I'd like to think that 'Don't Mean Nothing' had a shot at becoming a hit song based on the merit of the craft," Marx explains. "But I managed to get three of the Eagles on that record. It had been seven years since *The Long Run*, which was the last Eagles album. It was Joe Walsh, Randy Meisner, and Timothy B. Schmitt. Meisner and Schmitt [who sang backing vocals] had never worked together. When Joe came and played the solo, I realized we had created a mini-Eagles reunion."

With ace musicians backing an expertly written song, it's understandable how "Don't Mean Nothing" did so well. Walsh brings the edge with his lead, while the groove is winningly gritty. But what really hits home is the detail of Marx's lyrics. "It's never what, but who it is you know" is a notion that everyone who has felt stuck behind unqualified idiots has felt at one time or another.

It's also important that there's no real victory in the song; otherwise it would have felt unrealistic. The would-be starlet doesn't take a stand against the injustice of it all, but swallows her pride and capitulates in the hopes it will get her ahead. "Don't you open your heart," Marx warns, suggesting that you can at least keep that part of yourself safe from the disappointment of it all. It's a stinger of a song wrapped in an inviting package.

The success of "Don't Mean Nothing" started an avalanche of hits for Marx, an unreal seven straight in the Top 5 to start his career, which is still going strong as a performer and an in-demand songwriter. To think that it all began with a song about failure, the import of which Marx has come to truly appreciate:

> For thirty years now, I've been asked by journalists the stock question, "So what's your favorite song you've ever written?" It's an unfair and ridiculous question. And I have always demurred on that. Then, a couple months ago, I was doing a gig somewhere, and I was closing that night with "Don't Mean Nothing." And I said to the audience, "You know I've been asked this question for thirty years, and I've always been irritated by the question because I didn't have an answer for it. And I realize now that the answer is this next song. Yeah, I'm proud of it, it's really well written. But it's because it's the song that introduced us to each other. It's the song that changed everything for me."

"One" by Metallica

... AND JUSTICE FOR ALL (1988)

In the late 1980s, there was a pure demarcation line that bifurcated the world of heavy metal. On the one side, there were the bands that received a lot of airplay on radio and MTV, bands who traded in fist-pumping party anthems and lighter-waving power ballads and whose appearances were distinguished by unruly manes of hair and extensive makeup. These were the so-called hair metal bands, and they enjoyed a pretty impressive run of success until grunge knocked most of them out of circulation in the early 90s.

On the other side of that line were the bands that shunned all the frills and concentrated instead on the intricacy and potency of the music, which was played loud and, perhaps more importantly, fast. These bands for the most part remained underground and off mainstream radio and MTV, save for the wee hours of the weekend. Metallica was one of the leading lights of that community, a band that could have stayed underground and done just fine for the rest of their career. But their ambition and their talent carried them across that line into the mainstream, and the single "One" was the catalyst.

"One" appeared on the 1988 album . . . *And Justice for All*, which was the first that the band released in the wake of the death of bassist Cliff Burton in a 1986 bus accident; he was replaced by Jason Newsted. Metallica (which also consisted of guitarist and lead singer James Hetfield, lead guitarist Kirk Hammett, and drummer Lars Ullrich) was also intending to forge on with a new producer. Flemming Rasmussen, who had produced the band's previous two landmark albums, *Ride the Lightning* and *Master of Puppets*, was caught up in scheduling conflicts, so it was Mike Clink, famous for his work with Guns N' Roses, at the helm for the beginning of the . . . *And Justice for All* sessions in January of 1988.

That is, until Rasmussen received a fateful phone call a few weeks later. "Lars called me up," the Danish producer says:

I had also recently become a dad; I had my daughter on December 10, so I wasn't too keen on leaving her. He called me, and one sentence: "Hi, Flemming, it's Lars. When can you be here?" It just didn't work out with Mike Clink. Not that he's not a good producer. It was just, for Metallica at that time and where they were heading, probably not the direction he was going with his productions.

In any case, they wanted me to come. And I sat down and pushed all my sessions together, worked through the weekends so that on February 14, I could fly over there. And [Clink] basically got sacked the same day, which I don't think was a big surprise to him, because when you're in the studio and you're that close, you can feel when it's not working.

Work on "One," cowritten by Hetfield and Ullrich, was one of the first orders of business. It was a song epic in scope, intertwining the band's typical jackhammering fury with introspective sections that resembled the folkier side of Led Zeppelin. Rasmussen, who had been impressed by a demo the band had sent him of the song before he arrived, explains the long process of bringing all the distinct passages together:

> Me, Lars, and James would sit down. And they would play through the different parts of the song. From scratch, we built some guide guitars that would have the right feel and the right tempo, with me manually punching in a Linn drum click track. You didn't have computers to do stuff. It would have been a piece of cake today. In those days, it took most of the day to get that done. But also, while playing the transitions from one part to the other, we would kind of decide what the next part would be and how quick the rise should be and all that stuff. There was a lot of stuff to consider. And me and Lars dug our heads into the darkness of the studio and spent three days doing the ultimate drum track for that song.

Hammett's majestic lead guitar was the last musical piece added after Hetfield's rhythm guitar, Ullrich's drums, and Newsted's bass. "He'd always come in with everything worked out," Rasmussen remembers. "Meanwhile Lars has got really good feel for what the flow should be in a song. So me, Lars, and Kirk kind of reconstructed all the solos like, 'You should play some chords there.' In my opinion, the solo that Kirk plays on 'One' is probably one of the ten best guitar solos ever done. I think it's really fantastic."

As for Newsted's bass, well, don't think your ears are going bad if you can't quite distinguish it. "That was done in the mix," Rasmussen says. "Because I got in so late on the session, they'd already hired somebody to mix it. They made like a mix that Lars and James came and listened to. As far as the story goes, they went, 'Take the bass down so you can barely hear it.' And after that was done, 'Take it down another three notches.' Whether it was just to piss Jason off or whether they just wanted the guitars and drums so loud, I don't know."

In any case, the musical flow is seamless, peaking in a frenzied combination of kick-drum and guitar that evoked a machine gun. That dovetailed with the song's story, inspired by the Dalton Trumbo novel *Johnny Got His Gun*, about a wounded soldier left trapped in a hospital bed without the ability to see or speak. "I cannot live, I cannot die," Hetfield shouts, capturing the soldier's terrible limbo world with harrowing honesty.

A video for the song didn't skimp on the horrors of the soldier's situation, but it touched a nerve and helped push the song into the Top 40 in 1989. Hearing Hetfield intoning "Hold my breath as I wish for death" amid the other hits of the day was a somewhat surreal experience, but it nonetheless was the payoff for the efforts the band always gave in the studio. "On . . . *And Justice for All* and songs like 'One,' Metallica actually put the bar really high," Rasmussen says. "To reach that level of performance and perfection, it simply took a lot of hard work. We wanted it to be as perfect as possible."

Still, the mainstream success didn't mean Metallica went out to purchase eyeliner and rouge for their next video. "There were loads of hair metal pictures in the studio that were kind of filled with darts and shit," Rasmussen laughs. "They for sure did not want to go in any of the directions that these bands went." Which proves that heavy metal's most successful purveyors may have crossed that demarcation line with "One"—and would do so often in the next decade to court a much wider audience—but they never forgot where they stood in the first place.

"Under the Milky Way" by the Church

STARFISH (1988)

Throughout this book, we have encountered songs that practically jump out of the speakers and announce that they are hit song material. "Under the Milky Way" is not one of those songs. This is not to say it's not a great track, because it is: a cool, mysterious sonic world into which you dive for five minutes and let your mind wander through its intricacies and dark delights. But it isn't a song that you would envision being gobbled up for mass consumption. Unless you're Clive Davis, that is. (More on him in a bit.)

Steve Kilbey, who cowrote the song, played bass, and sang lead on the track for the Australian band the Church, says that such songs have a way of appearing, albeit rarely. "It's one of those songs where everybody congratulates themselves and says, 'Wow, we've finally got a cool song,'" Kilbey muses. "Every once in a while, some really cool song comes along that you wouldn't think would be a hit. Something breaks through. That's what that was. All the radio stations were like, 'Wow, we're right out on a limb playing this song 'cause it's sort of cool and ambiguous.'"

The Church had been a major player on the Australian rock scene since the beginning of the decade, but their 1988 album *Starfish* was intended to break the band worldwide. They recorded the album in Los Angeles, paired with veteran American producers Waddy Wachtel and Greg Ladanyi. But "Under the Milky Way" was a relatively unpopular entity during those sessions, an afterthought about which even its creator wasn't over the moon.

"The guitarists [Peter Koppes and Marty Willson-Piper] weren't really that mad on it," Kilbey says about his demo for the song. "We had a kind of a deal that we were going to write songs together. And I had already written a song on my own for the album. The producers weren't that mad on it, the guitarists weren't that mad on it, and I wasn't even really that mad on it. I didn't think that's where the focus of it all was."

175

"Under the Milky Way" began humbly enough, with a chord progression that Kilbey worked out on a piano at his mother's house on a warm evening. His then-girlfriend Karin Jansson came out to hear it and, after convincing Kilbey that he wasn't rewriting the Beatles' "While My Guitar Gently Weeps" with the somber chords, she helped him work out the words. Kilbey found when he transposed the song from piano to guitar and bass in his demo, something unique began to emanate, but he still wasn't too high on its prospects. He was convinced, however, to record it under the urging of his drummer (Richard Ploog, who was, ironically enough, replaced on the song's recording by American studio legend Russ Kunkel) and his manager.

To spice the hypnotic music up, Kilbey stumbled upon an odd instrumental fill for the break. "This is how random it is," he laughs. "On my demo, I left something like sixteen bars blank. There was just a drum beat there. So when were in the studio, they said, 'What are you gonna do here?' And I said, 'Oh, I'll think of something. Let me just put on those guitar chords: C, G, and A-minor.' And we were just f***ing around. They had this Synclavier. They said, 'What's your solo gonna be?' And I said, 'What have you got?' 'How about backwards African bagpipes?' And they put it on and we thought that was really funny. We gave it to the producers and they sort of took it seriously."

The lyrics to "Under the Milky Way" throw many intriguing images and word combinations at the listener, none of which are easy to grasp, which somehow makes them more alluring. We hear about "something that's shimmering and white" and are told about the somewhat oxymoronic "loveless fascination" that occupies the narrator's thoughts. In the chorus, the refrain of "Wish I knew what you were looking for/Might have known what you would find," hints that a relationship fissure is what has this guy out stargazing and pondering the imponderable.

Still, "Under the Milky Way" didn't really seem to bowl anyone over. "No one had even considered it a contender for a single or a hit or anything at all actually," Kilbey says. "They were trying to sequence it and put it on the album as the second-last song, which is the graveyard spot. It was just sort of an unloved song on an album."

All that changed when the brass of Arista, led by Clive Davis, came in to hear the finished *Starfish* album. "When the album was ready, the record company came in and they listened to all the other songs, and went 'Yeah, yeah, yeah,' Kilbey recalls. "When 'Under the Milky Way' came on, Clive Davis came over and went, 'That's a hit! Congratulations!' And he walked off. They were all slapping each other on the back and the Arista reps were all certain that it was going to be a monster hit."

And so it was, reaching number 24 in the United States and performing well around the world. But while Arista's initial push might have helped the song out, that doesn't account for why the song has lasted as long as it has in the public consciousness. Kilbey has his own clear-eyed ideas for why it has. "Ambiguity," he says:

> It's a completely universal song. You know, I've seen it in movies. It gets played at weddings, it gets played at funerals, it gets played at f***ing raves. Everybody has a go in doing it. It's universal. It's ambiguous. It's so ambiguous, it's almost meaningless. People find meaning in it because it's a portal, like all my songs. It's a portal for you to enter into the song and do whatever you like with it. Imagine whatever you like.
>
> You hear people saying it's about a hash bar in Amsterdam, the Milky Way Club. Some people are saying it's about Australia. I had a game warden in Australia say, "I sit out there in the Outback looking up at the stars. I know you wrote this about that." And I'm like, "Yeah, sure, whatever you think." I don't contradict people. It's like an abstract painting. Whatever it is, it is. And I don't try and f*** with it.

The Church continue to tour and release albums, and Kilbey pursues a lot of other creative avenues. So it's understandable that, when he considers "Under the Milky Way," he's a bit ambivalent about the unambiguous staying power of this ambiguous song. "I'm glad it was that song," he says:

> It could have been a lot worse. I know I'm gonna have to play that song for the rest of my f***ing life, wherever I go. It will probably be written on my gravestone. Seeing it is that song, I'm relatively happy with it.
>
> It's hard to know what to do with it. In one way, I resent being considered a one-hit wonder, so I have mixed emotions with the song. I resent it a bit, I'm proud of it a bit. Most of the time, I just don't f***ing think about it. I've written like a thousand songs now and it's one of them. It's just the most successful.

"Cult of Personality" by Living Colour

VIVID (1988)

When Vernon Reid first came up with the idea for the band Living Colour, he wasn't thinking, for the most part, that a band of black musicians playing hard rock and roll that was far more intelligent and musically adventurous than the prevailing hard rock of the time would have a tremendous impact on the 1980s musical scene. He actually was thinking in terms of the elements that comprised some of his favorite rock bands.

"Literally all I knew was that the form factor—guitar, bass, drums, and lead singer—and the trio factor were viable factors," Reid says. "I felt that it was possible to do it. I was thinking about the Who. I was thinking about Led Zeppelin. I was thinking about the Police. Those kinds of bands are very individualized in their approach. So those were the things that kind of told me that this could actually happen."

It took awhile before Reid, a virtuoso lead guitarist whose love of thunderous rock and roll—intertwined with jazz, funk, and rhythm and blues influences—found the right combination of talent to fill those predetermined roles. After some trial and error, Living Colour came together when Reid was joined by a rhythm section (bassist Muzz Skillings and drummer Will Calhoun) that could swing and pummel with equal dexterity, and a singer (Corey Glover) with a booming voice and an actor's knack for the dramatic moment. After the quartet played one show together at the legendary New York City club CBGB, Reid knew his search was over.

After about two years of honing their scorching sound, putting together some original songs was next on the agenda. As it turned out, a single rehearsal session produced "Cult of Personality," which would become the band's signature track and breakthrough hit. As Reid remembers,

> Corey said, "Hey man, why don't you play this?" He was trying to
> hum something to me, he was singing something to me. And I liter-
> ally stumbled onto the riff, which wasn't what he was singing. That
> was the impetus. I stumbled onto the riff and I said, "Man!" Will put
> a beat to this, then Muzz picked it up and it just kind of started to
> unfold from there.
>
> We were just playing the first phrase, and then I was like, you
> know, this has gotta go somewhere and [sings the extended guitar
> riff]. That was the thing. And Muzz kept the bassline going. I played
> that first nine chord on top of it. I like to say that the song kind of
> wrote itself and we didn't get in the way of it.

The final step that the band had to accomplish was to find some lyrics that
matched the incendiary tone of the music, which was ferocious and sure-footed
all at once. That's when Reid dug into a notebook of lyrics and told Glover to
try the phrase "Look in my eyes, what do you see/The cult of personality" as an
opening verse. Glover belted out the couplet and "Cult of Personality" was born
right there. And Reid couldn't believe how quickly it came together.

"It was funny," he says. "As we started the rehearsal, we had no 'Cult of Personality' and at the end of the rehearsal there was 'Cult of Personality.' The entire
rehearsal was about three, four hours, and it was the writing of one song. And we
played that song the next time that we played at CBGB's and people instantly dug
it. We started playing the riff and people started bouncing off the wall."

When it came time to record the song for the band's debut album, *Vivid*,
which would be released in 1988, Reid ran into a roadblock when he tried to
get some recorded quotes of famous leaders to tie in with the theme of the song:

> Originally we wanted Martin Luther King: "Free at last, free at last,
> thank God Almighty we are free at last," but the King foundation
> wanted $10,000 to use the quote, and we just couldn't do it. I was
> really bummed about this.
>
> I was walking around in Harlem and there was a guy who was
> selling tapes of Malcolm X. And there was a tape of "Message to
> the Grass Roots" at the beginning of it. Malcolm says, "We want to
> talk right down to earth in a language that everybody here can easily
> understand." And I thought we gotta use this.

Luckily for the band, one of Malcolm X's daughters was an early fan and gave
them the permission to use the speech.

Franklin Delano Roosevelt and John F. Kennedy also make appearances in
the song, but Reid's scorching lyrics, bellowed with piercing intensity by Glover,
are the centerpiece. As the song makes clear, the power of personality can be
used for nefarious purposes: "I exploit you, still you love me/I'll tell you one and

one makes three." The tradeoff is that such a powerful pulpit comes at a price: "When a leader speaks, that leader dies." When you add in the dynamics of the music, which shows off the band's chemistry and interplay while allowing for each member to shine when called upon, it's clear why "Cult of Personality" was so explosive then, and why it's still a powder keg today.

As Reid explains, he name-checked leaders of dubious reputation (Mussolini) alongside those who have been exalted (Gandhi) because their impact is similar. "There was something charismatic and there was something other-worldly that makes these people kind of rise above and become their voice of the generation, their voice of the moment," he says. "People that other people are willing to lay down their lives for."

Surprisingly, the song wasn't the first choice to introduce the band to the world, and it nearly cost them. "I felt it was the song," Reid says:

> But when we started out, the first single was "Middle Man." "Middle Man" got some radio play and we had a video for it. But it didn't catch on. It was like we would get late-night radio play from DJs who were super-adventurous.
> Back then, basically you got maybe two or three shots at the apple. A lot of it was politics. If your A&R man was politically connected in the company and was popular, you might get three bites at it.

"Cult of Personality" was the second bite, and it bit everyone who heard it. "The song broke on radio," Reid says. "People instantly were like, 'What the hell was that?' I think it was Boston that broke the song originally. It started to spread from there and then the video got placed on MTV. And then it just kind of took off."

"Cult of Personality" powered its way to the number 13 position on the *Billboard* charts in 1988 and cemented Living Colour as a purveyor of rock and roll that could make you think as well as it could make you move. The band still releases fierce music and tours to adoring fans today. Meanwhile, their most famous song seems to increase in relevance with each new presidential election. But Reid insists that it's likely to never go out of style, for good or bad.

"The process of charisma and celebrity is outside of politics," Reid says. "People come into the mix and they become divisive. They become celebrated and denigrated. There's a kid right now who's at his mother's breast who's going to be the world-famous fill-in-the-blank. That's always gonna happen."

"The Look" by Roxette

LOOK SHARP! (1988)

Luscious pop melodies have been one of the chief exports of Sweden ever since ABBA went worldwide in the 70s. The duo Roxette made for an interesting addition to the tradition. Per Gessle wrote the songs, showing that unerring sense of tunes and hooks that seems to exist in Sweden on a much higher per capita basis than anywhere else in the world. Marie Fredriksson did the belting, proving a powerhouse of a singer whose vocals betrayed just enough of her home accent to stand out from the pack on the charts.

Yet it was a song sung by Gessle that busted the band worldwide. "The Look" actually wasn't much for melody, but made up for it with synthetic rock heft. Meanwhile, Gessle's lyrics, which don't even try to hide the fact that English wasn't his go-to language, are idiosyncratically unforgettable.

Gessle was a member of a successful Swedish act (Gyllene Tider) in the early part of the 80s; Fredriksson was an occasional collaborator as well as a performer in her own right. "When I started out I was more interested in being a songwriter than an artist/singer, so working with someone like Marie was a dream coming true for me," Gessle explains of the partnership. "Marie and I had known each other since the late 70s, playing in various bands on the west coast of Sweden. Both of us worked primarily in Swedish. but we had this common ambition to try to make it happen internationally. When I say internationally, I actually mean Norway, Denmark, maybe northern Germany. Our dreams were not fluffier than that."

For a while, however, Gessle and Fredriksson looked like they would fall into the category of European favorites who would never crack the US market. "We never thought of crossing the Atlantic at all," Gessle explains. "It was like trying to land on the moon. We never thought we were good enough. Or had the legacy. Or the connections. We were just small-towners from a small country far away."

Yet the band were scoring hits overseas with no problem whatsoever. Most of these featured Fredriksson singing songs that were constructed on slow builds to anthemic choruses, all the better to show off her impressive instrument. "The Look," the third single off their second album—1988's *Look Sharp!*—was a completely different animal, however, and was based on a strategic decision that Gessle had made about the band's direction.

"After the domestic success of the first Roxette LP [*Pearls of Passion*] in 1986, I wanted to change our musical style a bit," remembers Gessle. "I didn't want to use the live band in the studio anymore. I wanted to go into a more technical and programmed direction. I wrote a lot of songs and bought a lot of synthesizers. One of them was an Ensoniq ESQ-1. Learning how to program it, I wrote 'The Look,' based on a pretty simple sequenced bass."

Gessle decided to demo the song without finished lyrics, which turned out to be a crucial factor in the song's eventual success. "The lyrics in the first verse were guide lyrics to begin with," he says. "I wrote them to remember the groove and the phrasing but eventually kept most of them. I liked the style and the vibe since they reminded me of 'I Am the Walrus'—phrases put together randomly that sounded really cool."

Hence the first lines: "Walkin' like a man/Hitting like a hammer/She's a juvenile scam/Never was a quitter." They grab you immediately, even though you have no idea where they're headed or what they signify. And so it goes from there. Some of the more memorable phrases that are sprinkled through the song: "Her lovin' is a wild dog," "Naked to the T-bone," "Shakin' like a mad bull." None are cliché even in the least, and, once you get on the song's wavelength, a couplet like "Lovin' is the ocean/And kissin' is the wet sand" reveals its odd profundity. It was as if listeners accustomed to English rock and pop idioms had the thrill of learning the language all over again.

Gessle admits that his unique approach had is advantages:

> Being Swedish, not having English as my native tongue, I probably encounter the English language differently. I notice different things, I might read too much into a phrase or even misunderstand it. Sometimes that can get interesting.
>
> Lots of people have told me over the years that hardly any English or American person could ever have written the lyrics to "The Look." Maybe they're right. I tried to find words that sounded and felt good, were catchy and easy to remember. And also, of course, made sense in a surreal kind of way, if you wanted them to.

Normally, Gessle would have turned the song over to his partner to sing, but this time Fredriksson insisted that the song be left as it was. She instead came aboard to sing the song's "na-na-na" hook and do some call-and-response work with Gessle in the chorus, her potent emoting nicely contrasting her partner's deadpan lead. It was like having a home run champ waiting to pinch hit at the most critical time of the game.

The guitar work of Jonas Isacsson added some extra edginess to the proceedings. "We asked him to play in a George Harrison style, a la 'Taxman' or 'I Want To Tell You,' and he came up with several riffs in that fashion that felt amazing," Gessle recalls. "If I remember things right, I don't think the guitar intro was an intro to begin with. We moved that guitar lick to the front of the song when we were mixing."

Gessle and Fredriksson knew what they had immediately once they heard the finished product. "It felt like an exceptional piece of pop music from the very first moment in the studio; everyone loved it," Gessle says. "There was something about it that sounded fresh, something you hadn't really heard before."

So how did the third single from the album become the one that wooed US audiences first? Dean Cushman, a Swedish expat living in the States, brought the song to the attention of a Minneapolis radio station; a program director heard it, loved it, and put it on the air; and a local phenomenon soon became a national one, until "The Look" landed at number 1.

Roxette had been launched internationally, but they didn't rest on their laurels. Gessle says,

> I was thirty years old, Marie was turning thirty-one, when "The Look" happened internationally. We've had ten years of domestic experience in the music industry which helped us tremendously. But nothing can prepare you for that kind of success.
>
> We knew we had done a great album. We knew we had more fab songs up our sleeve. We just kept on going and going with the antennas out. Traveling, touring, promoting, writing, recording. We didn't stop until 1995, when Marie had her second child. It was time to breathe.

Roxette earned that breath with their massive success, as "The Look" turned out to be far from a fluke. It was only the first of four number 1 songs Roxette would hang up on the *Billboard* charts. Health problems for Marie Fredriksson ended the band's touring days in 2016, but their legacy of hits speaks for itself. And Per Gessle, for one, can't quite believe it all.

"Marie and I have been musicians, songwriters and artists for over forty years, and that in itself is truly remarkable," he says. "We've been blessed. We were just music nerds trying to find a way to express ourselves. It's unbelievable. We basically came out of nowhere and, against all odds, made it. Roxette became so much bigger than we ever could imagine or even dream about."

"So Alive" by Love and Rockets

LOVE AND ROCKETS (1989)

Throughout this book, many artists interviewed about their 80s classics admit surprise that the song in question took off into the public consciousness the way it did—which makes the instant reaction that Love and Rockets members Daniel Ash and David J experienced to the first playback of their 1989 number 3 hit single "So Alive" so refreshing.

"When we finished recording it, David and I were sitting in the seats in the studio listening on the big speakers to it," Ash remembers. "And we looked at each other saying, 'If that isn't a hit, nothing is a hit. We've got one here.'"

That the members of this particular band (drummer Kevin Haskins rounded out the trio) would be feeling chuffed about the potential hit status of one of their songs should tell you something about the immediately striking nature of "So Alive." After all, the three had started their career together in the band Bauhaus, which was known for its brooding, gothic image and material. In the 80s, Ash and Haskins also moonlighted in the band Tones on Tail, another kind of underground project, and Love and Rockets was on their fourth album in 1989 without having garnered much in the way of mainstream recognition. What all these projects had in common was a willingness to experiment, to mix up genres, and to basically set an early template for what one day would be known as alt-rock. Commercial success, on the other hand, didn't seem like it would be their lot.

Nor was it a conscious decision that Love and Rockets' self-titled fourth album, released in 1989, would be a bid for wider acceptance. "It wasn't a matter of like, 'Oh, OK, it's 1989, let's write a hit single now,'" Ash explains. "It doesn't work that way at all. 'So Alive' wasn't an accident, as such, because I've never denied that I'm in love with the idea of three-and-a-half-minute hit singles. But it's nothing to do with, 'Okay, now it's time to reach a wider audience.' We wanted to reach the widest audience possible with the first thing we ever recorded with Bauhaus. We wanted 'Bela Lugosi's Dead' to be a hit single, but it was never gonna be because it was nine and a half minutes long and not commercial in the obvious sense."

Luckily for the band, Ash went out on the town one night and his eyes started wandering. "I actually went to a party with my wife at the time," he recalls. "It was peculiar. I was at this party and I completely fell in love with this girl who was on the other side of the room. I was completely transfixed. I can't explain it. It was just overwhelming. I mean I couldn't go up and talk to her, for obvious reasons. I was sort of starstruck with this person."

Those sublimated feelings of desire eventually made their way out. "[The party] was on a Saturday night," Ash continues:

> And then on Monday morning, we were going into the studio with the guys. We were gonna do one of Dave's songs and I said, "No, we've gotta record this one now. I've got this song and we gotta do it right now." And they said, "Can we hear it?" I said, "No, I haven't written it yet." That sounds ridiculous, but I knew I was gonna write something that morning.
>
> I had the two notes of the chord progression and the first line: "I don't know what color your eyes are." I said to them, "Gimme a half an hour. I'm going into the basement with a bottle of whiskey and some cigarettes. I'm gonna come out half an hour later and I'll have the song written." And I went downstairs sipping on this whiskey and I wrote the song, about half an hour, from start to finish. Looking back telling this story, it was quite a magical thing.

The recording process was equally rapid. "Half an hour later I came up and I'm a bit drunk," Ash laughs. "And I say, 'Okay, this is how it goes.' I started playing it and Kevin started doing that drum riff straightaway. And within an hour or two, we had it recorded."

Ash had been inspired by the backing vocals on the Lou Reed hit "Walk on the Wild Side," so the band hired a trio of girls to come in and second the singer's emotions. What emerged from the whiplash session is a song that veers niftily between 60s garage rock, thanks to David J's head bob of a bass line; dance music, courtesy of Haskins's crashing beat; and gospel uplift, emanating from the backing vocalists and Ash's testifying chorus.

Ash says that his band liked to sample different musical styles. "I can honestly say that none of us were purists as far as musical genres are concerned," he says. He also sums up well the effect of those disparate yet cohesive parts: "What it is with any hit single is every element of the track hits the mark. Every element, if you take it away from the whole song and analyze it, everything works really well. And you put it together and it equals hit song. Everything is in the right place."

The lyrics that Ash concocted in the spur of the moment keep away from linear predictability. They instead contrast the direct descriptions of the girl's physical characteristics (with her long and strong legs) with implications of the mystical transformation she has on him, even if he can't act on it: "My head is full of magic, baby/And I can't share this with you." Even as he feels like he's "on the cross," the simple potency of the chorus makes clear that she has engendered in him a spiritual awakening.

Ash understands that the lightning-bolt method by which the song came to him was ultimately beneficial. "I noticed through the years that all our best songs, no matter what band, were the quickest songs to write," he says. "They happened within a day, if not within a couple of hours. And then the ones that you labor over, they're either thrown to the side or they're not very good. I think it's almost like it's out of your hands. You're just like an aerial or antenna. I find that when you're not really working hard and you relax about it, this stuff comes through. When the human intellect is involved, as far as the arts go anyway, it f***s it all up."

Love and Rockets weren't the only ones who knew they had something special on their hands once "So Alive" was complete. "The record company [RCA], before the song was even released, they were putting stickers on the album saying, 'Including the hit single "So Alive,"'" laughs Ash. "That's how confident they were it was going to be a hit."

All of those expectations for "So Alive" were fulfilled and then some, making Love and Rockets that rare bunch of under-the-radar veterans to strike a chord with the wider public. And Daniel Ash, for one, has no problem with that: "If I can have twelve more of those before I kick the bucket, that wouldn't be bad."

"Free Fallin'" by Tom Petty

FULL MOON FEVER (1989)

In terms of rock superstars making the transition from the 70s to the 80s, nobody did it as smoothly as Tom Petty. Perhaps that was because, setting aside a few production flourishes here and there, he never strayed very far from what he did best: writing compact, compelling rock songs that owed something to the influence of the British Invasion and country rock but, because of his authenticity and clear-eyed point of view, always came out sounding distinctly Petty, which was inevitably a good thing.

Yet even Petty started to hit some bumps in the road as the decade progressed. The 1987 album *Let Me Up (I've Had Enough)* was the rare Petty album that felt like it had no reason to exist other than that it was next up in the recording cycle. Petty was also dealing with tensions within the Heartbreakers, the band that had accompanied him on his meteoric rise to stardom and elevated his material with their chemistry and soulful playing.

Phil Jones had served as a kind of extended member of the Heartbreakers, playing on tours and studio albums with Petty and the band as a percussionist in support of drummer Stan Lynch. His working relationship with Heartbreaker lead guitarist Mike Campbell landed him a place in Petty's search for new musical direction. "Mike Campbell and I would get together once or twice a month during the mid- and late 80s," Jones says. "I'd go over to his house and we would just play, he and I, in his studio."

As for Petty, he had recently struck up a friendship and songwriting partnership with Jeff Lynne, the mastermind behind the hitmaking British group ELO. They might have seemed like an odd pairing: Petty, the heartland American rocker, and Lynne, the orchestral pop auteur. But they immediately found themselves to be on the same page, especially on a stately ballad with lyrics that began as Petty's attempt to make Lynne laugh.

Jones takes the story from there: "Tom and Jeff had this song that they wanted to demo or work on. They knew and heard what Mike and I were doing so they decided let's just record it over at Mike's. They came over and we did the track. They played the track to a drum machine at first with acoustic guitars. And then I played [drums] over that. I actually played it before I heard the vocal. And that was 'Free Fallin'.' That was the first thing we did actually. It was very casual and pretty simple. It was just awesome, the track sound and everything."

"Free Fallin'" could have been a straightforward slow song, but Lynne kept adding intriguing little touches, including the breakdown in the final verse that featured cascading backing vocals and Jones's steady drumming patter around Petty's wistful ruminations. "Some guys play it as a march, but it's not really a march." Jones says of his shining moment on the song. "It's more straightforward. People want to put little rolls and fills in there when they cover that song. But that's not really what it was. In fact, Jeff's specific instructions were, 'No, don't do it like that. Just do it straight.'"

"Free Fallin'" is one of those elegiac tracks that Petty would occasionally drop amid all the peppy rockers to prove just how versatile his songwriting gifts could be—only this one somehow cut a little deeper, the fact that the singer was now more of a gritty veteran than a fierce upstart adding the weight of painful experience to the lyrics. The narrator surveys the sights of Southern California while painting a quick portrait of an American girl not unlike ones Petty had detailed in many other classics. But this is not a devotional love song, as the punch line to the second verse reveals: "I'm a bad boy 'cause I don't even miss her/I'm a bad boy for breaking her heart."

Lynne's backing vocals provide a dreamy touch to the proceedings, while Jones occasionally snaps us out of the reverie with his snare. Those touches are how you take a three-chord song and turn it into something dynamic and affecting. Meanwhile, the title is a double-edged sword. There is a sense of freedom in it, but there's also the notion that the narrator has reached a point in his life where there's nowhere to go but down.

Petty and Lynne were only just warming up, of course, with the eventual result being the stunning 1989 album *Full Moon Fever*. "They kept writing them and we kept recording them," Jones recalls. "And after a while it evolved into a Tom Petty solo album. It caused a little controversy within the Heartbreakers group. It was just really the four of us that did most of it, Jeff Lynne and Tom and Mike and myself. They added other things, but not much. It was mostly just real simple."

Lynne and Petty brought the sound back to a roots-based level that hearkened back to a much earlier era. "It was Jeff Lynne's process partly and it was also how they wanted to do it," Jones explains:

Lots of acoustic guitars. At first listen it seems less rock than the Heartbreakers stuff from earlier, although it does get into more rock elements. But I think the rootsy thing is because of all the acoustics on there that they used. Some of the tracks have six, eight acoustic guitars on them. That's how they got that sound.

They were building it from a blueprint, where you have a foundation and you're putting on stuff as it goes. It's a great way to make a record. It's not a live-band way. The end product, you couldn't do live unless you did like Phil Spector did, with six guitar players in the same room playing the same thing.

In one of the all-time examples of record company denseness, MCA was less than overwhelmed with the early results of the sessions. "What was interesting is that, after seven or eight songs, they took it to the record company and they said, 'Oh, I don't know, I don't really hear a single,'" Jones marvels. "They stopped for a while, and then they had to go back and do three or four more songs. On the first grouping of songs, 'I Won't Back Down,' 'Running Down a Dream' and 'Free Fallin'' were all in there. And the record company, in their infinite wisdom, said, 'I don't know if we want to put this out.'"

They were eventually convinced, of course, and Petty had one of the biggest hits of his career. It would eventually pave the way as well for Petty and Lynne's work with the Traveling Wilburys (whose first album was recorded after but released before *Full Moon Fever*). And *Full Moon Fever*, with "Free Fallin'" as its emotional centerpiece, looms large in Petty's catalog, which means it looms large in rock-and-roll history.

As for the guy who drummed on those unforgettable songs, his immense pride in the subject is understandable:

> I'll tell you, it's still one of the best records I've ever heard in years. One of the best records ever made, in my opinion. Even though I'm on it. It's hard to beat that record. When you hear that stuff, it still holds up. It's great songs and the sounds and everything. I'm honored to have been a part of it, and I learned a lot from doing it with those guys.
>
> When they [Petty and the Heartbreakers] did the Super Bowl, where you get four songs, they did "Free Fallin'," "Running Down a Dream," "I Won't Back Down" as three of them. That should tell you something.

"Love Shack" by the B-52's
COSMIC THING (1989)

It is the decade's ultimate party-starter, a song that DJs have put to extreme use in all the years since its 1989 release, whether they're providing the music for weddings, graduation parties, or any other gathering in need of some immediate livening up. Yet "Love Shack" came from a band that had only just decided to begin making music again together in the wake of profound tragedy.

The band was the B-52's, the Athens, Georgia, collective that had made a name for themselves beginning in the late 70s with music that wore its quirks on its sleeve and dared to be colorful while all the punks moped. They became college radio and critical darlings as well as a thrilling live act, even as mainstream radio really didn't know what to do with them.

The tragedy in question was the death of guitarist Ricky Wilson to complications from AIDS when he was just thirty-two years old. That left the remaining members—drummer Keith Strickland and vocalists Kate Pierson (who also plays keyboards), Cindy Wilson (Ricky's sister), and Fred Schneider—at a loss on how to proceed. "I think we just collectively assumed that it was over," Strickland says. "It was hard for us to imagine continuing the band without him. Everyone went their separate way."

Little by little, however, the B-52's found their way back together. "Eventually I resumed writing music, mostly as a way to cope with my own grief," Strickland remembers. "Several months later I met up with Cindy and Kate and played them a cassette tape of some music that I was working on. That's the first time that I can recall any of us discussing the possibility of writing together again."

But according to Strickland, there was still a healing process that the band needed to undergo. "Those writing sessions were cathartic," he says. "We often spent much of the time just talking. We became our own support group. We were doing it for ourselves at that point. We had to prove to ourselves that we could write without Ricky. Everything was different without him."

190

Whereas other bands might have come out of such somber sessions with soul-searching music, the B-52's emerged with their sound as offbeat and upbeat as ever as they prepared their comeback album *Cosmic Thing*. "Love Shack" in particular came from an idea of Schneider's, which he based on the Hawaiian Ha-Le, a dance club outside of Athens that the band frequented in their earlier days.

Strickland began putting together a backing track based on the kind of music they might have heard in those clubs, and then the four band members essentially jammed their way around that basic track until the song began to take shape. "In those days I would arrive with a tape cassette of music, and Cindy, Fred, and Kate would improvise lyrics, melodies, and harmonies over the music," Strickland explains. "We would record the jams then listen back and pick out parts we liked, and arrange them into a form that worked as a whole."

What emanated from this painstaking process was a song that eschewed the traditional pop song structure in favor of something more free-flowing and lovably loose. Strickland's surf guitar (he switched to the instrument in the wake of Ricky Wilson's passing) plays off the pummeling drumbeat of Charlie Drayton and the limber bass of Sara Lee. The only reason there's a refrain is because producer Don Was suggested a repeat of the "Love shack, baby, that's where it's at" section to orient listeners. The infectious groove is the constant even as the song springs in surprising directions.

The lyrics, like so many others from the B-52's, maintain their own cool, secret lingo that outsiders could never hope to replicate, what with Chryslers as big as whales and Pierson's immortal shout of "Tin roof . . . rusted!" (That last line has been the subject of wild theories since the day she bellowed it out, when it was actually just something she improvised when Strickland suddenly stopped the tape during a take.)

The song also has personality to spare, thanks to the vocalists. Schneider's amusing and exaggerated exclamations play off the harmonized cooing of Pierson and Wilson in endlessly engaging ways. This was a band that knew how to put a twist in a lyric that could make it mean so much more than it read on the page. Although, with the B-52's, even just reading the lyrics off the page could be a wild ride. As Strickland explains about the band's writing process, "Each song is like an adventure into our collective unconscious. We never know what's going to happen."

What the band realized about this particular adventure was that they had something special on their hands, especially once they began to receive some outside feedback on the song. "Don threw a small listening party at his home in LA after we finished mixing the tracks he'd produced," Strickland remembers. "When 'Love Shack' came on, everyone started dancing. The vibe in the room was like, this is a hit."

The vibe was dead-on: "Love Shack," which featured an effervescent video to help put it across, eventually worked its way to number 3 on the charts. Suddenly the B-52's were worldwide, crossing the globe on arena tours as follow-up songs like "Roam" and "Deadbeat Club" also dented the charts. But the whirlwind of success gave the band mixed feelings. "It was rather bittersweet that it was happening without Ricky," Strickland claims. "Even with all of the commercial success which was thrilling and gratifying, I still felt like we were outsiders."

If nothing else, "Love Shack" helped expose the B-52's and their unique musical charms to a much wider audience, something that has helped sustain them in all the time since. And Strickland tells a fascinating story about the song's strange, enduring power:

> In 2003, after moving to Key West, I was riding my bike around town one evening and heard "Love Shack" playing in the distance. I rode towards the sound, turned a corner and across the street was a Karaoke bar with about five young women on a small stage singing "Love Shack." It looked like everyone in the bar was singing along with them.
>
> I watched, thinking how at one time "Love Shack" was this funky little jam that the four of us just made up to make ourselves feel good and now it's their song, and they're feeling good, too. There's something mind-blowing about all of that.

It just goes to show that, no matter where you are when "Love Shack" is playing, that's where it's at.

"The Heart of the Matter" by Don Henley

THE END OF THE INNOCENCE (1989)

It is fitting, as we come to the end of this book, that "The Heart of the Matter" appears, as it is a song that is eerily apt for the end of an album, the end of a relationship, and, yes, the end of a decade. Poignance and profundity ooze from the song, the product of a lovely piece of music married to lyrics by two pros who had worked together often but perhaps had never before burrowed inside the human condition with such acuity and grace.

By 1989, Don Henley had already scored a slew of big hits in the decade, including one—"The Boys of Summer"—that, like "The Heart of the Matter," began with a homemade instrumental piece by Mike Campbell, renowned for his work as guitarist alongside Tom Petty in the Heartbreakers. When Campbell presented the music for what would become "The Heart of the Matter" to Henley, he knew just who to call to help him flesh out the lyrics.

JD Souther, in addition to being a successful singer-songwriter in his own right, was pretty much an unofficial member of the Eagles during Henley's time with the band, which combined country-tinged rock with alternately sweet and acidic takes on the West Coast scene to the tune of about a gajillion records sold in the 70s. Souther cowrote several songs, including hits like "Best of My Love," "New Kid in Town," and "The Sad Café," which were among the most wistful the band ever recorded.

When asked about this particular quality that tended to emerge whenever he worked with Henley, Souther doesn't deny it. "Wistful? Interesting choice of words for those songs, and you may be right," he says. "An easy place for us to go, I suppose. Maybe we're best suited to those themes and motifs. It seems to always be either that or a rant of some kind."

During the recording of 1989's *The End of the Innocence*, Henley and Souther collaborated on "Little Tin God" and "If Dirt Were Dollars," two songs of a more topical nature, before "The Heart of the Matter" ever entered the picture. "Don and I had already written two songs for that album with Danny Kortchmar, and I wasn't sure there would be more for those sessions," Souther says. "Then Don played me a late entry, the track that Mike Campbell had written and recorded, and it was just too good to resist, wonderfully familiar, and I couldn't think of any better music with those changes. I was honored to be invited. It was the perfect shape and superbly executed. We went to work immediately."

The music immediately suggested to Henley and Souther the theme of relationships and how they grow and, sadly, sometimes expire. But the two also tossed around big-picture ideas related to the seemingly misplaced priorities of the world at large:

> Undoubtedly, Mike Campbell's track set a perfect tone. But Don and I had both had recent breakups of serious relationships, which first focuses the mind and later expands its range.
>
> It was also impossible to ignore the trends of consumption, avarice, and superficiality that were afoot. A popular advertisement sneered: "Image is everything." So the fuse was already well lit for the [then-]current kleptocracy and we could smell it burning. It's not that people don't dream. But sometimes we are dreaming the wrong dreams, aren't we? Instead, what of higher dreams, those of peace, forgiveness, and safety for the innocent? What chance have we without the right dreams?

These notions come to the fore in the song's second verse, where Henley sings, "These times are so uncertain, there's a yearning undefined, people filled with rage/We all need a little tenderness, how can love survive in such a grace-less age?" Souther marvels at the breadth of those lines concocted by his writing partner when he hears the song these days. "Yesterday it caught me by surprise in a mall. The second verse killed me again and I think that's mostly all Don's lyric and very prescient. I listened to that and then set out in traffic to the murderous glare of rush-hour drivers," he laughs.

All of that is seamlessly intertwined with direct pleas to the heart, such as when Henley's voice arcs movingly upward to sing, "I'm learning to live with-out you now/But I miss you, sometimes." Sadly, the length of the song caused a radio edit to eliminate this part when it was released as a single, something that distressed Souther. "I had not heard the edit before it went to radio, so I was surprised and disappointed, as that section was my melody and lyric," he recalls. "Then I heard him perform it and it was back in, so I was surprised and delighted."

Through all of his heartbreak at the fact that his old love has found someone new, the narrator manages to collect his jumbled thoughts and focus on one recurring idea: "I think it's about forgiveness," Henley sings. "Even if you don't love me anymore." That word "forgiveness" is repeated like a mantra throughout the song. Souther again gives credit to Henley for this idea:

> I would love to say I thought of it. But Don surprised me with that refrain, repetition of the word "forgiveness," and with the title as well, brilliant gifts to this piece and spoken with fierce insight. He nailed it.
>
> We were sitting in my living room looking over Hollywood, legal tablets scribbled about, and he dropped that. Eureka? I didn't even catch it the first time he sang it to me. He was right on point, as usual, and stuck to his guns, thank goodness. I thank him for his courage and insight every time I hear it.

"The Heart of the Matter" was a modest hit, reaching number 21, which wasn't bad considering it was the third single off an album with two hits in front of it. But its resonance is undeniable. If ever a song contained words to live by, it is this one. And when sung by Henley so soulfully over those elegiac guitar chords of Campbell's, those words somehow take on even more import.

Souther explains that it is a song that took a certain bit of maturity to write, its deeper truths perhaps requiring difficult experience as payment before they would reveal themselves. "I certainly could not have come to that place in my twenties," he says. "Difficult? Well, yes, it seems improbable if not impossible to find perspective when you're hurting. But forgiveness is sacred and the first to benefit is the one who forgives. In my opinion it is also the only antivenom to anger and possession, devils of fear who are always out to steal our tenderness."

Wonderful music can also go a long way toward combating those devils, and the decade chronicled in these pages provided a lot of that. As someone who enjoyed them so much when they were released and still goes back to them often, it has been an honor to bring the stories of these songs to you. Now, whether you're experiencing it all for the first time or reliving the memories, it's time for you to go listen to the music and hear it all for yourself.

Index

About the Author

Jim Beviglia has been writing about music for more than fifteen years. He is a featured writer for both the print and online editions of *American Songwriter* magazine and contributes regular articles to CultureSonar and many other online music blogs. In addition, he is the author of four books in the Counting Down series: *Counting Down Bob Dylan: His 100 Finest Songs* (2013), *Counting Down Bruce Springsteen: His 100 Finest Songs* (2014), *Counting Down The Rolling Stones: Their 100 Finest Songs* (2015), and *Counting Down The Beatles: Their 100 Finest Songs* (2017). Beviglia was born and raised in Old Forge, Pennsylvania, where he currently resides with his daughter, Daniele, and his wife, Marie.